Gender, P gland

WOMEN AND MEN IN HISTORY

This series, published for students, scholars and interested general readers, will tackle themes in gender history from the early medieval period through to the present day. Gender issues are now an integral part of all history courses and yet many traditional text books do not reflect this change. Much exciting work is now being done to redress the gender imbalances of the past, and we hope that these books will make their own substantial contribution to that process. This is an open-ended series, which means that many new titles can be included. We hope that these will both synthesise and shape future developments in gender studies.

The General Editors of the series are *Patricia Skinner* (University of Southampton) for the medieval period; *Pamela Sharpe* (University of Bristol) for the early modern period; and *Margaret Walsh* (University of Nottingham) for the modern period.

Published books:

Masculinity in Medieval Europe
D.M. Hadley (ed.)

Gender and Society in Renaissance Italy
Judith C. Brown and Robert C. Davis (eds)

Gender, Church, and State in Early Modern Germany:
Essays by Merry E. Wiesner
Merry E. Wiesner

Gender, Power and the Unitarians in England, 1760–1860
Ruth Watts

Women and Work in Russia, 1880–1930:
A Study in Continuity through Change
Jane McDermid and Anna Hillyar

The Family Story: Blood, Contract and Intimacy, 1830–1960
Leonore Davidoff, Megan Doolittle, Janet Fink and Katherine Holden

Gender, Power and the Unitarians in England 1760–1860

RUTH WATTS

Longman
London and New York

Addison Wesley Longman Limited
Edinburgh Gate,
Harlow, Essex CM20 2JE,
United Kingdom
and Associated Companies throughout the world

*Published in the United States of America
by Addison Wesley Longman Inc., New York*

First published 1998

ISBN 0 582 0582 288266

Visit Addison Wesley Longman on the World Wide Web at
http://www.awl-he.com

British Library Cataloguing in Publication Data

A catalogue record for this book is available from the British Library

Library of Congress Cataloging-in-Publication Data

A catalogue record for this book is available from the British Library

Produced by Addison Wesley Longman Singapore (Pte) Ltd.,
Printed in Singapore

Contents

List of abbreviations

BAAS	British Association for the Advancement of Science
BJES	*British Journal of Educational Studies*
BL	British Library
CR	*Christian Reformer*
CW	Charles Wellbeloved
DMR	*Domestic Mission Report*
DNB	*Dictionary of National Biography*
DWL	Dr Williams's Library
GWW	George William Wood
HofE	*History of Education*
HP	High Pavement
JK	John Kenrick
MA	Manchester Academy
MC	Manchester College
MCO	Manchester College, Oxford
MCY	Manchester College, York
MI	Mechanics' Institutes
MNC	Manchester New College
MR	*Monthly Repository*
NS	New Series
PRO	Public Record Office
Roll	*Roll of Students, Manchester College, 1786–1867*
Thesis	R.E. Watts, 'The Unitarian contribution to education in England from the late eighteenth century to 1853' (Ph.D. thesis, University of Leicester, 1987)
THSLC	*Transactions of the Historic Society of Lancashire and Cheshire*
TUHS	*Transactions of the Unitarian Historical Society*
UC	*Unitarian Chronicle*
VASFE	*Vocational Aspect of Secondary and Further Education*

Place of publication is London, unless otherwise stated.

Glossary

Words defined in the Glossary are asterisked on their first appearance in the book.

ANTI-CORN LAW LEAGUE formed in 1839 to secure free trade and the abolition of the Corn Laws. Strongly supported by merchants and manufacturers, it was first based in Manchester

ANTI-TRINITARIAN opposed to the doctrine of the **Trinity**, that is the union of God the Father, Son and Holy Spirit in one Godhead. Unitarians believed this was added to Christian belief in the centuries after Christ

ARIANISM belief that Christ was pre-existent and divine but a subordinate messenger from God

ASSOCIATIONISM psychological theory which postulates that all mental phenomena arise from the association of ideas. These ideas are originally formed from sensations caused by the impression of external objects on the senses

ATONEMENT the expiation of human sin by Christ's death

BROAD CHURCH tolerant Anglicans favouring comprehension within the Church rather than insisting on rigid adherence to doctrine

CALVINIST Protestant believer in the doctrines of Calvin, particularly that of predestination, that is, God's ordaining in advance those chosen for salvation and eternal life

CHARTISM a working-class movement based on the 'People's Charter' of 1838 demanding universal manhood suffrage and five other points of political reform

CHRESTOMATHIC conducive to useful knowledge

COMMUNITARIANISM belief in living in communities which practise cooperative, even communist, principles

CONVENTICLE ACT the 1670 amended Act of 1664 providing penalties against people attending services not conducted according to the Book of Common Prayer

DEISM belief in the existence of God without accepting revelation

DISSENTERS those Protestants who from 1662 rejected the Thirty-nine Articles of the Church of England. They included Presbyterians,

Congregationalists/Independents, Baptists, Quakers and subsequently Methodists and Unitarians

EMPIRICISM reliance on experiment

ENVIRONMENTALISM belief that the environment has the prime influence on individual or group development

EVANGELICALISM Protestant movement that stressed the importance of individual salvation and the human soul and urged missionary work both at home and abroad

FIVE MILE ACT Act passed in 1665 forbidding nonconformist or unlicensed preachers to come within five miles of the parish where they had been incumbent or of any city or town

FROEBEL German pioneer of kindergarten teaching and of children's self-development through play

LATITUDINARIANISM tolerance towards particular creeds or forms of worship

LANCASTERIAN monitorial schools following the methods of Joseph Lancaster. The Lancasterian Association of 1808 became the British and Foreign Schools Society in 1815

MORAVIANS a Protestant sect founded in Saxony

MEETING a dissenting chapel

NECESSARIANISM theory that everything has a cause traceable to a first cause or God, a chain of cause and effect terminating in the greatest good of the universe

NONCONFORMISTS *see* dissenters

OWENISM communistic cooperation advocated by Robert Owen (sometimes called the 'father of English socialism')

PHRENOLOGY study of the external conformation of the cranium believing it shows the development and position of the organs of the individual's mental faculties

POSITIVISTS followers of the philosophical system of Auguste Comte, which recognized only positive facts and observable phenomena and rejected metaphysics and theism

RADICAL UNITARIANS term given by Kathryn Gleadle to the radicals of the 1830s and 1840s who grew from the group centred on William Johnson Fox, Unitarian minister at South Place, London. Many, but not all, were or had been Unitarians

RAGGED SCHOOL voluntary elementary school, often in makeshift accommodation, for vagrant and extremely deprived children. Often food and possibly lodging added

SOCINIANISM rejection of belief in the divinity of Jesus (who was nevertheless seen as the most perfect human being)

TEST AND CORPORATION ACTS Acts of Parliament from the reign of Charles II excluding from public or municipal office all those in Britain who would not swear the oaths of supremacy and allegiance or take Anglican sacraments

THEISM belief in existence of a god supernaturally revealed to humanity and having a personal relation to those he/she created

TRACTARIAN MOVEMENT English High Church movement wanting changes in the Anglican Church akin to sacramental Catholicism and based on the ninety *Tracts for the Times* published in Oxford in 1833–4 by Newman, Keble and others

UTILITARIANISM the radical philosophy arising from Bentham's doctrine of utility especially as transmitted by the Scot, James Mill

Acknowledgements

I am indebted to many people for their support over a number of years. My initial research was stimulated by the work of Brian Simon who has continued to encourage me since I wrote the original dissertation and thesis on which this work is based. I have been helped greatly in the development of my ideas by members of the History of Education Society and the gender group of the International Standing Group of History of Education. In particular, I have benefited from the constructive advice and support of Richard Aldrich, Joyce Goodman and Sylvia Harrop.

Harris Manchester College, Oxford, together with Dr Williams' Library in London, have been unfailingly supportive of my research throughout. In particular Barbara Smith, former librarian at Manchester College, gave me many fruitful suggestions. Amongst the many individual Unitarians who have helped me I must thank Dr David Wykes above all for his valuable advice on many occasions.

I am grateful to librarians in many places especially in the universities of Leicester, Manchester and Birmingham, to Brenda Cox and Louise Hutchins for their copy-editing and proof-reading respectively and to Ian Grosvenor and my colleagues at the University of Birmingham for their general support. My cheerful, efficient editors, Hilary Shaw, Maggie Walsh and Terka Bagley have given me excellent advice. Any faults in the book are mine not theirs.

Throughout the years I have relied on the loving and often humorous encouragement of Mark and Jane and, above all Rob, who has always supported me in every way. I dedicate this book to him.

Introduction

> In memory of Anna Laetitia Barbauld . . . endowed by the giver of all good with wit, genius, poetic talent, and a vigorous understanding, she employed those high gifts in promoting the cause of humanity, peace and justice, of civil and religious liberty . . .[1]

> By the learned and studious, it has often been objected to female company, that it so enervates and relaxes the mind, and gives it such a turn for trifling, levity and dissipation, as renders it altogether unfit for that application which is necessary in order to become eminent in any of the sciences . . .[2]

These two quotations, one from the epitaph of a famous eighteenth-century female poet and writer who died in 1825 and one a view of why male achievement is weakened by the very presence of women, indicate contrasting attitudes towards women's mental capacity and role in society in the late eighteenth century. Such a contrast is at the basis of gendered conceptions of female identity in the period 1760 to 1860, gender being a social and variable construct of what it means to be female or male and a 'primary way of signifying relationships of power'.[3] The famous woman was Anna Barbauld, a Unitarian, and thus a member of a rational Protestant dissenting group, famous, or infamous, for its radical views on religious, political and social issues. It will be the contention of this book that Unitarians played a significant role in changing ideas on women's abilities and what they could do. This, in turn, was an important

1. Grace Ellis, *A Memoir of Anna Laetitia Barbauld*, 2 vols (Boston, 1874), I, p. 320.
2. William Alexander, 'The History of Women' (1779), quoted in Bridget Hill, *Eighteenth-Century Women: An Anthology* (1984), p. 50.
3. See Joan Wallace Scott, *Gender and the Politics of History* (New York, 1988), pp. 28–49.

basis from which the balance of power within gender relationships could be changed.

On the surface at least, evidence would seem to show clearly that Unitarians played a prime role in the emancipation of women from the late eighteenth century onwards. Mary Wollstonecraft was much influenced by Unitarians both at Newington Green and in the progressive circle around her Unitarian publisher and mentor Joseph Johnson, a circle which included Anna Barbauld. In the nineteenth century Thomas Talfourd was largely responsible for the Act of Parliament which first began to break down the almost absolute rights which a father had over his children. Unitarian lawyers such as Matthew Davenport Hill and William Shaen helped Barbara Leigh-Smith (later Bodichon) draft the first bill to attempt to win property rights for married women in 1854. Others in the Women's Movement of the 1850s were, like the leaders Bessie Rayner Parkes and Barbara Leigh-Smith, either Unitarians or from strong Unitarian families.

It was not only a question of fighting directly for women's rights: Unitarian women, as well as men, were prominent in such causes as anti-slavery and all sorts of educational reform. Many leading female figures of the day either began as Unitarians or were drawn into the movement – for instance, Harriet Martineau, well-known sociologist and feminist, Mary Carpenter, pioneering social reformer for children, Elizabeth Gaskell, novelist and Mary Somerville, scientist. Others such as Marian Evans (George Eliot) and Florence Nightingale were strongly influenced by Unitarians or came from Unitarian families respectively. It would be easy to give further examples, especially in the later nineteenth century with the fight for the suffrage and against the Contagious Diseases Acts. The circumstantial evidence certainly seems to indicate that Unitarians both actively strove to improve the lot of women and themselves provided role models of what women could achieve. In recent years such conclusions have been strengthened by many writings on women's history, such as those of Jane Rendall, Clare Midgely, Kathryn Gleadle and my own, although at the same time limiting factors on Unitarian progressive ideals have been recognized.[4] The questions to explore are how far

4. Clare Midgley, *Women against Slavery* (1992); Jane Rendall, *Women in an Industrializing Society: England 1750–1880* (Oxford, 1990); Jane Rendall (ed.), *Equal or Different* (Oxford, 1987); K. Gleadle, *The Early Feminists: Radical Unitarians and the Emergence of the Women's Rights Movement, 1831–51* (1995); Ruth Watts, 'Knowledge is Power – Unitarians, gender and education in the eighteenth and early nineteenth centuries', *Gender and Education* I (1989), no. 1, pp. 35–50.

and why this group was in the vanguard of ideas on women and able to produce so many outstanding examples of them.

Unitarianism

First of all it is important to establish the identity of Unitarians. Unitarianism derived chiefly from Protestant dissent of the eighteenth century, that is it emerged from Protestants who were not members of the Church of England. In the eighteenth century, indeed, many 'Unitarians' could more accurately be called rational dissenters who, like other 'enlightened' thinkers of the day, denied the doctrine of original sin as the key to man's true nature and agreed that humanity and its environment were best understood by reason, experience and experiment. Unlike similar Continental thinkers, they were not secularists, an important factor at a time when religious belief was assumed, certainly by those above the ranks of the poor. Scholarly criticism brought to bear upon the Bible – held by all dissenters to be the all-sufficient basis of faith – had led Unitarians to reject some long-held Christian beliefs, including the Trinity. Such revolutionary theology made the most impact amongst Presbyterians and some other dissenters, particularly through the more liberal of the dissenting academies which many of the men attended. The teaching of these academies fused religion with philosophy and science in a supreme confidence that science was a way of understanding the rationality of God's creation and that only good could result from the growth of knowledge and open, free enquiry. Such attitudes were to be important in opening up ideas on gender.

Joseph Priestley, a brilliant former tutor at Warrington Academy, was largely responsible for a Unitarian form of Christianity which denied the Trinity and the *Atonement and sought to establish a pure, simple, optimistic religion which upheld the humanity of a perfect Jesus and strove for similar moral perfection. A former Anglican, Theophilus Lindsey, opened the first recognized Unitarian chapel in Essex Street, London, in 1774, and many Presbyterian and General Baptist chapels gradually, imperceptibly almost, became Unitarian. On the other hand, more conservative members turned to orthodox dissent whilst some outstanding Unitarians – Priestley himself and Thomas Belsham – came from Congregational ranks.

Since the movement was, in principle, an open, ever-developing religion, with no subscription to articles of faith, it is difficult to define Unitarianism accurately. There were differences between *Arians and *Socinians for example, but by 1813 most *anti-Trinitarians accepted the generic term 'Unitarian' to cover their beliefs. Few, however, openly called themselves such as the appellation was both illegal and considered blasphemous before 1813. Indeed, throughout this period it was often used as a term of abuse by outsiders. Similarly, Unitarians did not call their chapels Unitarian, especially since these, like their educational institutions, were open to all. They were also extremely individualistic, a factor which some Unitarians feared made them disunited and consequently ineffective. Unitarian identity was therefore often difficult to discern, especially as not all remained Unitarians throughout their life. Here, as far as possible, reference has been made to such individuals only when they still called themselves Unitarian.

Who were the Unitarians?

For the same reasons as their beliefs are hard to define precisely it is difficult to quantify the number of Unitarians. Even as late as the census count in 1851, when their membership had grown as a result of the regrouping of the more unorthodox Presbyterians and General Baptists, they only totalled 50,000. This compared with 490,000 Methodists and 165,000 Congregationalists (Independents), although in 1801 Methodists had totalled 189,777 and Congregationalists 35,000. The Quakers, who tended to come from the same sections of society as the Unitarians, numbered 19,800 in 1800 and 15,345 in 1847.[5] Unitarianism was an ideal refuge for liberal, independently minded men and women whose religious commitment might be deep but who preferred rational ethics to dogma. Such were a minority, however, and though Unitarians hoped to be a focus for all Christians in a more rational age, orthodox dissenters had little room for the minority of radical 'infidels' who had risen in their midst. Unitarians did cooperate with other dissenters on some social and educational reforms, but in their moderate attitudes to general living, at least, they were sometimes closer to liberal Anglicans, some of whom they attracted to their schools. Theophilus Lindsey, a leading Unitarian of the late eighteenth century, like some others, originated from Cambridge and the more tolerant wing of

5. A.D. Gilbert, *Religion and Society in Industrial England* (1976), pp. 31, 37, 40–1.

the Anglican Church, a factor which strengthened Unitarianism at the expense of the latter.[6]

Unitarians came almost completely from the middle-class to artisan sections of society. They were a small group, drawing most heavily on the merchant 'princes', the wealthier industrialists and intelligentsia of the commercial and textile manufacturing centres in the south-west of England, the industrial north and midlands, London and East Anglia. The Unitarian chapel, the New *Meeting, Birmingham, exemplified developments elsewhere in the late eighteenth century, when its congregation of many metal workers saw a gradual increase of more substantial manufacturers and professional people such as solicitors, surgeons and architects – the lower rather than the higher echelons of the professions.[7] Within the emergent social structure of 1780 to 1860, Unitarians were pleased to be in the vanguard of a new class. Unitarians such as Priestley and John Aikin were among the first to single out the 'middle sort' or 'class' as the 'golden mean', 'the most virtuous, the most enlightened, the most independent part of the community'.[8] Within this group, Unitarian nonconformity of an open and socially superior type was attractive to liberals, intellectuals and independently minded people who opposed the traditional establishment in Church and state, aristocratic power, the gentry and the old middle class. They were foremost amongst entrepreneurs of all kinds in a dynamic age and proud of their tolerant ethics, their rational religion, superb education and liberal tradition.

The historian Eric Hobsbawm, in contrast, called the majority of these middle-class businessmen self-righteous, hypocritical, unintellectual empiricists, yet even he admitted that there were some who were exceptionally 'intelligent, experimentally minded and even cultured'. He named four examples, of whom two – Josiah Wedgwood and Priestley – were Unitarians. Sylvia Harrop's depiction of the responsible, enlightened cotton masters of Hyde, Staleybridge and Dukinfield, and absorbing studies by historians such as John Seed on class and power relationships in Victorian towns and cities,

6. John Gascoigne, 'Anglican Latitudinarianism and political radicalism in the late eighteenth century', *History* (Feb. 1986), 71, no. 231, pp. 22–38.

7. John Seed, 'Theologies of power: Unitarianism and the social relations of religious discourse, 1800–50', in R.J. Morris (ed.), *Class, Power and Social Structure in British Nineteenth Century Towns* (Leicester, 1986), pp. 121, 123, *passim*; Emily Bushrod, 'The history of Unitarianism in Birmingham from the middle of the eighteenth century to 1893' (MA thesis, Birmingham University, 1954), pp. 206–19.

8. P.J. Corfield, 'Class by name and number in eighteenth century Britain', *History* (Feb. 1987), 72, no. 234, pp. 55–6.

reinforce the view of the role of Unitarians as a political and cultural élite within certain urban localities using new cultural institutions to assert what they saw as their rightful status.[9] Unitarian consciousness of the low culture of the new industrial middle class stimulated their desire to be its enlightened leaders. In such an aim education was to play a significant part. So too did women, although their role in this has been much neglected by historians.

Unitarians and reform

Before they could take any leadership role, however, Unitarians had to overcome the religious and political disabilities which beset them and, indeed, all dissenters. As the most disadvantaged until the 1813 Act removed the penalties on anti-Trinitarians, Unitarians were often the local and national leaders in the fight against the *Test and Corporation Acts, with Richard Price and Joseph Priestley becoming notorious for the part they played. Priestley particularly emphasized the necessity for civil liberty, that is, the rights of all to freedom of conscience, education and religion, and saw no need for an established Church. Both he and Price believed in the rights of man and full, free and equal citizenship; both disliked the aristocracy and hereditary power, preferring the morality and capabilities of the middle classes. Their beliefs, abhorred by conservatives as revolutionary and generally winning them odium as radical fanatics, went no further than demanding that men of independent judgement, and thus with education and status, should be able to participate in political life. Such beliefs appear entirely male-orientated, and, indeed, in the context of the day, Priestley's wish for all careers to be open to talent instead of being based on hierarchy and privilege was likely to widen the difference between the opportunities available to middle-class men and women. On the other hand, such reformist thinking could be applied to gender issues. George Philips and William Shepherd, for example, asked for female suffrage.[10]

9. Eric Hobsbawm, *The Age of Revolution* (1977), pp. 228–30; Sylvia Harrop, 'The place of education in the genesis of the industrial revolution with particular reference to Stalybridge, Dukinfield and Hyde' (MA thesis, Manchester University, 1976), pp. 37–9, 150, 234–5; John Seed, 'Unitarianism, political economy and the antinomies of liberal culture in Manchester, 1830–50', *Social History* (Jan. 1982), 7, no. 1, pp. 1–25.

10. Martin Fitzpatrick, 'Rational Dissent and the Enlightenment', *Faith and Freedom* (Summer 1985), 38, part 2, no. 113, pp. 91–101; R.V. Holt, *The Unitarian Contribution to Social Progress in England* (1952), pp. 96–7.

Such a mixture of reformism and radicalism roused fierce reaction and fears that the constitution would be undermined by change. In the heady days of the French Revolution great excitement and optimism on the dissenting and reformist side were matched by great alarm and bitterness on the part of the Church and aristocracy, whose deeply entrenched interests proved far better at mobilizing popular support than those who represented nonconformity and business. It was not until 1812–13 that the *Five Mile Act and the *Conventicle Act and then penalties against anti-Trinitarianism were repealed, and 1828 before the Test Acts went too.

Unitarians, however, also enthusiastically supported both American and French Revolutions, although they became increasingly isolated in the middle classes of society for so doing. Indeed, the sharp counter-revolution in England turned particularly against them, with many of them suffering persecution or even imprisonment as a result. Confusion eventually grew even in Unitarian ranks as the French Revolution became first more violent and thence thrust Napoleon into power. Some Unitarians eschewed political radicalism but others consistently opposed the war and, after it, most were prominently active in the Reform Movement. In the nineteenth century, indeed, they played a leading part in many reform campaigns, for example for the *Anti-Corn Law League and against religious disabilities – that is, penal laws against those who refused to conform to the established church, the Church of England. By then a number of them had become some of the most substantial industrialists and commercial men and progressive doctors and lawyers in many of the leading urban areas of England. Not least they were foremost in the campaign for municipal reform and, having helped achieve it, led local government in many of England's most dynamic towns such as Manchester and Birmingham. Their power locally belied the abhorrence in which their religious opinions were still held and this hatred was paralleled in industrial areas by working-class scorn of the economic imperatives which many Unitarians upheld. Such dislike often militated against their social and educational initiatives.

Unitarians and education

The Unitarians were consistently and deeply concerned in education. Their educational ideals, aspirations and practices were an integral part of their character, gave them the confidence and resources to wage their various battles and, not least, did this for their women as well as men. Their open attitudes and educational psychology allowed them to question time-honoured assumptions about women. They argued that differences between people were not innate but were based on education in its widest sense, encompassing upbringing and formal schooling. Thus they were more inclined to equate the male and female intellectual capacities and to see the need for women to be well educated both for their own moral and spiritual development and to fulfil their traditional maternal and caring roles. This more egalitarian concept of gender, vital for enlarging opportunities for women, led them to give females a much better education than the norm. Thus women could expand their own and other women's opportunities and give role models for the future. At the same time, however, because of the huge resources and effort that Unitarians put into male education, while men of the family achieved that status and power in society which they so eagerly sought, gendered notions of propriety limited women's opportunities. The complexity of this needs exploration.

The education, whether formal or informal, experienced by women in any period of history is a significant factor in both how they were regarded by their society and what they could achieve within it. It thus deserves serious attention. However, many studies to date have largely focused on the period after 1860. This contribution argues that the Unitarians, albeit small in numbers and largely from the white middle class, sowed seeds which, through both thought and action, potentially affected all women and their position in society. Unitarians were also important in that their views on education and gender were integral to their religion, and this emphasizes the significant interplay of issues of gender with different ideas in religion which endemically has both constrained and liberated women.

This book aims to analyse how far a progressive educational philosophy and its effects were fully realized. It is divided into two parts, the first covering 1760 to 1815, the period which saw vigorous Unitarian challenge to religious, political, economic, social and educational norms, the seeming failure of that challenge and how Unitarian ideals lived on, especially through education. The first chapter examines the general context of ideas on women and their education, while the following two investigate the educational ideals of the Unitarians and how they put these into practice. Chapter 4 analyses the effects of these ideals and of membership of the lively, extensive yet close Unitarian familial networks both on individuals and on ideas on women's rights.

Part II begins by examining the general context of Unitarianism and Unitarians between 1816 and 1860, paying attention to their contribution to political changes, cultural developments and the ideas on education and gender which were interrelated with these. Chapters 6 and 7 focus on Unitarian struggles to reform middle-class schooling and higher education and their own provision of these for both women and men. They demonstrate both the importance of the pioneering Unitarian contribution and how this was limited by class and religious struggles and gender constraints. The following two chapters examine how gender and class concepts intertwined within the Unitarian involvement in working-class education in this period. The final chapter explores further the gender issues raised and the significant effects that Unitarian education and ideas had had on women's rights and the Women's Movement by 1860.

In a work of this size it has been impossible to do justice to some of the issues raised. Not all Unitarians were middle-class, for example, but the focus has been kept largely on those who were, with a fairly brief analysis of Unitarian involvement in working-class education as it reflects on gender issues. It has not been possible either to do more than use examples of other religious groups in education for purposes of comparison. Lastly, although to understand the gender issue fully, it is necessary to see the whole context of Unitarian aspiration and action, especially the interrelationship between female and male education, the emphasis here is on girls and women. Nevertheless, the study contends that the Unitarians did play a significant part in changing assumptions about the capacities and role of women and thus gender conceptions. 'Knowledge is power' was the Unitarians' overt key to change in society. They wished to give the knowledge and thus power to women as well as men: in this they helped open the door to female emancipation.

PART ONE

1760–1815

CHAPTER ONE

The eighteenth-century context: ideas on women and their education

. . . if you happen to have any learning, keep it a profound secret, especially from the men, who generally look with a jealous and malignant eye on a woman of great parts, and a cultivated understanding.

DR JOHN GREGORY, 1774[1]

[Women should be given] the highest [education] of which they were capable. . . . the learned and the modern languages . . . mathematics and philosophy. Certainly, the minds of women are capable of the same improvement and the same furniture as those of men . . .

DR JOSEPH PRIESTLEY[2]

[Women] should be led to distrust their own judgement; they should learn not to murmur at expostulation, but should be accustomed to expect and endure opposition.

HANNAH MORE[3]

. . . from exercising my thoughts with freedom, I seemed to acquire new strength and dignity of character.

MARY HAYS[4]

The above four quotations, written in turn between 1774 and 1799 by an Anglican clergyman, a Unitarian minister, an evangelical Anglican and a radical Unitarian, demonstrate how diverse opinions were in the late eighteenth century concerning the learning and education of women. The four writers all belonged to the middle ranks

1. Vivien Jones (ed.), *Women in the Eighteenth Century* (1990), p. 46.
2. Joseph Priestley, 'Reflections on death' (1790), *The Theological and Miscellaneous Works of Joseph Priestley*, ed. J.T. Rutt, 25 vols (1817–31), XV, p. 419.
3. Hannah More, *Strictures on the Modern System of Female Education* (1799), I, p. 142.
4. Mary Hays, *Emma Courtney*, 2 vols (Oxford, 1995; 1st edn 1796), I, p. 40.

of society yet mixed in different social circles and varied in religion. This sample suggests, therefore, that, even within these middle ranks, social difference and religion might affect attitudes towards women's education in this period. The two Unitarians, Priestley and Hays, though of different sexes, had similar attitudes towards women. This chapter examines both the context of eighteenth-century education and differing attitudes towards women.

The structure of society and religion

In this period England was dominated by an established order of aristocracy, landed gentry and Church, but beneath this there was massive social, economic, intellectual and cultural change. The aristocracy, great landowners holding leading positions at court and in the Church of England, had an 'unshakeable grip' on political power and, with the gentry, ran local government. The middle ranks in society, however, including at the top both merchant princes rich from tobacco and slave-trading and new industrialists making fortunes in coal, iron and cotton, were growing in size and confidence.[5] The term 'middle class' did not actually appear until about 1812. Historians such as Eric Hobsbawm, Asa Briggs and R.J. Morris have shown how industrial and urban change and the economic, political and social struggles from the 1790s to the 1840s helped new blocs of 'bourgeois', new men from the provinces, become 'increasingly conscious of themselves as a *class* rather than a "middle rank" bridging the gap between the lower and upper orders'. Morris argued this was more complex than Marx's three-class model since the importance of sub-groups coming together through religion, influential institutions, status and political party has to be recognized.[6]

These discussions of class are entirely male-orientated. Women did assume the rank or class of their father or husband, but the connotations of class had very different effects on them than on their brothers, especially if they were single and/or had to earn their own living. Below the ranks of the very wealthy, all women worked, for the most part within the house or the family economy.

5. Roy Porter, *English Society in the Eighteenth Century* (1990), *passim.*

6. E.J. Hobsbawm, *The Age of Revolution* (1977), pp. 227–8; Asa Briggs, 'Middle-class consciousness in English politics', *Past and Present* (Apr. 1956), pp. 65–8; R.J. Morris, *Class and Class Consciousness in the Industrial Revolution* (1979), pp. 18, 29, 45, 62–9.

Whether or not they were paid for this affected their status in society and consequently could reflect badly on their relatives. Within the categories of paid work there were huge differences of rank between, say, 'lady governesses' and scullery maids, but teaching, like writing, although permissible for women of the middle ranks, was still contested territory for 'ladies'.

The beginnings of industrialization and urbanization were creating new tensions and groupings in society. Such tensions were reflected in religion, where those people who refused to conform to the established Church, the Church of England, were called *dissenters or *nonconformists. In the earlier part of the eighteenth century these had comprised just over 6 per cent of the English population, half of them being Presbyterians, who were particularly strong in Lancashire. Although the Presbyterians had to forgo their commitment to become a national Church and had developed more like the Independents (or Congregationalists) and Baptists in structure, they had less tightly disciplined communities than the others, drew from a wider spectrum of society and, like the society of Friends, or Quakers as they were more commonly known, had higher-ranking and wealthier members. Nevertheless, all dissenters cooperated to defend their civil rights against the penal laws which still debarred conscientious members from corporate, civil and military office and, even when not enforced, hung over their heads. Roman Catholics suffered even greater disabilities, but until the 1790s were a declining group in England.

A gradual decline in the number of dissenters and their influence was reversed in the later eighteenth and early nineteenth centuries by the spectacular growth of Methodism and the rise of *Evangelicalism, which stressed the importance of individual salvation and the human soul and urged missionary work both at home and abroad. Evangelicalism affected not only a minority of Anglicans but also spread swiftly through the ranks of *Calvinist dissenters, particularly Congregationalists and many Baptists. The enthusiastic, spiritual emotionalism of Evangelical 'new' dissent offered a strong challenge to 'old' dissent – Quakers, General Baptists and Presbyterians. The last of these groups particularly was transformed by rationalism, many of its adherents becoming Unitarians, although Unitarianism, as already shown, drew from other Protestant sects as well. The Quakers were steadily declining in numbers but, like rational dissenters, drew increasingly from the upper ranks of the middle classes, from among the wealthier and more highly educated manufacturers and merchants of industrial England.

Education, work and gender

Within the diversity of social ranks and religious groups, education was to play an increasingly significant role. It both helped reproduce social distinctions and helped people to change their inherited social status; it served to preserve religious peculiarities and to initiate people into new ways of thinking; in the case of the lower ranks in society it was both feared by their 'superiors' as likely to foment revolution and heralded as a way to aid social control. Education too was undergoing many challenges in the late eighteenth century. England's traditional educational system, indeed, was in a parlous state. The only two English universities, Oxford and Cambridge, had become somewhat ossified, complacent and self-contained, reflecting in their traditional, largely classical studies both clerical dominance and exclusion of dissenters and an increasing reliance on the governing classes. The public schools had a justified reputation for corruption, dissipation and lawlessness. The grammar schools which provided the age-old classical education for boys from the middle ranks suffered from neglect, poverty and competition with private schools offering a more modern curriculum. Academic conservatism tended to prevent change, so many parents in the commercial classes preferred to send their sons to one of the many private schools which offered more useful mathematical and vocational subjects. Some of the aristocracy, squirearchy and clergy preferred private tutors or private classical schools which provided a classical education, the all-important attribute of being a 'gentleman'. Farmers and craftsmen also used these in their locality because they provided a 'gentleman's education' at a low cost.

The daughters of middle-class families had an even worse deal. There was little desire that females should be well-educated, for few men of the day considered women capable of an intellectual education or of having any use for one if they were. There were no public schools or academies for girls, although in the late eighteenth century there was a proliferation of schools, particularly boarding schools for girls of the wealthier classes. These were of mushroom growth and short duration with even the best usually teaching no mathematics or science (nor would these be taught in boys' grammar schools). School-teaching may have become an increasingly viable option for middle-class women in the late eighteenth century, but girls' schools were still of indifferent quality. For girls and boys of the poor there was no state schooling, and charity schools, which had only ever catered for a few, were increasingly insufficient in a time of rapid population growth. In the late eighteenth century, apparently, literacy rates for men were slightly less than two-thirds and for women just below a half, but such figures give little guide to the quality or extent of education available. What is certain is that many children had no, or next to no, formal education. Despite the growing demand for skilled men in the retail and foreign trades and among such crafts as machine-making, the ruling élite feared that too much literacy for the masses would threaten the established order and many industrialists still preferred an uneducated, cheap, subservient workforce. The alternative view of evangelicals such as Hannah More from the 1780s, that if the poor could read the Bible they would learn 'habits of industry and piety', due deference and subordination, horrified conservatives.[7]

Such considerations also applied to the education of girls and women. The amount and content of a girl's education was generally determined by her perceived domestic character and familial role and by her assumed inferiority of intellect and body. All women were expected to marry and bear children, although significant numbers achieved neither or only one of these aims. Variations of social rank and religion might well affect significant differences in attitudes towards women's status and role and thus their education, but all women had to accept or contend with a predominantly male culture in which women had no political rights, no legal existence if they were married with a living husband, and little way of earning an independent living. Agricultural and industrial changes increasingly removed from the home many of women's former functions within the family economy, making women more dependent on men. These changes began to destroy the working partnerships, albeit usually unequal ones, between husbands and wives and led to wealthy women having less to do. Yet tightening perceptions of what was or was not ladylike debarred them from most forms of public or professional life. Notions of gentility often affected the education and use of leisure time of those of middle rank too, although these ranks ranged from those managing households on incomes of about £100 or even less to families of wealthy industrialists and merchants who lived in sumptuous style. By contrast, in the new textile factory areas, working women began to go out of the

7. Nicholas Hans, *New Trends in Education in the Eighteenth Century* (1951), pp. 194–208; Susan Skedd, 'Women teachers and the expansion of girls' schooling in England, c.1760–1820', in Hannah Barker and Elaine Chalus (eds), *Gender in Eighteenth Century England* (1997), pp. 101–25; John Lawson and Harold Silver, *A Social History of Education in England* (1973), pp. 235–40.

home into disciplined waged work, though, at most, at half the rate of men. Other women played a significant role both within the workforce and the family economy, although their work was traditionally seen as unskilled and their contribution has been unsung by historians. The realities of their working life and family responsibilities, like those of servants – an increasingly large occupational group amongst women – greatly affected the context for their education.[8]

The family basis of the social relations of production and the increasingly distinctive sexual division of labour were important for the evolving middle-class domestic ideology. They were also partly a result of long-held notions about women often drawn from the disciplines of theology, law and medicine. Some medical traditions, for example, depicted femaleness as a weakness and female bodily functions as an aberration. At the same time the growing tendency for male doctors to replace female midwives in attendance on childbirth meant that even in this most personal area women became dependent upon men.[9]

Legally, many of the disabilities of women stemmed from property laws made in feudal times, although both civil and criminal law were affected by common assumptions about the dependency and frailties of women. Husband murder, for example, was considered petty treason whilst rape offences were often hard to prove.[10] Most importantly, in an age when most professed a religion, theologians used the scriptures to prove that God willed women's subservience and inferior position in marriage and society.[11] Not all Christian sects stressed inequality to the same degree. Unitarians did not; whilst Quakers gloried more in the 'equality of men and women in spiritual privilege and responsibility'. Nevertheless, men dominated Quaker public meetings and business concerns, and, although from 1784 a Women's Yearly Meeting was established in England, its powers were strictly limited.[12] Yet Quakers were still recognized as being different in principle on the position of women. In the Methodist revival, for example, some women took enthusiastically to preaching, albeit outside the church so that Pauline injunctions were respected. Their leader John Wesley reluctantly but pragmatically accepted

8. Maxine Berg, *The Age of Manufacturers* (1994; 1st edn. 1985), pp. 4–9, 136–65.

9. Alice Browne, *The Eighteenth Century Feminist Mind* (1987), pp. 18–19; Jones, *Women*, pp. 60, 93–5.

10. Browne, *Feminist Mind*, pp. 15–17.

11. e.g. 1 Corinthians 14: 34–5; 11; 7–8; 1 Timothy 2: 11–13.

12. William C. Braithwaite, *The Second Period of Quakerism* (Cambridge, 1961), pp. 270–88; Sheila Wright, *Friends in York: The Dynamics of the Quaker Revival 1780–1860* (Keele, 1995), pp. 15–17, 31–49.

this as a way of reaching some 'sinners' who would not be caught in other ways; he was clear, however, that this was not breaking biblical injunctions in the way Quakers did: 'The difference between us and the Quakers in this respect is manifest. They flatly deny the rule itself, although it stands clear in the Bible. We allow the rule: only we believe it admits of some exceptions.'[13] For more orthodox Christians even such exceptions were going too far: Dr Samuel Johnson famously likened a woman preacher to 'a dog walking on his hind legs'.[14] Women were not to have positions of authority in religion. Even when proposals were made intermittently throughout the eighteenth century for Protestant nunneries they were usually intended for the economic relief of impoverished but genteel middle-class women.[15]

Yet women were expected to be religious, and female goodness was very much couched in terms of Christian morality. Ideas of female perfection were based on assumptions of the differences between the sexes and female virtue was seen almost exclusively in sexual terms – 'modesty, restraint, passivity, compliance, submission, delicacy and, most important of all, chastity'. These ideas were drawn not only from religious injunctions but also from customary male-dominated views that had long intermingled with the latter. Such views are well illustrated in Dr John Gregory's *A Father's Legacy to his Daughters* (1774), which became the most popular of the many conduct manuals for females. Gregory praised virtuous females and assured them that women were intended to be not slaves of men's homes or pleasure but 'companions and equals'. This, however, did not prevent him from limiting the whole of the conduct, behaviour, dress and pursuits of such equals by the light in which men would regard them. Similarly, the Rev. John Bennet expressed the need for women to be religious somewhat ambiguously as 'the only true and unfailing resource' left when, as *naturally* happens, tender, devout, sensitive women were depressed or bored in the 'many lonely hours' left at home whilst their menfolk sought 'health and pleasure in the field'.[16]

Theologians, lawyers and doctors were all professional men whose utterances gave authority to customary views on woman and

13. D. Colin Dews, 'Ann Carr and the Female Revivalists of Leeds', in Gail Malmgreen (ed.), *Religion in the Lives of English Women, 1760–1930* (Indiana, 1986), pp. 68–9.

14. Porter, *English Society*, p. 22. 15. Browne, *Feminist Mind*, pp. 132–4.

16. Bridget Hill (ed.), *Eighteenth Century Women: An Anthology* (1984), pp. 17, 22–43; Jones, *Women*, pp. 44–53; Hill, *Anthology*, p. 22.

her role. With their arguments to prove female inferiority and weakness and a legal system which debarred married women especially from active participation even in their own affairs, women had no way into the professions or public life. Nor was it generally considered that they would have the intellect to cope in such situations. Thomas Gisborne, in *An Enquiry into the Duties of the Female Sex* (1798), for example, was sure that God had not given women male powers of 'close and comprehensive reasoning', because men needed such powers for the abstract learning and variety of skilled concerns 'assigned' to them. Women, who had different duties, were endowed with 'the most amiable tendencies and affections implanted in human nature' instead. Dr James Fordyce, when examining *The Character and Conduct of the Female Sex*, indulgently asked 'gentlemen . . . to make more allowance for the imbecility of those who were formed to delight us', although William Alexander in his *History of Women* warned that female company so 'enervates and relaxes the mind' that it made *men* unfit for serious study.[17]

Furthermore, in contemporary literature of all kinds, women were not usually differentiated as men were but were constantly and 'confidently identified' as a group. As such they were generally depicted either as passive, submissive, domestic and deferential or as needing an education which would make them so. The written culture was ordered by men although, particularly in the later decades, a significant number of women became writers, especially of fiction.[18] Traditionally females had learnt moral and religious precepts and, according to social rank, either to run a household or work in one. Education in behaviour and relationships was always given a higher priority than intellectual development. There was little encouragement anywhere to study deeply or seriously. Standards were low and emphasis was placed primarily on those accomplishments which were seen by some as indispensable in civilized society. In 1813, in *Pride and Prejudice*, Jane Austen described these as 'a thorough knowledge of music, singing, dancing, drawing and the modern languages . . . a certain something in her air and manner of walking, the tone of her voice, her address and expressions'.[19] How far 'a thorough knowledge' of anything was normally given is debatable. Modern languages usually meant a little French, except for aristocrats who might well learn more. Drawing was an elegant accomplishment provided it was kept within 'proper' limits, preferably

17. Ibid., pp. 50–1. 18. Jones, *Women*, pp. 6–11.

19. Jane Austen, *Pride and Prejudice* (London, 1952), p. 46. Originally published 1813.

not landscapes or portraits. Such acquirements, together with ornamental needlework and crafts, reading and basic grammar, arithmetic and geography, became the hallmark of genteel female education and that of the lower middle ranks who had social aspirations. Gentry and aristocracy often preferred lower-ranking females to concentrate on useful household skills, but the additional accomplishments were valued as a means of catching husbands, the one most important career move in a woman's life, or at least, if it were necessary, as a way of earning a living by teaching others.

There were alternative educational opportunities. Public lectures were generally open to women and some, such as those on medicine and midwifery, were primarily intended for them. The new dictionaries and encyclopaedias of this period were written for both sexes. A more practical education was demonstrated in 1785 in the Quaker School for girls in York, which was to last until 1814. Its 519 pupils in those years included the most familiar Quaker names of the nineteenth century. The school was the brainchild of Esther Tuke, who with her husband William aimed principally at simplicity of manners and the religious improvement of the girls' minds mainly through a sympathetic atmosphere. The curriculum was very basic, with useful history and geography as extras. When Ann and Mary Darby from Coalbrookdale were there from 1791 to 1793, they made shirts and collars for their brothers and cut pens. Not a very academic diet, seemingly, although grammar was certainly thoroughly taught. Importantly, however, the proprietors were nominally nine women, all Quakers, who, with their husbands, met once a year in committee.[20] Another girls' school in Yorkshire which won a prestigious reputation was the Unitarian Richmall Mangnall's Crofton Hall, which had about 70 boarders and celebrated useful knowledge of a more academic kind. Both of these schools appealed particularly to the radical sects from which they had sprung.[21]

A girl's schooling did depend very much on the inclinations and expertise of her family. Only a minority attended school. Indeed, some were educated at home precisely because parents disliked not only the expense but also the frivolity of a boarding-school education. Critics of the latter went further and blamed the likely lack of decent facilities and overcrowded bedrooms as sources of disease of both body and mind. The fears expressed of immodesty, even vice, had much to do with a snobbish dread of social mixing, but it fed

20. H. Winifred Sturge, *The Mount School, York* (1931), pp. 3–30.

21. G.M. Ramsden, *A Record of the Kay Family of Bury, Lancashire* (Gift to MCO, 1979), pp. 52–3.

into the growing belief among the professional middle ranks that domestic education was morally and intellectually better than schooling for all children.[22]

Importantly, too, of the many women educated at home, a few received an excellent academic education, especially from their fathers. Anna Barbauld (née Aikin), Hannah More and Anna Seward, each of whom became a famous writer, all had fathers whose profession was teaching. More's father taught her Latin and mathematics, although he dropped the latter when her progress seemed too rapid to be 'feminine'! Seward learnt Milton's poetry at home at the age of three.[23]

It was women such as these, chiefly coming from the professional and mercantile middle class, that the wealthy widow Elizabeth Robinson Montagu encouraged to attend her London home where she held the first 'salon' in England. Those attending included Aikin, More, Fanny Burney, a famed novelist, and Hester Chapone, a brilliant conversationalist, teacher and Greek translator (although she publicly denied the need for women to read Greek). Such women had shown it was possible to win public recognition for their abilities and were glad to gain a unique opportunity to participate in equal intellectual discussion with men. Montagu's circle became known as the 'bluestockings', so called because some of the gentlemen who visited the salon wore ordinary blue, not dress, stockings. But although this salon, with two others, was more of a first, tentative assembly of individually distinguished females than anything like the nineteenth-century women's rights groups, it won no favour generally.[24] Indeed, to be a 'blue' became a term of abuse for a women.

Nevertheless, it is significant that women were pushing into the public world of writing. Their output and the significance of the growth of female readership was largely ignored by both literary and social historians until the 1980s and 1990s, but it has now been demonstrated that there was a substantial rise in novels written by women. Stereotypical notions of women's power of sympathetic sensitivity to individual situations could be utilized to justify their participation in this relatively new genre. This might lower the status

22. Browne, *Feminist Mind*, pp. 42–3; F. Musgrove, 'Middle-class families and schools, 1780–1889: interaction and exchange between institutions', in P.W. Musgrave (ed.), *Sociology, History and Education* (1970), pp. 117–25.

23. Mary R. Mahl and Helene Koon (eds), *The Female Spectator* (1977), pp. 258, 273, 297.

24. Ibid., p. 10; Cheryl Turner, *Living by the Pen: Women Writers in the Eighteenth Century* (1994), pp. 107–8.

of novel writing, yet in becoming writers women upset notions of their role and capabilities. Publishing might bring a liberating sense of individual achievement, financial reward and possibly public acclaim, but it might equally well stimulate public abuse, often of a nasty and virulent type, and ambivalent personal feelings.[25]

Awareness of the delicacy of their position prevented most female authors from deviating much from the common assumptions about gender roles and 'natural' characteristics which prevailed in society. Thus, fiction written and read by women often reinforced the private and inferior position that women were expected to keep. Nevertheless, some questioned women's position in society. For example, Fanny Burney, despite her outward correctness and propriety, seethed with rage at the dangerous ignorance enjoined upon women. *Evelina*, read enthusiastically by the reading public from the court downwards, has much to say about the disastrous education, or lack of it, given to girls.[26]

Similarly, in other literary genres which women either read or began to write in themselves – conduct manuals, devotional books, religious autobiographies and didactic books – the injustices women suffered were increasingly aired, although their weaknesses and 'natural' subordination were commonly accepted. On the other hand, a growing deference to women's supposed moral superiority actually restricted how women expressed themselves in public. This superiority was confined by class. Both male and female writers were of, and addressed themselves largely to, the middle and upper ranks of society, where female virtue was often maintained at the expense of that of women in the lower ranks. The domestic ideal of femininity, emphasizing morality and feeling, was to become the hallmark of middle-class identity in the nineteenth century and to enshrine gendered power relations.[27]

Educational reformers

Constant debate about educational reform for both sexes took place in this context of domesticity. The famous political economist Adam Smith, for example, preferred the basic premise of female education to that of males, because girls were taught only what was judged

25. Ibid., pp. 1–16; Jones, *Women*, pp. 6–12.

26. Julia Epstein, *The Iron Pen: Frances Burney and the Politics of Women's Writing* (Bristol, 1989), pp. 3–5, 14–16, 95, 99, 112, 140 and *passim*.

27. Browne, *Feminist Mind*, pp. 23–9; Hill, *Anthology*, p. 50; Leonore Davidoff and Catherine Hall, *Family Fortunes* (1987), *passim*.

necessary or useful for them to learn for their future roles in life. His somewhat optimistic opinion, whilst maintaining a specifically gendered view of education as what women needed to learn, also contained severe reservations about the useless or absurd education he believed boys received in their public institutions.[28]

Such comments were typical of the large literature on education from 1760. This stemmed partly from the influence of the 'Enlightenment', a term used loosely to cover the philosophic and cultural ferment of eighteenth-century Europe, in which rational understanding or human omniscience was the ultimate goal. Various political, religious and scientific developments had stimulated faith in human progress by using reason to understand humanity and its environment rather than resting solely on classical learning and Church theology. In the post-Newtonian world, reason signified the scientific method, both the deductive one of mathematics and the inductive empiricism of the natural sciences. Such an emphasis obviously had implications for education; but so did the belief of 'enlightened' thinkers that men and women were not innately sinful or weak but made so by their environment and circumstances. If the latter could be better understood by observation and experiment they could be changed. Such beliefs led to enthusiastic criticism of many time-honoured political, legal and religious institutions and an eager championing of science and scientific method by reformers. Both facets had within them the potential to revolutionize educational thinking and traditional assumptions about women.

Undoubtedly one of the most important educationists in this period was Jean-Jacques Rousseau, whose *La Nouvelle Héloïse* (1761) and *Émile* (1762) were as influential in England as they were in France and elsewhere. He radically posited that childhood was a separate phase of human development with its own rights and experience, that each child required suitable individual education and that parents and teachers should concentrate most on the growth of healthy bodies in children until the age of twelve. His belief that children learnt imperceptibly through the senses and therefore through experience was drawn from the *environmentalist theories of Locke and was thus in keeping with progressive educational reform in England, as was his stress that all humans are originally good but go wrong through faulty upbringing. Rousseau's insistence, however, that children should not be given an intellectual education until twelve, when they had reached the age of reason,

28. Hill, *Anthology*, p. 53.

was new. Before this age he wished boys, at least, to have a 'natural' education under the absolute authority of their tutor or parent and isolated, if possible, from others who might destroy their ignorant innocence. He deeply desired that they should learn to be useful, independent and self-sufficient, knowing the real importance of things, unlike the generality of the rich. He opposed the formal education of his day or any purely intellectual education divorced from moral and physical development.[29]

All these ideas, seemingly rational, yet accompanied by Rousseau's extreme sensibility and sentimentality, were heady stuff in an age of reason, stimulating a number of reformers to experiment eagerly with them. His ideals gave more respect both to children and to those in charge of them, and promised a new world once people had been educated without the false notions and superstitious and ignorant fancies of the past. In two notable experiments in England, however, by Richard Edgeworth and his friend Thomas Day, the success eagerly anticipated failed to materialize. What was significant here was that Day did not bring up the two female orphans he adopted as an educational experiment in the same way as Edgeworth's son. The latter was 'left as much as possible to the education of nature and of accident', but Day strictly controlled the education of Sabrina and Lucretia in keeping with Rousseau's depiction of different systems of education for males and females.[30] Over and above his obvious writing for an upper-class audience and his impracticalities, therefore, Rousseau's ideas posed problems.

Rousseau did urge that 'the earliest education is most important and it undoubtedly is woman's work', a pronouncement which gave a central role to women. He also insisted on the sexes being different with qualities appropriate to them rather than unequal in kind. Both convictions enabled women to seize his educational philosophy as life-enhancing. At the same time, however, the education Rousseau would give to Sophy, Émile's intended partner, was essentially different, seeming even to contradict Rousseau's basic principles at times. The mother was never more than a nurse acting under the instructions of the child's preceptor. Girls, although permitted to enjoy proper exercise and sensible clothes, were allowed these only as part of their central aims in life – to please men and to become a mother (and the latter as often as possible). They were

29. All references to these here are taken from W. Boyd (ed.), *The Minor Writings of Jean-Jacques Rousseau* (1962) and Jean-Jacques Rousseau, *Émile* (1974).

30. R.L. and Maria Edgeworth, *Memoirs of Richard Lowell Edgeworth Esq.*, 2 vols (1821), I, pp. 173–4, 208–21, 268–74, 332–5; II, pp. 92–7.

to have their minds cultivated only so far as this would enable their husbands to teach them. They were to be ruled by authority in all things, leaving matters of morality, understanding, religion, principles and abstract truths for men to judge. Rousseau claimed that women were naturally dependent, then took great pains to show how they might be made so. He stressed woman's virtue and modesty, yet encouraged her to use her 'natural' wit and cunning to defeat nature's object of making man the master. Extolling the reason of men, he wallowed in sickly sentimentalism and sensuality when it came to women. Easily unconventional in his radical views on male education, religion and politics, he remained bound by traditional patriarchal assumptions on women, asserting: 'The man should be strong and active; the woman should be weak and passive; the one must have both the power and the will; it is enough that the other should offer little resistance.'[31]

Sophy and her kind had the appeal of being simple, gentle and virtuous and of being free of the timorous fears associated with women – Day had dropped melting sealing-wax on Sabrina's arms and fired loaded pistols at her skirts to fortify her mind![32] Nevertheless, some writers, particularly women, were anxious to demonstrate Rousseau's sexist fallacies. Catherine Macaulay Graham, famed for her eight-volume, republican *History of England*, eagerly accepted in her 1790 *Letters on Education* that girls should have physical exercise and gain health instead of that 'feebleness of constitution' generally forced upon them by the constraints of a 'false idea of female excellence'. She utterly rejected, however, the idea that 'the education of females should be of an opposite kind to that of the male', courageously urging coeducation even in sports and play. She justified herself by arguing that since the same moral law governed all rational beings, 'true virtue in one sex must be equally so in the other'. To develop this, true wisdom not ignorance was needed, especially since our happiness in the next world might depend on the degree of perfection attained in this.[33]

Such religious themes were to be argued more cogently by rational dissenters, but Macaulay's rare plea for coeducation was to be taken up by another radical who, like her, was affected by both Rousseau and by the *empiricist psychology of Enlightenment rationalism. Mary Wollstonecraft's first novel, *Mary*, was much influenced by the 'sensibility' of Rousseau, but as she became more

31. Rousseau, *Émile*, pp. 322 and *passim*.
32. Dorothy Gardiner, *English Girlhood at School* (1929), p. 451.
33. Ibid., pp. 54, 455; Hill, *Anthology*, pp. 54, 249–50, 46.

aware of the trap into which women could fall if they gloried in Rousseau's stress on their feelings, she turned contemptuously against his ideas. In particular, she argued against founding women's conduct on different principles and aims from those of men so that they could not be considered as moral beings in the same way. Kept from useful and rational knowledge, how could women be expected to be 'virtuous and constant when reason is neither allowed to be the foundation of their virtue, nor truth the object of their inquiries?'[34] In her later book, *The Wrongs of Women*, Wollstonecraft explicitly denounced the excessive sensibility stimulated by Rousseau and the false morality which depicted female virtue as merely 'chastity, obedience and the forgiveness of injuries'.[35]

Wollstonecraft's increasing emphasis on reason exemplified her place in late eighteenth-century Enlightenment thinking. Influenced by rational dissenters, she became part of that literary circle centred around Joseph Johnson which had radical ideas for changing society in many ways. Johnson published thinkers such as William Godwin and many 'rational' educationists – for example, Erasmus Darwin, Maria and Richard Edgeworth, Joseph Priestley, John Aikin and Anna Barbauld.[36] All of these were attracted by the thought of children enjoying a useful scientific and rational education, appropriate to their age, where they learnt to think and experiment for themselves. Richard Edgeworth, for example, was closely involved in the education of his own nineteen children and both he and his eldest daughter Maria, who worked with him and became an author and educationist in her own right, used this experience to elucidate practical education for others. Their partial agreement with Rousseau did not include his strictures on female education, as Maria's first published work, *Letters for Literary Ladies*, in 1793, illustrated. Both Edgeworths wanted all women to cultivate fully their powers of reasoning and judgement. Thus they included many illustrations of girls making experiments and reasoning well in their prime book on education, *Practical Education*. They derided the popular wish for women to have only superficial knowledge which simply rendered women 'arrogant and ignorant'. A proper education from a mother or a governess of a 'sound, discriminating and enlarged understanding', however, would generate young women fit to marry worthy husbands, educate their own family, run the

34. Mary Wollstonecraft, *A Vindication of the Rights of Women* (Harmondsworth, 1975), pp. 189, 177–91; *Mary* and *The Wrongs of Woman* (Oxford, 1980).

35. Ibid., pp. 88–9, 98–9, 153, 193, 196–7.

36. Gerald Tyson, *Joseph Johnson: A Liberal Publisher* (Iowa, 1979), *passim*.

family finances, argue intelligently in company and, if necessary, become an able governess. The Edgeworths, indeed, were well ahead of their times in wanting teaching to become a 'liberal profession' for women. They even argued for pay of £300 a year, ten times the salary which might be expected even half a century later. Thus, despite the ways in which they urged women to adapt to the society in which they lived (and despite the way Richard Edgeworth ran through wives!), the Edgeworths both gave greater respect to women than was the norm and wanted women themselves to have greater self-esteem. This was instanced not least in their apology for usually using the masculine pronoun as a matter of grammatical convenience.[37]

The Edgeworths' friend, Erasmus Darwin, although more sentimental, agreed with their aims. Writing for his own two illegitimate daughters, who established a school in spacious surroundings in Ashbourne in 1792, he was attentive to the health and real understanding of girls and advocated using a wide range of teaching methods and visual aids. He also wished older girls to be taken by their parents to see the wonders of modern English arts and manufacturing – the cotton, pottery, iron and other industries of the midlands and the north, both for their own enjoyment and to make them more interesting future companions for men educated in the 'more useful . . . modern sciences'.[38]

The type of education which these rationalist educators (vaguely Anglican and atheist respectively) preferred for girls can be seen by examining how their friends, the Quaker manufacturer and chemist Samuel Galton and his wife, educated their daughter Mary. She enjoyed a wide education in science, classics, languages, literature, history and modern politics. A lonely child, she taught her magpie and parrot Latin! She learnt to carve wood, bind books, make charts and models and imbibed morals and religious principles from her mother. In 1802 she became a *Moravian and subsequently criticized her early education for its licence and its corrupting influences. She blamed her father for allowing her to read indiscriminately and believed that the various rationalists frequenting her home, including her friends the Unitarian Priestleys, were led astray by their over-dependence on human reason. She also came to believe

37. Maria and R.L. Edgeworth, *Practical Education*, 3 vols (1801), I, pp. 179, 258–60, 272–3, 258; III, pp. 1–26, 48, 53–5, 229, 272, 279–80, 300, 311; O. Elizabeth McWhorter Harden, *Maria Edgeworth's Art of Prose Fiction* (Monton, 1971), pp. 13–15.

38. Erasmus Darwin, *A Plan for the Conduct of Female Education in Boarding Schools* (Derby, 1797), *passim*.

that female education should be, albeit thorough and wide, essentially different from that of males who were to rule 'in the affairs of life'. Such views depended deeply on her religious acceptance of woman being 'the means of the fall' and Pauline edicts on female subservience.[39]

The differing emphases which Mary Galton (later Schimmelpennick) felt in education in different phases of her life are symptomatic of disparities felt between female educational reformers in the late eighteenth century. Many of her emphatic wishes are reminiscent of Hannah More, the evangelical reformer. More and her four sisters ran a school in the 1750s and 1760s in Bristol which had an advanced curriculum for the day, including Italian and Spanish. In the 1770s More became a celebrated playwright, but her growing adherence to evangelical Anglicanism turned her away from society life in London and, from the late 1780s, she and her sisters lived in Cheddar where they concentrated on the education of the poor.[40] More's religious convictions pervaded her views, helping her become both a conservative and a reformer. It was her assurance that the women of the upper classes did have great influence which led her to direct her *Strictures on the Modern System of Female Education* to them in 1799. Hating contemporary female education and the useless accomplishments which led to vanity and 'French' principles, More argued that it was 'unreasonable and unjust' to castigate women for becoming precisely the type of character for which it would be evident to an 'unprejudiced' bystander that the 'whole scope and tenor of their instruction had been systematically preparing them'.[41]

More preferred to educate 'not only rational, but accountable beings' who would be helpful wives of 'judgment' and 'discrimination'. Since the first lesson she counselled for girls, however, was 'to learn to distrust their own judgment . . . not to murmur at expostulation, but . . . be accustomed to expect and to endure opposition', it is difficult to know how such 'reasoning' beings were supposed to emerge. Yet despite her depiction of a compliant 'Sophy', Hannah More despised Rousseau and his sublimation of feeling over justice and duty. She both resented the corruptions of German literature, which held out to women 'the same allurement . . . which was employed by the original tempter of our first parent . . . Knowledge',

39. Christina C. Hankin (ed.), *The Life of Mary Anne Schimmelpennick* (1858), *passim.*
40. Mahl and Koon, *Female Spectator*, pp. 273–4.
41. Hannah More, *Strictures on the Modern System of Female Education*, 2 vols (1799), I, p. ix.

and disliked 'that vulgar system of education which rounded the little circle of female acquirements within the limits of the sampler and the receipt book'. Instead she recommended invigorating reading and a thorough diet of history and biography, geography and natural history, modern languages and, above all, lively and practical lessons in religious knowledge so that women should have a thorough understanding of the principles and morality of Christianity and be positively attracted to its 'truths'. Such would help women excel in their profession, that is, to be the daughters, wives, mothers and mistresses of families.[42]

In these ways Hannah More postulated an improved education for women, although, apart from religious truth, they were to be taught solely with their expected future familial role in mind. Religion itself frequently seemed to stimulate women's endorsement of their inferior function. Another evangelical reformer, Sarah Trimmer, had even found her moral inspiration in reading misogynist satire.[43] Nevertheless, neither was daunted from writing publicly. Indeed, Hannah More sold 2,000,000 of her *Cheap Repository Tracts* for the rural and urban working class in one year. But More could defend this work as Christianizing the poor. Her very emphasis on the moral and religious influence of women was to be important in the development of the concept of women as guardians of morality *provided* they kept to their separate sphere. This concept both inflated and limited woman's role, for increasingly greater respect for rational motherhood kept married women subservient as the father of their children was head of the household. Enormously influential herself, More deprecated women entering into religious or political controversy and chastised women like Mary Wollstonecraft as sources of corruption.[44] The unfortunate reputation, indeed, which Wollstonecraft had over generations was not just the product of what was seen as an unsavoury lifestyle but derived from what was castigated as an amoral philosophy by evangelicals.

Wollstonecraft applied to women the theory of rights, developed to such telling effect by the male French Revolutionaries. Her arguments for women to be seen equally with men as active and moral agents were persuasive but could have drawbacks if woman was perceived merely as an inferior model of man. Similar ideas were expounded also by Priscilla Wakefield and Mary Hays, the one a Quaker and the other a Unitarian. Mary Wollstonecraft moved freely

42. Ibid., pp. 42, 69, 97–8, 105, 162–230 and *passim*.
43. Browne, *Feminist Mind*, p. 22. 44. Turner, *Living by the Pen*, pp. 54–5, 140–1.

in Unitarian circles and so it might be concluded that all in Old Dissent proclaimed the rights of women. It was not so simple. Wakefield wanted a rational education for females but she also postulated that they had a different intelligence from men. Hays even dared to describe the sexual longings of women, yet harped on her disadvantages as an 'unlearned' woman when writing on political matters.[45] She did so write, however, unlike the Anglican Anna Seward of Lichfield, a prolific poet and author and a copious correspondent of many major literary figures, who would not contribute to the *Analytical Review* because her own 'stock of knowledge [was] so limited'.[46]

In some areas it was difficult to separate conservative and radical females. Anna Barbauld, Priscilla Wakefield, Maria Edgeworth, Hannah More and Mary Wollstonecraft were all pioneers in writing specifically for children, and all argued for a rational education for women in the 1790s. This, in itself, was a significant change from the early eighteenth century when it was debated whether women were capable of any rational thought at all. Mostly these women wrote about the education of the middle and upper ranks but they differed in how they wished women to use their education, despite the fact that they all, Wollstonecraft included, assumed that most women would marry and that caring for husband and family would be their primary duty. For example, Wollstonecraft and Wakefield wanted greater career opportunities for unmarried women. The more conservative, however, preferred spinsters to keep only to philanthropy and charitable education of the poor – an emphasis that was developed to considerable lengths in the nineteenth century.[47]

These significant shifts of emphasis were noticeable in the public campaigns against the slave trade in which women played a vital part. Here all women reformers could fight together, but essentially the educational philosophies they followed pulled them in different directions. Evangelical beliefs on female sensitivity were enlisted in a sentimental way in the anti-slavery cause, and More's fear of French Revolutionary doctrines undermined her hitherto outspoken opposition to slavery. Barbauld, on the other hand, delighted that freedom's victory in France might herald the same

45. Ibid., pp. 26, 73, 74–5, 78; Hill, *Anthology*, pp. 54–5; Hays, *Emma Courtney*, *passim*; Mary Hays, *Cursory Remarks on an Enquiry into the Expediency and Propriety of Public or Social Worship inscribed to Gilbert Wakefield BA* (1792), pp. 3–4, 21, 27.

46. Mahl and Koon, *Female Spectator*, pp. 297–8; Tyson, *Johnson*, p. 98.

47. Browne, *Feminist Mind*, pp. 158–9, 162, 166–7; Turner, *Living by the Pen*, pp. 54–6.

for 'poor Africans'. Wollstonecraft went further and likened the oppression of women to that of the slaves.[48] It could be said, indeed, that the conservative, evangelical philosophy had potentialities for the evolution of a responsible *feminine* role but it was the environmental, rationalist philosophy which held the seeds of women's rights. Both had repercussions for women's education and therefore opportunities, as the educational ideas and practice of the dynamic rationalist group, the Unitarians will demonstrate.

48. Clare Midgley, *Women against Slavery* (1992), pp. 14–17, 25–40; Grace Ellis, *A Memoir of Mrs Anne Laetitia Barbauld* (Boston, 1874), pp. 80–1, 109–11, 192, 223–4, 279–80.

CHAPTER TWO

Unitarianism and education

In the late eighteenth century Unitarians were leaders in promoting religious, political and social change. Education was the crucial agency of change leading to the growth of Unitarianism and giving its adherents the tools to forge the power they craved. Unitarians eagerly sought knowledge of all aspects of existence, optimistically certain that a millenary dawn of peace, brotherhood and justice could be won by the unrestrained pursuit and propagation of truth. They had their own distinct philosophy of education, most clearly established and expounded by Joseph Priestley but also developed by other Unitarian educationists. This chapter will explore this philosophy, its effects on the methods and subjects of teaching and learning advocated for both sexes, and the significant implications of these on gender issues.

Priestley, Hartley and the associationist psychology

Confronted by an educational system which neither satisfied their perceived needs or aspirations nor allowed them access to its higher prizes, Unitarians turned to their own alternative avenues of education. In higher education, like other dissenters, Unitarian men either went to Scotland or the University of Leyden in Holland, or attended dissenting academies. The latter had been established since 1662 to educate those who were averse to the ethos of Oxford and Cambridge or who were denied a degree at Cambridge or even matriculation at Oxford because, in conscience, they could not subscribe to the Thirty-nine Articles of the Church of England. At first these academies were very small, private institutions concentrating on providing dissent with an educated ministry, but by 1760 some had dropped the traditional university method of teaching in Latin and had developed their curriculum by adding more modern studies and stimulating open questioning of every issue. Like the universities, these academies took students from the age of sixteen, and the more progressive included laymen as well as intending ministers. From mid-century a few academies were run by governing boards rather than individual owners and these grew in staff, students and learning, offering a dynamic challenge to the hierarchical and apparently moribund universities.

The most outstanding of the academies was Warrington, which from 1757 to 1786 attracted a galaxy of brilliant staff and students. Many previous academies had not survived the retirement or death of their owners. Warrington, therefore, had been established as a deliberate attempt to maintain a permanent college, resting on secure financial foundations with backing from subscribers principally from the north-west, Birmingham and London. The aims of the academy were to educate ministers who would be free to follow their own search for truth and to educate laymen for the professions and commercial life in the 'useful branches of literature' and the 'true principles of religious liberty, of which principles they must, in future life, be the supporters'.[1]

In 1761, Joseph Priestley was invited to become tutor in languages and belles-lettres (literature). A mild, gentle, private man but an acerbic public polemicist, he had already been running a school for boys and girls where he had successfully introduced lessons in both practical science and modern history. He had also begun the long line of educational works based on his own teaching which helped so brilliantly to redress the dearth of suitable textbooks. Inspired by the most progressive academies, his wide-ranging lectures at Warrington, particularly on history and law, furthered a broadening of the curriculum in an already innovative institution. His personal preference was for science and he gave some lectures on anatomy. From his activities at Warrington emerged an incredible range of publications, including the *Chart of History* which earned him an LL D from the University of Edinburgh and *A History of Electricity* which gained him a fellowship from the Royal Society. He remained a fluent publicist of educational reform

1. William Turner, *Warrington Academy, 1757–86* (Warrington, 1957; first printed in *The Monthly Repository*, 1813–15, vols VIII, IX, X), p. 4.

throughout the following years when he became the leading figure in English pneumatic chemistry, a formidable adversary in religious debate and a widely feared protagonist for civil and religious liberties. He ardently believed education was fundamental to these other issues. In later years, from 1791 to 1795, Priestley delivered his Warrington lectures on chemistry and history at the New College, Hackney, one of Warrington's two successors. Priestley was no mere theorist in education, therefore.

Priestley's educational writings were also influenced, however, by his studies in rationalist philosophy, particularly that concerning the working of the human mind. John Locke had influenced most dissenting educationists of the eighteenth century, but Priestley went further. He was absorbed by David Hartley's *Observations on Man*, which he reissued in condensed form and developed to become the cornerstone of Unitarian educational thought in the eighteenth and early nineteenth centuries. Like other eighteenth-century thinkers, he hoped that scientific methods used on philosophical questions would lead to the generation of a few basic, wide-ranging general laws which would clear a path through ignorance, superstition, confusion and unfounded authority as they had done in Newtonian physics. Thus he welcomed Hartley's attempt to use Newtonian techniques to formulate a succinct and clear theory of the mind. The result was a full *associationist psychology which argued that all complex or 'intellectual' ideas arise from simple ones, which, in turn, 'arise from the impressions made by external objects upon the several parts of our bodies'. Hartley postulated a physiological basis to this in line with empirically observed facts,[2] but Priestley, although excited by such a theory, decided that it might discourage people from recognizing the value of Hartley's theory of the human mind and so left out all reference to it in the version he publicized.

Hartley's thesis had profound implications for education. He argued that impressions give rise to sensations which, if often repeated, stimulate ideas. Thence, any series of sensations, if associated with each other sufficiently, often have such 'power over the corresponding ideas . . . that any one of the sensations when impressed alone, shall be able to excite in the mind the ideas of the rest'. Such associations of ideas, particularly if further associated with pleasure or pain, would combine and coalesce into complex intellectual ideas and abstractions until the original simple ideas or

2. David Hartley, *Observations on Man*, 2 vols (New York, 1976) I, pp. 65, iv, 7–72, 416.

sensations could be forgotten. For instance, many human prejudices, customs and emotional feelings arose in such a way. If, however, such complex ideas could, again through association, be analysed into their simple component parts, then educators could take care that only good associations would be built up.[3] Priestley thus eagerly welcomed this analysis of complex ideas whereby 'our external senses furnish the materials of all the ideas of which we are ever possessed'. It was, he said, environment and 'the influence of such circumstances as [they had] actually been exposed to' which made people what they were and therefore careful education from birth was all-important for 'children may be formed or moulded as we pleased'.[4] All vice and virtue arose from this basic law of association. Moral, religious and intellectual development, even perfection, therefore could be realized, but only through reflection, experience and extensive intellectual education, and not through innate cause or divine intervention. Through association, intellectual, physical and moral education became interdependent, so a healthy body was important too (although 'muscular habits' were not conducive to sensibility of mind!).[5]

The inference of this educational philosophy was egalitarian: all people of both sexes should receive the same, careful, wide education from well-educated parents and teachers who fully understood the law of association themselves. Since it was education not sex which made people what they were, women were not, as usually assumed, inferior in mental capacity. Priestley praised the Rev. Robert Robinson of Cambridge, for example, who, eschewing a 'vulgar and debasing prejudice (that women, being designed for domestic cares, should be taught nothing beyond them)', gave his daughters the same extensive education in classics, modern languages, mathematics and science as his sons. Women, indeed, he said, should be given 'the highest [education] of which they were capable . . . the learned and the modern languages . . . mathematics and philosophy. Certainly, the minds of women are capable of the same improvement and the same furniture as those of men.'[6]

3. Ibid., I, pp. i–ii, 65, 75, 81, 368.

4. Joseph Priestley, 'Introductory essays to Hartley's theory of the human mind' (1790), *The Theological and Miscellaneous Works of Joseph Priestley*, ed. J.T. Rutt, 25 vols (1817–31), III, p. 184; 'The doctrine of philosophic necessity illustrated' (1782), III, p. 521.

5. Priestley, 'Preface and dedication to heads of lectures on a course of experimental philosophy' (1794), *Works*, XXV, p. 389; 'Philosophic necessity' (1782), p. 515.

6. Priestley, 'Reflections on death' (1790), *Works*, XV, p. 419.

Besides, since morality and virtue were improved by intellectual culture, women had as much right to the latter as men. Priestley was certain that where women were utterly subservient and without education they would become degraded creatures unworthy of trust. But to be respected in a happy marriage it was vital for husband and wife to be equally educated or the man would truly be marrying 'beneath himself'. Well-educated women would be admirable influences on men, good teachers of others and able to maintain themselves respectably if necessary.[7]

Thus Priestley preferred a similar education for both sexes. This type of education was new, for the law of association affected the curriculum and methods of teaching. Since for Priestley 'the most effectual discipline of the mind' was experience, those subjects whose content or methods were based on experience and inductive reasoning were favoured. In human sciences history was the outstanding example of this,[8] and his introduction of modern history as an academic discipline as opposed to ancient history in higher education was a revolutionary innovation. Similarly, the methods of study of the physical sciences delighted Priestley, the leading English chemist of the time, and the increase in scientific knowledge seemed to presage 'the security and happiness of mankind'. With sublime optimism he concluded that both science and history proved that Divine providence was 'gradually conducting things to a more perfect and glorious state'.[9] He thus encouraged experimental science especially, and stressed the need for a scientific investigation and questioning of the scriptures.[10]

Eager to promote clear knowledge, Priestley emphasized that all studies should be adapted to the age and the capacity of the learner. He urged teachers to illustrate and exemplify their ideas and to use systematic methods and visual aids as he did himself, for example, in his own *Chart(s) of History* and *Biography*. Indeed, he applied his science of psychology to all subjects. In history he debated with students the multifarious kinds of sources which historians use; in science, he insisted on experiment as the key to understanding and clear thinking; in English he proved associationism to be the basis

7. Ibid.; Priestley, 'A comparison of the institution of Moses, with those of the Hindoos and other nations' (1799), *Works*, XVII, p. 230; 'Miscellaneous observations relating to education' (1780), XXV, pp. 137–8, 147–8, 166–79.

8. Priestley, Lectures on history and general policy (Philadelphia, 1803), *Works*, XXIV, pp. 29 and *passim*.

9. Priestley, 'The history and present state of electricity, with original experiments' (1767), *Works*, XXV, p. 342.

10. Priestley, 'Experimental philosophy', p. 385.

of good speaking, writing and, indeed, teaching, and to be influential in the formation of imagination and taste. His own teaching and writings helped the acceptance of English and its literature as an academic subject in both schools and academies. In this he was emulated by two other tutors at Warrington, the deeply loved Dr John Aikin, whose attractive teaching of English literature first established it as a subject in its own right in higher education, and William Enfield, whose scholarship in English literature was illustrated by his elegant, repeatedly published anthology *The Speaker.*[11]

Priestley's motivation in modernizing the curriculum came from his perception of knowledge as power – power both to create virtuous beings and to control the forces of nature for good. Like Hartley, his acceptance that all intellectual, affective and moral capacities were reducible to external impressions, thereafter developed by association, led him to believe that everything had a cause traceable to a first cause or God, a chain of cause and effect terminating in the greatest good of the universe. This *necessarianism, as it was termed, was not fatalism – people could make conscious choices to join the chain of causes leading to unbounded knowledge, pure happiness, the love of God and perfect virtue, but they needed correct nurture, education and environment to allow the right associations to develop.[12] Thus Priestley's psychological and educational philosophy dovetailed with his primary preoccupations as a Unitarian minister.

Priestley's philosophy also matched his perception of the needs of that rising industrial and commercial middle class in which most of the enterprising Unitarians were found. He dismissed as useless public distinctions originating from force, superstition or hereditary factors, sure that only those based on merit and good understandings were beneficial. Happily convinced that it was an era of dramatic change and progress for humanity, he exhorted the students of Hackney College to help obtain a 'flourishing state of science, arts, manufactures and commerce; [and] everything that makes nations secure and happy'.[13]

11. Priestley, 'A course of lectures on oratory and criticism' (1777), *Works,* XXIII, p. 259; 'Miscellaneous observations', p. 219; 'History', pp. 54–202, 463–83; *A Familiar Introduction to the Study of Electricity* (1769), p. 10; 'Oratory'; pp. 257–482; 'The rudiments of English grammar' (1798), XXIII, pp. 3–118; Turner, *Warrington,* pp. 16–17, 35–40.

12. Hartley, *Observations,* I, pp. 80–3, 371–403, 416–99, 511–12; II, pp. 5–337; Priestley, 'Introductory essays', pp. 184–8; 'Philosophic necessity', pp. 146–51, 221, 244–9, 447–540.

13. Priestley, 'Oratory', p. 255; 'The proper objects of education in the present state of the world' (1791a), *Works,* XV, p. 434.

For such reasons Priestley published his seminal educational treatise, *An Essay on a Course of Liberal Education for Civil and Active Life*, in 1780 explicitly to outline a liberal education suitable for the modern world and for those who he believed should be its leaders. He included with this his *Course of Lectures on the Study of History*, eager to make plain his views on the place of economic activity in society, as well as every aspect of civil government including law and the principles of commerce and taxation. The latter subjects were usually omitted from a gentleman's or 'liberal' education because trade and commerce were seen as activities of the lower orders of society. Science too was denoted as merely a hobby for amateurs and a study for dissenters and for classes below the rank of 'gentlemen'. But Priestley's friends and colleagues were forging Britain into the first modern industrial nation. His own brother-in-law was 'iron-mad' Wilkinson, whose accurate cylinders enabled the Boulton and Watt steam engine to be so successful. Priestley, positive that future leaders would come from those who had mastered the sources of knowledge which had changed the world, was convinced of Britain's need to modernize higher education. He emphasized the very scientific and industrial interests scorned in traditional education, as the just basis of a prosperous meritocracy. He saw uses in the classics and pure mathematics so important at Oxford and Cambridge. Yet, whereas at the universities these were prized almost exclusively because they were seen as liberal subjects which generally broadened the human mind and brought all its facets into play, Priestley upheld science as providing the liberalizing and humanizing role in education. For him, a 'truly liberal education' needed literary *and* scientific excellence, accompanied, of course, by a proper moral development.[14]

Indeed, all Priestley's reforms at Warrington, including his upgrading of the teaching of modern languages and encouragement of elocution lessons, stemmed from his desire for rational thought and religion and his ardent wish to produce enlightened leaders of the middle class whose culture and status they would raise. He argued that, 'In fact it is *knowledge* that finally governs mankind, and *power*, though ever so refractory, must at length yield to it.' He did not admire the hereditary aristocracy and condemned their public schools as immoral and their universities as repressive. In contrast he depicted middle-class dissenting academies as liberal

14. Priestley, 'Miscellaneous observations', pp. 185–95, 206–18, *passim*; 'History', pp. 5, 22, 311–17, 403–15, 471–5; 'Electricity', p. 345; 'Experimental philosophy', p. 389; 'Proper objects', pp. 420–1; *Autobiography*, pp. 88–9.

and enlightened, open to all, less expensive, teaching liberal principles in both religion and politics and resembling 'rivers, which taking their natural course, fertilise a whole country', unlike the universities – 'pools of stagnant water . . . offensive to the neighbourhood' and inculcating 'slavish and illiberal' principles.[15] These were hardly sentiments likely to induce admiration from members of England's most prestigious institutions.

Priestley's involvement in education, therefore, was an integral part of his major preoccupations. A liberal and useful education based on the principles and methods of Hartleyan psychology served the interests both of rational religion and of the new industrial and commercial classes. Priestley tried to popularize his ideas through his prolific writings, by making difficult subjects like electricity understandable and by making the sources of knowledge more accessible. For example, he promoted libraries in both Leeds and Birmingham. He was not alone in his ideals. His friends the Edgeworths, Erasmus Darwin and Thomas Day shared his stress on the supreme importance of environment and upbringing, the interdependence of intellectual, moral and physical education and active methods of learning. Thomas Day differed from them on women's role, but his fictional attacks on the selfish values of the arrogant, idle, dependent rich delighted them, for they all aimed at imbuing the middle class generally with rational values of humanity and usefulness and enabling it to give enlightened leadership to society. None were as radical as Unitarians in politics, however, and they differed over religious education, which Priestley's friends left to a similarly rational but secular morality.[16] Two other leading (though hardly popular) rational educationists of the day, Mary Wollstonecraft and David Williams, a *Deist, were much closer to Unitarianism and in essential agreement with its principles of education.

Unitarianism and associationism

It was the Unitarians as a group who were most influenced and inspired by Priestley, not least because he typified as well as led their enthusiasm for education and 'Enlightenment' optimism. He

15. Priestley, 'Proper objects', pp. 439, 425, 431; 'Miscellaneous observations', pp. 50–2, 111–19; 'A letter to the Right Honorable William Pitt' (1787), *Works*, XIX, p. 128.

16. Thomas Day, *The History of Sandford and Merton*, 2 vols (1812 edn; 1st edn 3 vols, 1783–89), *passim*; R.E. Schofield, *The Lunar Society of Birmingham* (Oxford, 1963), pp. 212 ff.

was successful in the first place in winning their adherence to associationism. So close became the relationship between Hartleyan philosophy and Unitarianism at this time that acceptance of the former was often a prime factor in leading to conversion to the latter. This was seen when both Thomas Belsham and his students at Daventry Academy, from 1781 to 1789, were unable to withstand the logic of Belsham's teaching on Hartley and became enthusiastic Unitarians. Belsham subsequently became divinity tutor at New College, Hackney.[17] Other tutors like Hugh Worthington recognized that goodness depended upon knowledge. It was chiefly in the progressive academies that Hartley's works were studied and his philosophy eagerly adopted, but others like Catherine Cappe, a Unitarian social worker, were similarly convinced.[18]

Conversely, when some Unitarians like William Hazlitt and Samuel Taylor Coleridge rejected Hartley's philosophy they turned away from Unitarianism too.[19] On the other hand, even Arian Unitarians who accepted an 'original difference of minds' contended that 'the far deeper and bolder lines of distinction are drawn by early culture', and some like Richard Price who retained a belief in intuitive morality were still counted in the Unitarian camp.[20] The physician Dr John Aikin, who had taught at Warrington for twelve years, wrote, like his sister Anna Barbauld, many educational books for children under sixteen, an age group mentioned less by Priestley. He drew an analogy between bodily and mental disease, showing how bad characters are almost inevitably created out of bad conditions, whether those of the poverty-stricken area of St Giles in London or those of the rich boy, flattered and indulged through a public school, university and grand tour education, nurtured on guns and hounds and allowed to be the uncontrolled master of an estate and probably thus a 'low-minded, brutal, tyrannical debauchee'. The only means of effecting a change, argued this ardent middle-class reformer, would be to alter the habits by means as powerful

17. Thomas Belsham, *Memoirs of the Late Rev. Theophilus Lindsey* (1873; 1st edn 1812), pp. 190–5, 301; John Williams, *Memoirs of the Late Rev. Thomas Belsham* (1833), pp. 244–7 ff.

18. Hugh Worthington, *A Sermon . . . to the Supporters of a New Academic Institution among Protestant Dissenters* (6 May 1789), pp. 15–17; Catherine Cappe, *Memoirs of the Life of the Late Mrs Catherine Cappe* (1822), pp. 158–60, 360–1, 456–8.

19. William Hazlitt, 'Remarks on the system of Hartley and Helvetius', *Complete Works*, 21 vols (1930), I, pp. 65–6, 73 and *passim*; Samuel Taylor Coleridge, 'Biographia Literaria', in D.A. Stauffer (ed.), *Selected Poetry and Prose of Coleridge* (New York, 1951), pp. 168 and *passim*.

20. Thomas Barnes, *A Discourse Delivered at the Commencement of the Manchester Academy* (14 Sept. 1786), pp. 6–7; Martin Fitzpatrick, 'Rational dissent and the Enlightenment', *Faith and Freedom* (Summer 1985), 38, part 2, no. 113, p. 87.

and as long contrived as the first. His sister, Anna Barbauld, in her very popular *Hymns in Prose for Children*, used association to inculcate religious habits and piety through pleasurable play on the imagination and feelings. She further emphasized that wisdom could only come from a combination of learning and goodness. The Aikins, like some other Unitarians, did not deny some innate characteristics, but they stressed how these were modified by association and the habits and principles this induces.[21]

Lant Carpenter, early in his teaching career, eagerly endorsed the modern curriculum promoted by Unitarians. He loved both classics and science but thought mental philosophy the highest study of all, essential for developing one's own intellect and heart and for knowing how to form the mental and moral characteristics of others. For such reasons Carpenter was particularly concerned that females should know Hartleyan psychology.[22] This was interesting because some Unitarians were most concerned in enlightening young men in the 'hazardous' period between leaving home and settling down. Nevertheless, the principles of education and all the books written for those under sixteen were directed at both sexes. This was true also of teaching. For instance, although open-mindedness in belief was the avowed intention, as the Rev. Andrew Kippis said, rational religion had to depend on knowledge and understanding. Much attention was thus given to the education in rational religion of different age groups in congregations, as for example that of Newcastle upon Tyne. Priestley, who particularly promoted such teaching in his congregations in Leeds, Birmingham and London, had special evening classes for young men and women between eighteen and thirty to study religious history, theology and disputed questions in Christianity. Timothy Kenrick only worried that some 'moral obligations' which young men ought to learn would be neglected before a mixed audience. Lant Carpenter, however, had an extra vestry built for him at Exeter to lecture to young men and women.[23]

21. John Aikin, *Letters from a Father to his Son* (1793), pp. 174–85; 'Thoughts on the Formation of Character', in Lucy Aikin (ed.), *Memoir of John Aikin MD*, 2 vols (1823), II, pp. 362–86; Anna Laetitia Barbauld, *Hymns in Prose for Children* (1819), p. v; Philip le Breton (ed.), *Memoir, Miscellanies and Letters of the Late Lucy Aikin* (1864), pp. 21–8.

22. *MR* (1806), I, pp. 291–2, 354–7; (1811), VI, pp. 145–8, 275–80, 532–7.

23. Andrew Kippis, *A Sermon . . . on the Occasion of a New Academical Institution among Protestant Dissenters* (Apr. 1786), pp. 1, 11, 29–32; William Turner, *A Short Sketch of the History of Protestant Nonconformity and of the Society assembling in Hanover Square, Newcastle* (Newcastle upon Tyne, 1811), pp. 33–6; Priestley, 'A particular attention to the instruction of the young', (1791) *Works*, XV, pp. 458–74, 581–4; Russell Carpenter, *A Short Account of the Rev. Lant Carpenter LL.D*, 2 vols (Bristol, 1848), I, p. 22.

Thus for Unitarians it was important for the young of both sexes to be educated in a particular view of rational religion and society. Furthermore, the knowledge desired did not come from a cramming of facts, as this contradicted associationist theories. It was gathered by a careful education through example, a good home and rational and useful studies. This hopefully would produce an enlightened middle class, humane, tolerant, benevolent, useful, high-minded, pure, self-controlled and with a deep sense of public spirit.

A new education for both sexes

Unitarians' adherence to associationism, together with their religious and political objectives, greatly affected their educational curriculum. They shared Priestley's attitude of valuing classics as a basic subject, especially for intending clergy and professional men, but believed that they should only be part of learning. The liberal dissenting academies after 1780 also gave less prominence to classics than it received in grammar schools and universities, much to the despair of Gilbert Wakefield, who taught classics at both Warrington and Hackney after leaving Anglicanism and Cambridge. At Manchester Academy in 1795, the classical tutor himself, William Stevenson, the father of Elizabeth Gaskell, wrote a pamphlet entitled *Remarks on the Very Inferior Utility of Classical Learning.*[24]

Yet John Aikin, the revered classics and then divinity tutor at Warrington from 1758 to 1780, was an eminent classical scholar, as were many of his students, including his son John, who delighted in modern Latin authors. Significantly, however, the latter referred to Alexander the Great as a robber and Achilles as a brute in the popular book for children he wrote with his sister Anna.[25] She in turn thought that the French Revolution would inspire a revolution in education

> and particularly be the ruin of classical learning, the importance of which must be lessening every day; while the other sciences, particularly that of politics and government must rise in value, afford an immediate introduction to active life, and be necessary in some

24. John Aikin, *Letters*, pp. 4–6, 18, 27–48; Gilbert Wakefield, *Memoirs*, 2 vols (1792), I, pp. 71–8, 198, 203–7, 337–40, 348–75; Herbert McLachlan, *English Education under the Test Acts* (Manchester, 1931), pp. 159, 168, 204–10, 233, 240, 242, 256–7.

25. J. Aikin and Mrs Barbauld, *Evenings at Home* (Edinburgh, 1868; 1st edn 1793), pp. 116–18, 266–8.

> degree to everybody. All the kindred studies of the cloister must sink, and we shall live no longer on the lean relics of antiquity.[26]

Mrs Barbauld's own writings were peppered with classical allusions, nevertheless, and she was sure that the classics were the foundation of learning and culture.[27] The point was that Unitarians wanted the best of traditional education whilst reforming the latter to suit the needs of the present times. The long agonizing of Josiah Wedgwood over his sons' education illustrates this central point. Wedgwood made much use of classical art in his pottery. He wanted his sons to have good grammar and classical knowledge to give them polish in society, but since they could gain these from learning their own language and reading 'excellent translations' he feared that for future businessmen to spend too much time on classics could be a case of 'diamonds' being 'too dearly purchased'. In the end he did have them taught Latin and the eldest learnt Greek. Appropriately enough, none of his sons remained in business.[28]

In the equally thriving industrial Greg family of Styal in Cheshire, it was the mother Hannah who insisted that all her children, girls as well as boys, had one of the best liberal dissenting educations. She thus sent them to a private school run by the Rev. James Tayler in Nottingham where Greek and Latin were a staple part of the curriculum – much to the delight of Tayler's son John. Later an excellent Latinist, he became a Unitarian minister and scholar. He and his father debated their interests with the ex-pupils Robert Hyde Greg and Samuel Robinson, to whom John wrote youthful letters full of classical allusions and questions such as whether Troy had ever existed. Robinson and Greg were to become two of the biggest cotton manufacturers of the day, with factories in Dukinfield and Styal respectively. Robinson later produced five books on Persian poetry whilst Greg wrote articles on Greece. After Nottingham, Hannah Greg had sent the boys on to Lant Carpenter's school in Exeter, where they would have continued with an excellent education in classics alongside modern subjects including science. The girls had excellent teachers at home.[29]

26. Lucy Aikin (ed.), *The Works of Anna Laetitia Barbauld*, 2 vols (1825), II, pp. 158–9.

27. Anna Laetitia Barbauld, *A Legacy for Young Ladies* (1826), pp. 73–94.

28. J.W. Wedgwood, *Letters of Josiah Wedgwood 1771–1780*, 2 vols (1903), II, pp. 542, 549–50, 562.

29. Peter Spencer, *A Portrait of Samuel Greg* (Styal, 1982), pp. 25–8; J.H. Thom (ed.), *Letters Embracing his Life of John James Tayler BA*, 2 vols (1872), I, pp. 1–8; *DNB* (1897), XLIX, p. 44; Mary B. Rose, *The Gregs of Quarry Bank Mill* (Cambridge, 1986), pp. 47–9.

Perhaps it was in this area of classical education more than any other that the complexities of Unitarian thinking on gender emerge. The dilemmas they experienced in working out how much time future middle-class 'gentlemen' should spend on the classics had an extra dimension when they considered 'gentlewomen'. Classical studies comprised the education *par excellence* which both marked out society's élite from the rest and further differentiated well-educated gentlemen from their ladies. Hannah More's father stopped her learning Latin when he realized how good she was at it, and even Dr Aikin had been dubious at first about teaching Anna the 'unfeminine branches of knowledge'.[30] The important point, however, is that he did and she, in turn, supported girls with the time and the opportunity to learn Latin, although she considered Greek took too much time. Her niece, Lucy Aikin, and girls such as Louisa Kay learnt Latin. Arthur Aikin later said of his sister-in-law, Anne, that she learnt classics from her father Gilbert Wakefield not to be ostentatious but to acquire 'refined taste' and the 'high principles' inculcated by the 'great ethical writers of the ancient world'.[31]

In 1815, when the Unitarian schoolteacher John Morell published his book *Reasons for the Classical Education of Children of both Sexes*, the reviewer in the Unitarian *Monthly Repository* stressed the importance of girls gaining such a deep knowledge of language and thus being enabled to develop and activate their mental powers. The reviewer was glad that Morell paid attention to the usually neglected subject of female education and considered that edited editions would overcome expected objections to the immorality of the classics not only for girls but also for boys. Furthermore, the reviewer added, such an education would hasten the time when women were rightly valued by 'generous and enlightened' men and became true rational helpmeets. The sting, however, was in the tail. Such a woman, apparently, would be happy to employ her talents as the 'mainspring of order and happiness in her little community', and would not seek to be 'the rival of man in power and worldly influence'.[32]

In modern languages priorities were usually changed. Here the Unitarians were modern in stressing the need for males to learn these as an integral part of a gentleman's education. Wedgwood

30. Shirley Nelson Kersey, *Classics in the Education of Girls and Women* (1981), p. 204; Lucy Aikin, *Anna Barbauld*, I, pp. vi–vii.

31. Barbauld, *Legacy*, pp. 45–6; le Breton, *Lucy Aikin*, p. xix; Louisa Potter, 'Eighty years ago: a Manchester lady's memories', *Manchester Guardian* (6 Aug. 1896); *Inquirer* (1821), pp. 623–4.

32. *MR* (1815), X, pp. 242–4.

certainly showed more confidence in all his children, both boys and girls, learning French.[33] Priestley, like friends of his in the Lunar Society, sent his sons, destined to be businessmen, to the Continent to learn modern languages (and science).[34] Coleridge, in his somewhat misty way, and later Carlyle, became famous for diffusing German thought in England, but it was the Unitarians William Taylor and Henry Crabb Robinson who had spearheaded the actual introduction of German works into England from the 1790s and 1800s. Anna Barbauld, admired by both of these men, argued that French was as necessary to a girl as Latin was to her brother. She preferred reading it to the usual emphasis on speaking it, however, unless the learner was going to spend some time in France. Once French was learnt she thought Italian would be easy. Her niece Lucy followed her in being proficient in both.[35] Italian was enjoyed and promoted by a number of Unitarians, especially William Roscoe, whose book *The Life of Lorenzo de Medici* celebrated an earlier period of humanist and commercial endeavour.[36] In the academies which Unitarian men largely attended, Hackney offered the option of French and modern languages, Warrington those of French and Italian. Manchester Academy was definitely teaching modern languages from 1801 to 1802 and certainly intended to from 1786.[37]

But it was education in their own language which Unitarians stressed. Anna Barbauld, a well-known poet herself, her brother John Aikin and his daughter Lucy all produced books for young people introducing them to English poetry and prose. Barbauld, editor in 1811 of *The Female Speaker*, was certain that good writing and speaking could best be learnt through studying one's own language. She proved this not only in her own brilliant essays but also in her teaching at the boys' school which she ran with her husband. John Aikin blended experimental and natural sciences and literature together in his books in a way which is still rare in an English classroom, but his own educational philosophy drew from both and he wished children to perceive the 'easy' connection between them. A number of Unitarians either used Priestley's works or, like Thomas Bowen, master of an academy in Walsall, brought out their own books to help the teaching of English grammar and literature.[38]

33. Wedgwood, *Wedgwood*, II, pp. 561–3.

34. A.H.G. Armytage, 'The Lunar Society and its contributions to education', *University of Birmingham Historical Journal* (1967/68), 5, p. 65.

35. Barbauld, *Legacy*, pp. 47–50; le Breton, *Lucy Aikin*, p. xix.

36. G. Chandler, *William Roscoe of Liverpool* (1953), pp. xxxiii, 88, 93–4, 97.

37. McLachlan, *English Education*, pp. 157, 211, 219; MCO, *Prospectus, Manchester Academy* (22 Feb. 1786), p. 2; G.M. Ditchfield, 'The Early History of Manchester College', *THSLC* (1972), pp. 123, 92.

The Unitarians' predisposition towards writing and literature rather than music or art bears out Noel Annan's thesis on the small, interrelated intellectual aristocracy of late eighteenth- and nineteenth-century England whose 'good manners appeared in their prose' but whose 'response to art was at best uncertain'. This proposition was interesting particularly with regard to female education. In the eyes of reforming educationists art as a mere accomplishment often played far too large a part in the education of upper- and middle-class girls and it appears to have featured little in the education of most of the Unitarians studied. On the other hand the wealthy Sukey Wedgwood had drawing lessons along with more academic work, whilst Jane Marcet put the thorough artistic training she had enjoyed to excellent use in the clear line drawings of apparatus which accompanied her *Conversations on Chemistry*. A similar cross-fertilization of subjects was seen when Josiah Wedgwood superbly fused industry, science and art and patronized the sculptors Roubiliac and Flaxman while the Derby painter Joseph Wright romanticized science and industry in his paintings.[39]

Unitarians were showing the world a new culture. In the same way, not only did they teach and write about modern history but their emphasis was also different from the norm. John Aikin's ten-volume *General Biography* was chiefly devoted to scientists, inventors, philosophers and reformers rather than the usual generals, rulers and politicians. In all his books he upheld as heroes those who achieve through their own ability and self-control, not those called great because of birth or conquest. He publicly admired his friend John Howard, the prison reformer, and argued: 'How much higher, as an intelligent being, does a Brindley rank, directing the complex machinery of a canal, which he himself has invented, than an Alexander at the head of his army . . .'[40]

History was taught at Warrington, Hackney, Exeter and Manchester Academies,[41] but Unitarian educationists showed their interest in modern affairs as much by their active participation. Anna Barbauld's statement, for example, that history had many lessons for those

38. Lucy Aikin, *Barbauld*, pp. xxxvi–xxxvii, xxxix–xlii, xlix–li, xliv; McLachlan, *English Education*, p. 123; A.P.F. Sell, 'The social and literary contribution of three Unitarian ministers in nineteenth century Walsall', *TUHS* (Oct. 1973), p. 81.

39. N.G. Annan, 'The intellectual aristocracy', in J.H. Plumb (ed.), *Studies in Social History* (1955), 241–87; Wedgwood, *Wedgwood*, II, p. 433; Willie Henderson, 'Marcet's *Conversations on Political Economy*: a new interpretation', *HofE* (1994), 23, no. 4, p. 425.

40. Lucy Aikin, *John Aikin*, p. 194; J. Aikin and Mrs Barbauld, *Evenings*, pp. 266–8, 255–8, 293–6.

41. McLachlan, *English Education*, pp. 215, 217–18, 233, 248, 251, 257.

'whose actions may one day become the objects of it' was very pertinent. Such an emphasis did not mean that history was seen as a male subject. Barbauld justified the value of history as enlarging the mind, extending understanding of human nature under all circumstances, increasing rational but not prejudicial love of one's country and strengthening the moral feelings in much the way that Priestley had. She urged that for any man or woman 'of cultivated mind', 'to be ignorant of history is not permitted'. Her niece Lucy became a popular historian of the reigns of Elizabeth I and the early Stuarts.[42] A woman whose historical writing received both greater fame and obloquy was Richmall Mangnall, second cousin of Louisa Potter. Her *Historical and Miscellaneous Questions for the Use of Young People*, written in 1798 for the girls at her school, was in its twelfth edition in 1815. Her *Questions* remained popular with governesses throughout the nineteenth century, but as early as 1799 Hannah More slated such 'superficial *question-and-answer*-way[s]' of learning history, a criticism which has been echoed in the twentieth century. Their author's intention, however, had been the opposite, seeking to awaken curiosity through history, biography, astronomy and myth and including much modern history. Mangnall herself probably never intended her book to be used merely as a catechism of knowledge but saw it as an aid to teachers bereft of textbooks.[43] Other teachers like William Wood in his girls' school in Leeds used abridged versions of Gibbon and Goldsmith to help them deepen their pupils' understanding of history.[44]

Geography or 'the use of globes' was becoming a recognized subject for girls, although often linked to other subjects. John Aikin and Anna Barbauld promoted it for both sexes as a collateral to history and produced appropriate books for pupils. So did others such as Thomas Bowen, although elsewhere geography was not yet recognized as an academic subject. William Wood linked geographical and biological facts to the political and civil divisions of society.[45] Such linking of subjects to each other and to crucial issues of the day was seen by Unitarians as a natural part of education, a way

42. Barbauld, *Legacy*, pp. 121–37; le Breton, *Lucy Aikin*, pp. xix–xx.

43. Richmall Mangnall, *Historical and Miscellaneous Questions for the Use of Young People* (1822), *passim*; G.M. Ramsden, *A Record of the Kay Family of Bury, Lancashire* (Gift to MCO, 1979), pp. 52–3; Hannah More, *Strictures on the Modern System of Female Education*, 2 vols (1799), I, pp. 159–61.

44. Charles Wellbeloved, *Memoirs of the Life and Writings of the Late Rev. W. Wood FLS* (1809), pp. 72–3.

45. Ibid., pp. 75–6; Lucy Aikin, *John Aikin*, I, pp. 119, 244; John Aikin, *England Delineated* (1790), pp. iii–viii; Sell, *Unitarian Ministers*, p. 81.

to invigorate learning and to help not only students but also schoolchildren to realize the significance of their studies.

Science was similarly linked to current concerns. In line with their Puritan inheritance of wishing to master nature both to show God's glory and to 'relieve man's estate', and freshly stimulated by advances in science and technology within their own industrial and intellectual milieu, many Unitarian ministers showed a perhaps otherwise surprising involvement in science. Many of these were also teachers and tutors. For example, the Rev. William Wood, who succeeded Priestley at Leeds, was an original member of the Linnean Society, ran the department of natural history for Arthur Aikin's *Annual Review* in the early nineteenth century, contributed many articles for Rees' *Cyclopaedia* and enthusiastically taught much practical natural history at his school for girls.[46] Warrington's superb legacy to scientific and medical education in England was amply borne out by the scientific books written for both students and schoolchildren by the 'scholar-physician' John Aikin, who had been both student and tutor there. For example, his *Calendar of Nature* on animal and vegetable life, written for ten- to fourteen-year-olds, was such a successful compendium of natural science and poetry that in 1788 his son, Arthur Aikin, enlarged it for older readers into *The Natural History of the Year.* Many dialogues in *Evenings at Home* demonstrated the keen interest which Unitarians took in the very latest scientific thinking. One of them, for instance, acknowledged the gradual dawning of evolutionary theories emanating from men like Erasmus Darwin, a friend of Priestley and Wedgwood. Other dialogues emphasized the desire of Aikin and his sister Anna for people to understand their own environment, to know 'things not words', and through conversational methods introduced children to such topics as gravity, paper-making and manufactures. Even tea-making was used as an illustration of chemistry understandable to children.[47]

These books, like the rather less digestible offerings of Jeremiah Joyce and Thomas Dix Hincks, were written for children of both sexes. Outside of higher education at least, science was not being kept as a male preserve although gender differences were acknowledged within it. For example, in his *Arts of Life*, where he explained how humans have to learn the arts of subsistence and well-being, Aikin included cookery as one of his arts but stated that males were

46. Wellbeloved, *Wood*, pp. 79–81, 98–103.

47. Lucy Aikin, *John Aikin*, pp. 37–40, 60; J. Aikin and Mrs Barbauld, *Evenings*, pp. 6–11, 29–34, 87–91, 149–53, 206–9, 236–48, 258–63, 290–3.

'prohibited' in the kitchen. He outlined the details of food preparation, explaining that its intention was medicinal and its practice, chemistry. Aikin added simple moral touches to his writings, such as his thought on manure: 'Thus nothing is lost; but things the vilest in nature are made to contribute to the general good.' He admired the human skill and industry which could produce delicate Brussels lace from flax or tasty broths from animal or vegetable materials. In all these examples he tried to lead the young of both sexes to appreciate their dependence on the useful and practical arts of life and to adopt humane and liberal views at the same time.[48]

Another radical who attempted to mingle such a 'love of virtue; a taste for knowledge; and attentive observation of the works of nature' in writing for children was Thomas Percival, the first student at Warrington. Percival's *A Father's Instructions*, of which part of the subtitle is quoted above, would seem over-moralizing to modern children but it conveyed a lot of useful and interesting information, much of it in fictional form. His story cautioning against 'Cruelty to Insects', where a youth who tortured and killed flies learnt through the use of a microscope how beautiful they really were, was an example of rational literature for the young. In this short story many of the preoccupations of these radical educationists can be seen: dislike of ignorance and the unthinking cruelty it often leads to; an assured eagerness to dispel lack of knowledge by engaging in scientific discovery; the excited use of new scientific equipment and wonder at the revealed beauties of nature. Furthermore, even in a short story like this about biology, Percival managed to insert a reference to the rights of 'life, liberty and happiness', which had been recently upheld in the American Declaration of Independence and were supported by radicals like the Unitarians against the hostility of the established ruling classes.[49]

Female Unitarian authors exhibited similar enthusiasm. Anna Barbauld in her dialogues in *Evenings at Home*, and more playfully in her poetry, equally testified to such principles. 'The mouse's petition' (to Priestley), for example, not only saved a mouse from experiments with oxygen but appealed to liberal political principles:

> If e'er thy breast with freedom glowed,
> And spurned a tyrant's chain,
> Let not thy strong oppressive force
> A free-born mouse detain!

48. John Aikin, *The Arts of Life* (1802), pp. 87–101, 41–2, 112, *passim.*
49. Thomas Percival, *A Father's Instructions* (1806), pp. 19–20.

Barbauld believed it was 'unpardonable' for young ladies not to know natural history, astronomy, botany, experimental science, chemistry and physics, although she urged the understanding rather than the investigation of science upon females.[50] Nevertheless, such writings acknowledged no difference between boys and girls in their need to be interested in science. Jane Marcet's *Conversations on Chemistry*, famed for their influence on Michael Faraday, actually took the form of conversations between a woman and two intelligent, perceptive girls. A modern scientific journal recently praised Marcet for 'the charm and depth of intellectual argument . . . concisely expressed' and the realism of the characterization and discussion.[51]

It was indeed through their writings that Unitarians sought to disseminate their educational philosophy. The establishment of William Eyres' printing press in Warrington stimulated many tutors there to publish their work. Many Unitarians wrote educational works often linked closely to their religious, political and economic outlook. To Unitarians how subjects were learned was as important as what was learned. They thus wrote poetry, drama and story books as well as textbooks for children of different ages so that knowledge could be built up from an early age. They were amongst the first to write specifically for children, and although some critics such as Charles Lamb disliked their didacticism, the many editions published suggest considerable popularity. (Lucy Aikin feared that the novel-like tales which had succeeded superstitious fairy stories gave an equally false picture of the world, so she brought out a simple selection of *Poetry for Children* which she thought better than either. William Roscoe, refreshingly, wrote *The Butterfly's Ball* just for fun.) Many teachers, like Thomas Bowen of Walsall, wrote and published their own school-books.[52]

Unitarians, therefore, favoured certain educational methods and subjects based on a particular psychology as an integral part of their deep religious and political commitment. Significantly, they promoted this rational education for both sexes. They believed all needed it to reach perfection. They also considered it vital for future educators of children to understand fully the law of associationism, which, in turn, demanded investigative methods of

50. J. Aikin and Mrs Barbauld, *Evenings*, pp. 97–116; Lucy Aikin, *Barbauld*, I, pp. 35–8, 55–8; *Legacy*, 51–2.

51. 'Mrs Marcet's column', *Education in Chemistry* (Jan. 1995), p. 5.

52. Betsy Rogers, *Georgian Chronicle* (1958), p. 123; Lucy Aikin, *Poetry for Children* (1825; 1st edn 1801); Chandler, *William Roscoe*, pp. xxxi–xxxii; Sell, *Unitarian Ministers*, p. 81.

learning. Therefore girls, like boys, had to have an education which taught them to think for themselves. Likewise, when pioneering modern history and science, they taught them to females as well as men. Thus they reserved neither education for citizenship nor an understanding of the scientific principles on which a brighter future hopefully rested, to men only. Nor did they withhold classics from females, the subject which above all usually demonstrated male, as well as class, superiority. The methods and curriculum of education are supremely important factors in class and gender issues, as many twentieth-century battles have illustrated. Although a few others in England, often friends, supported similar ideas, Unitarians as a whole consistently favoured rational education. How influential their educational philosophy might be depended on how far they were able to put it into practice.

CHAPTER THREE

Ideals into practice: Unitarians in education

Education led to the growth of Unitarianism in the eighteenth century and Unitarians hoped it would enable its adherents to win religious and intellectual leadership and political and social standing. Furthermore, their educational philosophy implied a much greater equality of provision for females and males than had ever been the case hitherto. Since there was a dearth of good educational institutions for both sexes, however, Unitarians would either have to establish better ones themselves or reform the old if they were to succeed in their aims. Given particularly the complete lack of higher education for females, any change would be an improvement. This chapter explores the extent to which Unitarians were successful in their educational provision for both boys and girls and how far women themselves participated in educational and social initiatives.

Education at home and school

The Unitarian educational ideal was disseminated in both informal and formal ways. Some Unitarians, like the Wedgwood and younger Aikin children, were largely educated at home, with mothers and sisters playing a leading role especially in the early years. William Greg's early education, for example, was 'under the auspices of an elder sister'.[1] Many, however, attended schools run by Unitarians, often ministers who saw school-keeping as a necessary part of their work and a means to supplement their often meagre salaries. These

1. Julia Wedgwood, *The Personal Life of Josiah Wedgwood the Potter*, 2 vols (Manchester, 1915), II, pp. 433, 547–8, 555–6; Philip le Breton (ed.), *Memoirs, Miscellanies and Letters of the Late Lucy Aikin* (1864), pp. xi–xviii; John Morley, 'W.R. Greg: a sketch', *Macmillan's Magazine* XLVIII (1883), p. 111.

schools compared with and, indeed, might be better than the grammar schools used by upper- and middle-class boys. Unitarian parents certainly usually preferred them to the grammar schools, disliking the orthodox religion, lack of individual attention and perceived brutish and low ethical standards of the latter.[2]

Unitarians ran many schools according to their own principles, although never establishing them as 'Unitarian' and often, indeed, like the Rev. Ralph Harrison, attracting the children of liberal Anglicans. Many were very successful. For instance, the boys' school run by the Rev. William Turner in Newcastle from 1785 to 1802 was reopened in 1813 at the request of parents, many of whom were professional men, especially doctors. One or two schools, like Joseph Bretland's in Exeter and John Ludd Fenner's at Devizes, kept to a traditional curriculum but these were unusual. Most offered science and English as well as classics, as in the case of the Rev. Philip Holland's school, whose pupils included the three sons of Josiah Wedgwood and future schoolteachers such as William Turner and William Shepherd.[3] Such schools produced many well-educated people (not all dissenters) eminent especially in the law, medicine, science and the arts. They were also likely to impart radical ideas, an important factor when considering the future positions some ex-pupils would hold Michael Maurice's school near Lowestoft, for example, leaned towards 'republican theories of government'; William Shepherd's school at Gateacre was visited by his friend, the 'infamous' Jeremiah Joyce, only six months after his imprisonment for high treason for attacking government reaction to the French Revolution; in 1798, Shepherd's language teacher, Thomas Lloyd, was imprisoned for two years for sedition. Prominent ex-pupils included Benjamin Gaskell MP, William Duckworth, Master in Chancery and Richard Vaughan Yates, the Liverpool philanthropist.[4]

Most of these schools were for boys up to sixteen. Others, like the boarding school at Palgrave, Sussex run by Anna Barbauld and

2. Herbert McLachlan, *The Unitarian Movement in the Religious Life of England* (1934), pp. 101–40; Thomas Barnes, 'A brief comparison of some of the principal arguments in favour of public and private education' (7 May 1783), *Memoirs of the Manchester Literary and Philosophical Society* (Manchester, 1785), II, pp. 1–15.

3. Sir Thomas Baker, *Memorials of a Dissenting Chapel* (1884), p. 45; M.M. Bowery, 'William Turner's contribution to educational developments in Newcastle (1782–1841)' (MA thesis, Newcastle on Tyne University, 1980), pp. 105–15; *DNB*, VI, pp. 274–5; Thomas Saddler (ed.), *Diary, Reminiscences and Correspondence of Henry Crabb Robinson* (1872), p. 6; McLachlan, *Unitarian Movement*, pp. 111–12, 118, 123–4.

4. J.W. Robberds (ed.), *A Memoir of the Life and Writings of the Late William Taylor of Norwich* (1843), pp. 234–5; Hannah Ridyard, *A Selection from the Early Letters of the Late Rev. William Shepherd, LL.D* (Liverpool, 1855), pp. 45–6, 60–2.

her husband Rochemont from 1774 to 1785, catered for younger boys, although they certainly had some as old as fourteen. Mrs Barbauld gained a reputation for teaching, future eminent scholars commenting on her enthusiasm and humour and how she cultivated their taste for poetry writing and interest in topical subjects.[5] Although details are often lacking on other schools, many of which were small, short-lived or with pupils who attended for a short time, Unitarian educationists obviously tried to carry out the ideal of a new type of liberal and useful education so eagerly promoted by Priestley and Aikin.

What little evidence there is on girls' schools suggests that they were run on similar lines. The Rev. William Wood of Leeds, for example, taught girls modern history, geography (exploring differences in governments and cultures), science, psychology, literature (English and classics in translation), grammar, moral philosophy and the evidences of natural and revealed religion. Encouraging experiment and active learning, he abridged and edited the best authors of the day for his pupils, including many textbooks written by Unitarians. Wood deliberately chose to open a school for girls rather than boys because he wished to educate 'those whose early and powerful influence over the infant mind renders it in the highest degree desirable that they should be well furnished with useful knowledge'.[6]

At least two other girls' schools run by Unitarians flourished. The Lawrence sisters and their mother set up a girls' school in Birmingham when their father lost his money in the financial crisis of 1793, establishing a pattern which was to be emulated by their more famous great-nieces at Roedean in the late nineteenth century. From 1807 to 1839 they had a school at Gateacre, near Liverpool. They were highly accomplished teachers, attracting the daughters of leading Unitarian families to their school. Sarah Lawrence, a writer, poet and good Horatian scholar, was principal. Another able teacher was Richmall Mangnall, who became the owner of Crofton Hall, near Wakefield, a leading girls' school in Yorkshire. Her various publications, including books of poetry, earned her a large fortune.[7]

5. Robberds, *William Taylor*, pp. 7–10; Grace Ellis, *A Memoir of Mrs Anna Laetitia Barbauld*, 2 vols (1874), I, pp. 62–8, 70–4, 96–8, 113.

6. Charles Wellbeloved, *Memoirs of the Life and Writings of the Late Rev. W. Wood FLS* (1809), pp. 68, 70–82.

7. Dorothy E. de Zouche, *Roedean School 1885–1955* (printed for private circulation, 1955), pp. 15–17; 'Notes of an octogenarian minister', *The Christian Life* (3.10.1910), XXXVI, p. 609; G.M. Ramsden, *A Record of the Kay Family of Bury, Lancashire* (Gift to MCO, 1979), pp. 52–3.

From her vantage point in the thick of the advance guard of Unitarian education, Lucy Aikin certainly believed that female education at the turn of the century had changed much from the days of backboards, tight-lacing, little exercise and an educational spread of the three Rs, sewing, cookery, pickling, preserving, wine-making and washing, considered essential learning for all middle-class girls. In a fictional dialogue she also noted significantly, 'Well-bred ease was then very rare indeed': the middle class were mere beginners in learning it.[8] Unitarians were seeking to acquire such polish along with their formal education, but their experience in this varied according to both gender and wealth. Both Unitarian boys and girls appear to have known a variety of home, school and tutorial education along liberal lines, but after the age of about sixteen their education differed, the males receiving further stimulus either through higher education or work outside the home.

Higher education for men

Progressive educational ideals flourished in the liberal academies of rational dissenters, the most outstanding of which was Warrington from 1757 to 1786. This one academy alone had an enormous effect on the religious, political and cultural proclivities of rational dissenters. From it came a stream of Unitarian ministers and laymen, many of whose families, such as the Gaskells, Hibberts, Heywoods, Robinsons, gave pivotal support for rational dissent and radical and scientific education in their communities for a century to come. Others included industrial names in Manchester such as Potter and Kennedy. With a stream of excellent and innovative tutors the academy inspired its students and bravely forged new paths in the curriculum. Many of the most important contributions to English medicine and science in the eighteenth century, for example, came from Warrington. This owed much to the teaching of John Aikin, who was both a student and later, after qualifying in medicine at Edinburgh, taught chemistry and anatomy and pioneered works on medical hygiene such as *Thoughts on Hospitals* (1771). Similarly the first student, Thomas Percival, became a distinguished medical practitioner and renowned writer on medical ethics, influential in both England and America. He achieved much for public medicine in Manchester including establishing a local

8. le Breton, *Lucy Aikin*, pp. 11–20.

Board of Health. Above all, perhaps, Warrington stood for free enquiry into the scriptures, its theological tutors bravely exhorting their students not to assent to any principle taught them unless they could support it by proper evidence or reason. It was no wonder that those who experienced Warrington remembered it with reverent affection.[9] Anna Barbauld (née Aikin) summed up Warrington's ethos:

> Lo there the seats where science loved to dwell,
> Where Liberty her ardent spirit breathed.[10]

From 1786, however, only a few liberal academies remained, largely because Unitarianism spread so easily in them that they lost the support of liberal Anglicans and orthodox dissenters. Warrington, beset by financial and disciplinary problems, closed in 1786; Daventry closed in 1789, succeeded by Northampton which ended in 1798. The two new academies, Hackney and Manchester of 1786, each saw itself as the successor to Warrington. Hackney inherited Warrington's scientific apparatus, Manchester its library. The greater number of Warrington trustees favoured London, however, and thus Hackney had far richer and wider support.[11]

Both new academies began with high hopes. Amid great excitement, New College, Hackney was opened to educate future learned ministers, virtuous, 'enlightened, useful and active citizens' and professional men of rational religion and the type of knowledge 'which invigorates the understanding [and] inspires noble and enlarged sentiments of liberty'. Manchester Academy opened with similar sentiments. Its first principal, Dr Thomas Barnes, dedicated the academy 'to TRUTH! to LIBERTY! to RELIGION!'[12]

These liberal academies were never called Unitarian by their supporters and *would not be on principle.* As William Turner Junior later said, they did not wish to seem 'to promote the interests of *Unitarianism* in preference to those of *truth.* We value and pursue the former, only because we believe it to be an important portion

9. MCO MS c2. J.R. Wreford, *Statistics on Dissenting Colleges* (1820), pp. 1–9; William Turner, *Warrington Academy, 1757–86* (Warrington, 1957; first printed in *The Monthly Repository*, 1813–15, vols VIII, IX, X), pp. 16–17, 26, 40, 42.

10. Lucy Aikin (ed.), *The Works of Anna Laetitia Barbauld*, 2 vols (1825), I, p. 169.

11. Herbert McLachlan, *English Education under the Test Acts* (Manchester, 1931), pp. 124, 163–9, 180; David Wykes, 'Sons and subscribers: lay support and the college', in Barbara Smith (ed.), *Truth, Liberty, Religion* (1986), pp. 41–2.

12. Hugh Worthington, *A Sermon . . . to the Supporters of a New Academical Institution among Protestant Dissenters* (6 May 1789), p. 49; Thomas Barnes, *A Discourse Delivered at the Commencement of Manchester Academy* (14 Sept. 1786), pp. 55, 59–73.

of the latter . . .'[13] Tutors genuinely tried to provide unbiased theological teaching and investigation of the scriptures (although they often happily believed that this in itself might lead students to Unitarianism). Even so, since the majority of the trustees and tutors at both Hackney and Manchester were either Arian or Socinian Unitarians, the public judged them accordingly. This was especially so at Hackney, where, of the three contemporary outstanding leaders of Unitarianism, Priestley and Belsham were both tutors and Lindsey was on the committee.[14]

The cream of intellect in rational dissent was attracted to these academies as tutors, especially men of proven academic worth and modern scholarship and often associated with Warrington. The subjects offered combined to make that broad curriculum so desired by Priestley. Science was important, even though it was not the cornerstone, and this commitment ensured that the academies differed from Oxbridge, where modern science was not part of the basic studies despite some stimulating university professors. Manchester Academy's promotion of science was demonstrated through its close links with the Literary and Philosophical Society and the short-lived Manchester College of Arts and Sciences, while from Hackney came a stream of men who did much to extend scientific education in England. For example, John Corrie FRS became Vice-President of the British Association for the Advancement of Science and Arthur Aikin was a founder and later honorary secretary of the Geological Society and secretary of the Society of Arts from 1817 to 1839. Between them these two academies had as tutors two of the leading chemical scientists in England – Priestley lecturing at Hackney from 1791 to 1794 and the Quaker John Dalton lecturing at Manchester in mathematics and science from 1793 to 1800, the very years he began publishing his renowned discoveries.[15]

There was in fact a wide variety of subjects, including classics, taught over five years for divinity students and three for lay students. The tutors were expected to be versatile and, in straitened times particularly, could be overloaded – as the students themselves might be – but generally the tutors defended the system as a preparation for later specialization and for stimulating thought on relevant and

13. William Turner [Jnr.], *Lives of Eminent Unitarians* (1840), p. 353.

14. DWL 38.14, *Hackney College Minutes* (1785–91), 23; MCO, *Report of the Committee of Manchester Academy* (22.2.1786), 1.

15. H.W. Stephenson, 'Hackney College and William Hazlitt' (1929), *TUHS*, IV, no. 3, pp. 225, 239–42; Betsy Rogers, *Georgian Chronicle* (1958), pp. 156–60, 173–8, 190–1.

useful subjects.[16] In these ways, although there were private schools offering modern subjects, the liberal dissenting academies were the most reputable scholastically and the only institutions in England to challenge the traditional curriculum in higher education.

Upholders of that traditional curriculum, however, were very hostile to these new ideas of what a liberal education should be. These quarrels were not merely academic. Curriculum was a social class issue then as now. Traditionalists saw the new subjects offered at the dissenting academies as illiberal, comprising a narrow professionalism (that is, self-interested education) which could fragment and threaten the élitist culture of the upper classes, attract 'unsuitable' students or induce dissent.[17] But supporters of these academies, such as Thomas Barnes, followed Priestley in upholding their modern education as liberal and as giving both a broad, general acquaintance with important subjects which could be studied more in later life and stimulating enlarged, energetic, vigorous and clear mental powers. The latter, they argued, were as necessary to men of trade and leaders of civil life as to those in the upper classes and men of letters. By including subjects relevant to businessmen they did not envisage a specifically commercial or technical education but one enabling future industrialists, citizens and commercial men to understand scientific principles, direct new developments in the best interests of society and become useful, rational and progressive leaders of a cultured, powerful middle class.[18] No wonder, therefore, that many from the supposedly most prestigious institutions in England, including leaders of the established Church and state, condemned such self-assertive radical education.

Priestley and the liberal dissenting academies were also opposed as dangerous infidels trying to overthrow religion. The loathing they aroused was strengthened by the way they gloried in the fact that they imposed no religious tests, were so prominent in the fight against the Test and Corporation Acts and appeared in the 1790s at Hackney Academy to be leading some of the students into outright scepticism. Nor was it only Anglicans who were uneasy. Increasingly orthodox dissenters withdrew to orthodox academies which enforced

16. Andrew Kippis, *A Sermon . . . on the Occasion of a New Academical Institution . . .* (1786), pp. 16–19.

17. Ben Knights, *The Idea of the Clerisy in the Nineteenth Century* (Cambridge, 1978), pp. 190–3.

18. MCO Thomas Barnes, *A Discourse Delivered at the Commencement of the Manchester Academy*, 14 Sept. 1789 (printed with *Report on Hundredth Anniversary of MNC*, 1886), pp. 62–6; Ralph Harrison, *A Sermon Preached at the Dissenting Chapel in Cross St., Manchester* (Manchester, 26 Mar. 1786), pp. 8–10.

doctrinal subscription, taught intending ministers only and operated a narrower curriculum.[19]

Such reaction obviously prevented the remaining liberal academies from gaining the wide support they had hoped for, especially in the case of Hackney, where Unitarian converts, no longer welcome in more orthodox institutions, fled.[20] The situation was further exacerbated by the hatred poured on Unitarians because of their involvement in revolutionary politics, an activity engaged in by both tutors and committee members at Hackney College. Not only was their opposition to established religion perceived as an attack on the state, since the two were seen as inseparably bound, but many Unitarians, not least Priestley and Richard Price, both tutors at Hackney College, were leading middle-class polemicists for civil rights and parliamentary reform and ardent supporters of the nascent French Revolution. Many students from Hackney listened eagerly to Price's passionate cry in 1789 that the 'oppressors of the world' could no longer 'hold the world in darkness'. They enthusiastically attended controversial debates in the House of Commons, circulating incendiary pamphlets and excitedly cheering on those in conflict with the government. As William Hazlitt, a student at Hackney from 1793 recalled, 'A new world was opening to the astonished sight.'[21] Such enthusiasm did not win friends at a time when the excesses of the French Revolution steadily alienated even many former adherents.

The increasing isolation of the Unitarians affected the viability of the academies of which they had expected so much. Extravagant expenditure on buildings and a rather belated proper management of discipline exacerbated Hackney's problems and the academy was forced to close in 1796. This disaster was greeted gleefully by its opponents, who chortled that 'the slaughterhouse of Christianity' or 'Babylon' had fallen – 'a striking proof' that the English were 'not disposed to encourage the modern philosophers in their attempts to undermine the constitution'.[22] Nor could Unitarians take any comfort in the continued existence of Manchester Academy since it too was hit by discipline problems and a serious shortfall in subscription, a factor not helped by public castigation of seven of

19. McLachlan, *English Education*, pp. 199–203, 237–40.

20. Kenrick, *Wellbeloved*, pp. 10–11.

21. Richard Price, *A Discourse on the Love of our Country, Nov. 4th 1789* (1790), p. 49; Stephenson, *Hazlitt*, pp. 376–94; William Hazlitt, 'Memoirs of the Late Thomas Holcroft' (1932), *Works*, III, p. 155.

22. Ibid., 235, 395, 397; John Williams, *Memoirs of the Late Thomas Belsham* (1833), pp. 443–67.

its committee as 'levellers and republicans'.[23] A small liberal academy was opened at Exeter from 1799 to 1805 but ended with the life of its principal, Timothy Kenrick, a strong Unitarian.[24]

By twentieth-century standards the ideals of Priestley and other Unitarians of that period hardly seem revolutionary, but their precepts were undermining the established order and thus the educational initiatives promoted in their academies were deemed subversive. In the 1790s, especially when Britain went to war with revolutionary France, bitter reaction against all those who stood for religious or political change led to the persecution of Priestley and other Unitarians and their ideals. Priestley, driven out of Birmingham by savage, destructive rioting, eventually found refuge in America, and many other Unitarians suffered public ostracism, financial ruin, violent attack or imprisonment.

Unitarian initiatives in higher education were not completely thwarted. Although Manchester Academy ground to a halt at the turn of the century, eventually the Rev. Charles Wellbeloved agreed to become principal if the college removed to York where he ministered. Wellbeloved, who had enjoyed the 'free light and air' of being at Hackney, publicly vindicated Unitarians from being either infidels or republicans in the 1800s, a time when even many Unitarians were disquieted by the violence of the later French Revolution and the tyrant it seemed to have spawned. For the first seven years at York his own ceaseless anxieties were about the viability of the college, but by 1810, and the securing of its finances, the college was able to proceed into a proud part of its history. Under Wellbeloved, its aim was primarily theological, but the real shift in emphasis, as David Wykes has brilliantly shown, had much to do with social and economic factors,[25] an important indication of the deep social and political considerations which underlay Unitarian educational concerns.

The academies were not the sole means of disseminating Unitarian ideals amongst adults since, quite apart from the fact that women did not attend them, neither did many men. Even amongst rational dissenters, unless their sons were divinity students paid for by the foundation, only the wealthiest parents could afford such an education despite the relatively low fees. Although in the booming commercial centre of Manchester the academy seemed well placed

23. Archibald Prentice, *Historical Sketches* (1851), pp. 423–4.
24. McLachlan, *English Education*, pp. 232–4; Mrs W. Byng Kenrick (ed.), *Chronicles of a Nonconformist Family* (Birmingham, 1932), pp. 113–15, 125–6 and *passim.*
25. Kenrick, *Wellbeloved*, pp. 6–98; Wykes, 'Sons and subscribers', pp. 31–77.

for educating the sons of the middle class, for most businessmen, except the wealthiest, formal schooling was customarily short and practical training in business was expected to begin at fourteen at the very latest. Only wealthy merchants and businessmen who wished to live like gentlemen and to be able to pursue cultured leisure interests were usually concerned about a liberal education for their offspring. Unitarians, not always rich, were prepared for their sons at least to absorb the ethos of a liberal academy but, all too often, sent their sons at sixteen only for one year or two. Between 1786 and 1796 at Manchester Academy, for example, only three of about 78 commercial students completed the three-year course. The remainder of the lay students (about 25 per cent) chiefly distinguished themselves in science or medicine.[26]

The removal of the college to York took it from the commercial centre of Manchester, where families of modest fortunes had been willing to enrol young men who could live at home, possibly attending part-time. More in the Warrington tradition, the York college catered for the wealthy, but was far more denominational in effect and its lay students were from industrial and professional families rather than merchant or landed. These factors signified Unitarians' growing isolation from mainstream orthodoxy and the increasing industrial wealth of some of their members. It was to such members that the liberal educational philosophy upheld by Manchester College at York particularly appealed. Even before 1815 sons from the huge cotton-spinning firms of Strutt, Houldsworth and Ashton attended the college, alongside those of prominent families such as the Potter, Philips and Kenrick families of Manchester, Liverpool and other leading industrial and commercial towns. By 1840 the names McConnel, Paget, Dawson and many others could be added to the list. An increasing number of these students, interestingly, entered professions such as the law where they could help the family business.[27] A small, Unitarian old boys' network at the top of industry, commerce and the new professions was being created which held to liberal political, religious, educational, social and economic principles of a particular kind.

Other Unitarians sent their sons to other countries where there were educational institutions sympathetic to their needs. Some used German or Dutch universities, but the Scottish were the most popular partly because of the common language and the excellent Scottish

26. Ibid., pp. 57–8, 34–7; Barnes, *Manchester Academy*, pp. 58, 66, 70–2; MCO, *Roll of Students . . . 1786–1803* (1868).

27. Ibid., *1803–15*; Wykes, 'Sons and subscribers', pp. 58–63.

university hospitals. In particular, late eighteenth-century Scottish universities, despite some criticisms of overcrowded lectures and indiscipline, were leaders of scientific learning. Many students from Warrington, an equally exciting centre of scientific education, subsequently went to Edinburgh to study medicine. John Aikin was one of these, as was his great friend Dr James Currie, who distilled political economy in the Roscoe circle in Liverpool. In this way intellectual Unitarian networks were further built up. Orthodox dissenters were at home theologically in Scotland; Unitarians were less so, but there was no doctrinal subscription and, at Glasgow especially, there was both a strong liberal movement and cheap education.[28]

Although defenders of the English university system derided the Scottish system as too philosophical and utilitarian and not sufficiently 'calculated to educate gentlemen', the broad curriculum was congenial to the active classes of the new industrial age. From Scotland to England came a stream of innovative industrialists, experimental scientists and significant educational reformers, not least the reformist Whigs and Utilitarians connected with Bentham. Unitarians figured much in all these categories: Benjamin Heywood, the Manchester banker, doctor Thomas Southwood Smith, scholar John Kenrick and educationist Lant Carpenter were prominent examples. The Wedgwoods, and later the Gregs, used Edinburgh university rather than Glasgow for their sons, a decision possibly based on their superior wealth.[29] Priestley, perhaps surprisingly, copied his fellow 'Lunaticks' (Members of the Lunar Society) in Birmingham, James Watt and Matthew Boulton, in by-passing British higher education altogether and sending his sons to France and Germany to learn science and languages, visit factories and meet eminent men of science.[30]

Culture and science for 'gentlemen'

Unitarians worried about the impact of commercial and industrial developments upon moral progress, and wishing to make up the

28. Lucy Aikin, *Memoir of John Aikin MD*, 2 vols (1823), I, pp. 7–8, 96–8; S.G. Checkland, 'Economic attitudes in Liverpool 1793–1807', *Economic History Review* (1952), 5, pp. 69–75; W.M. Matthews, 'The Origins and Occupations of Glasgow Students, 1740–1839', *Past and Present* (Apr. 1966), no. 33, pp. 76–94.

29. T. Heywood, *Memoir of Sir Benjamin Heywood*, printed privately, pp. 13–22; MSS MCO, *Letters and Testimonial to Lant Carpenter from Glasgow* (10.5.1810); Morley 'Greg', pp. 112–13; Wedgwood, *Josiah Wedgwood*, p. 314.

30. W.H.G. Armytage, 'The Lunar Society and its contributions to education', *University of Birmingham Historical Journal* (1967/68),V, p. 65.

shortfall in much middle-class education, had further initiatives for their sons. The Rev. Thomas Barnes and the apothecary Thomas Henry, for example, opened a College of Arts and Science in Manchester in 1783, for young men aged fourteen to eighteen, destined for some 'respectable' line of trade. They were unsuccessful, although they tried to break down the strong prejudices against future tradesmen indulging in a liberal education, arguing that tradesmen and manufacturers needed the latter no less than a 'gentleman'. To Barnes cultured and intelligent businessmen in the Wedgwood mould would bring honour to Manchester and 'contradict the disgraceful idea that a spirit of merchandise is incompatible with liberal sentiment, and that it only tends to contract and vulgarise the mind'.[31]

The founders of the college had longer-lasting success in the Manchester Literary and Philosophical Society, which, along with Dr Thomas Percival, they also founded. All three men were members of the Unitarian Cross Street Chapel, where the first meetings were held in 1781 and, like many other members, they were former students of Warrington, whose literary and scientific culture they sought to continue. Over half the original members were medical men but many others were businessmen and manufacturers. In 1785 over a third of the 43 members were connected to Cross Street Chapel and this proportion was to increase. In effect they expressed the cultural challenge through education of the small, vibrant, tightly knit Unitarian community in Manchester, the 'urban pace-maker of the industrial revolution'.[32]

This was neither the only urban centre of the late eighteenth century where both Unitarianism and provincial culture flourished nor the only one where Unitarians made their mark through a scientific society. There were some specialized societies like the Linnean Society in London to which John Aikin belonged, but the striking feature of provincial England from the late eighteenth century was the more general philosophical and literary societies, which nevertheless stressed the application of science to industry. They

31. T. Barnes, 'On the affinity subsisting between the arts with a plan for promoting and extending manufactures, by encouraging those arts on which manufactures principally depend' (1782), 'A plan for the improvement and extension of liberal education in Manchester' (1783), Thomas Henry, 'On the advantages of literature and philosophy in general, and especially on the consistency of literature and philosophy with commercial pursuits' (1781), *Memoirs Lit. and Phil.*, 1, pp. 7–28, 72–89; II, pp. 16–29.

32. Ibid., F. Nicholson, 'The Literary and Philosophical Society 1787–1851', *Memoirs Lit. and Phil.* (1923–4) 68, part 1, pp. 98–108; V.A.C. Gatrell, 'Incorporation and the pursuit of Liberal hegemony in Manchester 1790–1839', in Derek Fraser (ed.), *Municipal Reform and the Industrial City* (Leicester, 1982), pp. 28–9.

were open to all men irrespective of religion and attracted supporters from many different professions. In Leeds, Leicester and York, Unitarians were predominant in the founding of such societies, whilst in places such as Derby and London they played an important role.[33]

In Liverpool a wealth of Unitarian talent was centred around William Roscoe, who rose from work in a market garden to be a leading banker in Liverpool, a well-known poet and writer of historical and literary works on Renaissance Italy and owner of an outstanding art and book collection. He was a spirited, humane and generous man, courageously arguing against slavery and for the rights of dissenters and Roman Catholics. Despite the reactionary times of the late 1790s, Roscoe and his friends were able to initiate the establishment of the Athenaeum Club in 1798 and the Botanic Garden in 1802, an amalgam of élitism and popularism which was to be typical of Unitarian public life in the nineteenth century. Equally typical was his eagerness to reconcile private power and wealth with public well-being, albeit with no criticism of the economic realities of capitalism. Roscoe opposed 'degrading' inequalities, and believed that modern manufacturers were of far greater value than the previous leaders of society, the medieval knights and the landed gentry who 'neither toiled nor spun'.[34]

Birmingham too was a lively centre of progressive ideas especially when Priestley was there from 1781 to 1791. As a thriving unincorporated town, Birmingham was attractive to dissenters. One of its fast-expanding industrial concerns was that of Matthew Boulton and it was from his contacts that the extraordinary Lunar Society imperceptibly grew, meeting monthly over three decades. Comprising only fourteen members throughout its duration, the society nevertheless had an amazing galaxy of talent, including the inventor James Watt, the botanist William Withering, the manufacturers James Keir, Samuel Galton and the Unitarian Josiah Wedgwood, and the educationists Erasmus Darwin, Richard Edgeworth and Thomas Day. Its most brilliant years were those when Priestley was a member, although Birmingham itself seemed blithely unaware of its existence and, indeed, turned savagely against the radical politics and religion of Priestley and the Unitarians. Nevertheless, whilst the Lunar Society existed, the enthusiastic, intelligent cooperation

33. A.E. Musson and Eric Robinson, *Science and Technology in the Industrial Revolution* (Manchester, 1969), pp. 31–7, 78, 81, 85, 158–9, 163–4, 190–8; Lucy Aikin, *John Aikin*, I, p. 186.

34. George Chandler, *William Roscoe of Liverpool*, (1953), *passim*; Checkland, 'Liverpool', pp. 58–75.

of the members led to a stream of momentous inventions, important scientific and educational publications, science lectures in Birmingham and a science section in the library which Priestley had developed.[35]

The Newcastle Literary and Philosophical Society, established in 1793, was as important a cultural icon in the north-east as the Manchester Society in the north-west. It too centred around a Unitarian chapel – Hanover Square – its dominant force being the minister William Turner, another ex-student of Warrington and of Glasgow. Inspired by his links with both Priestley and the Manchester model, he successfully urged the scientific and cultural value of such a society in a developing mining and trading area. Although most of the debate and papers were scientific, the term 'literary' was used to demonstrate that this was a society which required calm discussion and communication. An excellent library and the beginnings of a museum were established and, in 1802, a 'New Institution' to run organized lectures which, in Baconian fashion, would apply science to exploit natural resources, particularly those of the locality. Turner, appointed as lecturer, eagerly sought not only to prepare men for further education but to bring science to those young people who had no other chance of an academic education and to provide an 'agreeable and instructive course of entertainment' for all ages and each sex. In this, there was a marked difference from other societies, but Turner justified women's inclusion on gendered lines. The various arts connected with domestic economy, he argued, 'are nothing else than different applications of Chemistry' and, more importantly to Turner, 'is it not from our parents of this sex that we obtain our earliest and most valuable knowledge?'[36]

Further education for women

Both Turner's inclusion of women and his reasons for so doing were significant. The liberal academies and the new literary and scientific societies which Unitarians so enthusiastically and energetically founded, promoted and supported were for men only. So were the new public libraries which they eagerly sponsored in places

35. R.E. Schofield, *The Lunar Society of Birmingham* (Oxford, 1963), *passim.*

36. Derek Orange, 'Rational dissent and provincial science: William Turner and the Newcastle Literary and Philosophical Society', in Ian Inkster and Jack Morrell (eds), *Metropolis and Province: Science in British Culture, 1780–1850* (1983), pp. 205–29; Bowery, *Turner*, pp. 148–242.

like Manchester, York, Leeds and Birmingham.[37] Not all Unitarian men received higher education, but they did gain knowledge, understanding and experience through work and often travel, and they could now extend themselves by attending these local societies. The women were usually only guests at certain meetings of these and then only attended by right of their male companion. Unitarian educational philosophy might seem egalitarian, but when it came to higher education or informal public education, Unitarians appeared to accept the social norms of society. Yet even here they made some inroads into the masculine domain. Lucy Aikin and her friends in Stoke Newington, for example, replied in kind in the early 1800s by discussing the latest quality books in their own Ladies Book Society, from which men were excluded.[38]

Generally, however, women with similar intellectual, literary and scientific interests as their male counterparts learned within the family circle or by themselves when beyond school age. In stimulating Unitarian circles such an option was viable. Indeed, it appears that daughters were often deliberately sent to visit relatives and friends within the tightly knit yet disparate intellectual and cultured Unitarian network in order to extend their education. For example, some visited Anna Barbauld for a time to perfect their education through her lessons and influence. Betsy Fletcher's mother, for instance, was satisfied that her daughter had achieved 'a high standard of intellectual and moral perfection' in this way. Priestley's granddaughter Anna Finch and 'the vain & bouncing' Sally Taylor (later Sarah Austin) were others who spent a similar culturally enhancing time. Construing Latin, reading a heavy diet of history and literature, writing essays on a variety of subjects were part of the intellectual side of the arrangement, but a further education was received through meeting the various notables who made their way to Anna Barbauld's house and the enjoyment of poetry, art, drama and music which enlivened it.[39]

Another important avenue of education for women was the new monthly and quarterly journals which played a significant part in the wider education of the middle classes in the nineteenth century. Unitarians did much to help develop these. For example, Priestley edited *The Theological Review*, and John Aikin edited the *Monthly Magazine* from 1796 to 1806 and the *Athenaeum* from 1807 to 1809. Anna Barbauld, Lucy Aikin, Mary Hays and Ann Jebb also

37. Musson and Robinson, *Science*, p. 113; Kenrick, *Wellbeloved*, p. 81.
38. le Breton, *Lucy Aikin*, p. 126.
39. Betsy Rodgers, *Georgian Chronicle: Mrs Barbauld and her Family* (1958), pp. 101–4.

wrote on a range of subjects in such journals. Mary Wollstonecraft was a key contributor from 1788 to 1792 to the widely ranging *Analytical Review,* largely written by Unitarians. Most of these journals were published by the unassuming Unitarian bookseller Joseph Johnson, who thus not only did much for rational religion, radical politics, science and medicine, progressive education and the increase of knowledge in this period, but was also significant for the way he promoted female authors.[40]

The educationist the Rev. Lant Carpenter actually tried to extend higher education to women. In the 1800s he enthusiastically taught history, philosophy and other subjects to young ladies in Liverpool who had finished school, sufficiently inspiring at least one twenty-year-old to sit up for three hours to finish her work after coming home from a ball at 1.00 a.m. Carpenter began his classes at the instigation of the Rev. John Yates, Unitarian minister at Paradise Street, who was keen to continue the education of such young women as he believed that without it their intellectual development might even recede. Yates (ex-Warrington) was part of the Roscoe circle in Liverpool, as was William Shepherd, who advocated female suffrage. Carpenter was, much to his own delight, linked to such circles; from 1806 he was in Exeter and subsequently Bristol.[41] In such ways educational ideas, including those on women, were forged and spread.

It was to be a long time, however, before such ideas stimulated much public education for women. Turner's specific wish for women to be participants at the New Institution was thus a step forward. He explained women's need for science within their traditional female roles but, nevertheless, he saw these roles as requiring the same depth of knowledge and understanding as he believed men should have for skilled and professional jobs. In this he was like John Aikin and Anna Barbauld. His daughter Mary, in fact, was a frequent visitor of the latter two when at eighteen she went on 'several pleasant and improving journeys' which included staying three months with John Wedgwood's family in London. Already having had a good education at schools in Manchester and Newcastle, in London Mary Turner attended lectures at the Royal Institution, saw many 'curious and beautiful things' and had lessons in singing and drawing. These she used to good effect in Newcastle, drawing diagrams on the blackboard for her father's lectures at the New

40. Lucy Aikin, *John Aikin*, pp. 233–54; Gerald Tyson, *Joseph Johnson: A Liberal Publisher* (Iowa, 1979), *passim*; McLachlan, *Unitarian Movement*, pp. 165–77.

41. Russell Lant Carpenter, *Memoir of the Rev. Lant Carpenter, LL.D* (1842), p. 99.

Institution. She said that this helped her to understand the lectures better, but she did them beforehand so there 'could be no objection' to her participation. Indeed, Mary's experience seems to have been a mixture of advanced views with nods to contemporary propriety. On further journeys to relations and other fellow Unitarians she met Dr Crompton in Lancashire, who professed amazement that William Turner's daughter did not understand Latin. Her brother was sufficiently highly educated, however, to be a tutor at Manchester College, York and in visiting him there Mary met John Gooch Robberds, whom she married in 1812 after he had become co-pastor at Cross Street Chapel, Manchester.[42]

The duties of wives

Turner's letter to Mary shortly after her marriage illustrates how a Unitarian woman was expected to use her talents. Gentle and affectionate, he agreed with the 'strong and often coarse, though too often well-founded, strictures of Mrs Wollstonecraft', which he knew Mary had read, that a wife should be a companion and helper, not merely an upper servant. He did expect that as a minister's wife Mary should do much, acting as her husband's proxy especially in cases of distress concerning women and children. She should also help in charity and Sunday schools, act as a mediator in the congregation and look after various public charities besides continuing to study herself and teaching her own family. He saw the more general wifely duties as being the 'refuge . . . comfort and counsellor' of her oft 'exhausted' husband, reading with him and aiding his plans. But if this seems a little one-sided, Turner also believed that the wife should 'admonish' her husband if he neglected or failed in any of his duties and that each should help and cooperate with the other.[43] He thus expected his daughter to be a well-educated and respected member of the community, working with her husband but to help his profession rather than hers. He put women's intellectual and cultural needs much closer to those of professional and skilled men than was the norm but saw these needs as allied to gendered roles. His delineation of the 'professional' housewife and mother anticipated that exaltation of these roles which was to prove both appealing and limiting to women in the nineteenth century.

42. Bowery, *Turner,* p. 234; Mary Robberds, 'Recollections of a long life', in J.A.V. Chapple and Anita Wilson (eds), *Private Voices* (Keele, 1996), pp. 105–13.
43. Ibid., pp. 115–20.

Women, philanthropy and class relations

A vital part of the work Turner assigned to the minister's wife was charity work. He specifically recommended, in fact, Catherine Cappe's 'excellent' paper on female visitors to public hospitals. This was a controversial issue. Catherine Harrison, a zealous 'convert' to Unitarianism from youth, had, long before her marriage to the cultured minister at York, Newcome Cappe, striven to help the poor through Sunday classes and female benefit clubs. In York she reformed the conditions of the girls at the Grey Coat School and later wrote about the constitution of charity schools and the establishment of female benefit clubs. Catherine, accepting that it was 'perhaps wisely' forbidden to women to take part in legislation or administration, nevertheless believed that organized charity work by ladies would help both observance of the laws and their own sex generally. Her own work amongst the poor convinced her that the female departments of all public institutions should be regularly visited and inspected by well-educated women officially appointed so to do. Against the hostility of the governors of the County Hospital, she managed to experiment in this work, but she and fellow Unitarian and Quaker reformers were forced to realize the bitter reaction to interference from reformers of any kind and especially women.[44]

Cappe demands attention in many ways. She established and reformed charity and educational institutions in the teeth of persistent difficulties; she particularly worked for the benefit of females at a time when benefit clubs were only just beginning for men; she campaigned for 'professional' female visitors almost a hundred years before such an idea became more generally acceptable; and she argued for the latter partly for the advantage of the visitors themselves, who, she believed, would be raised 'higher in the scale of moral and rational beings' by doing such work. Such views anticipated women's voluntary work in the nineteenth century and would have been very acceptable to her correspondent of many years, Dr Lant Carpenter, whose highly educated daughter Mary was to become famed for her work amongst the poor and outcasts of society.[45]

Unitarian struggles within and for the emergent middle class did not prevent involvement with the concerns and education of the working classes although it undoubtedly affected their attitudes and actions in this sphere. Their political and educational views, after

44. Catherine Cappe, *Memoir of the Life of the Late Mrs Catherine Cappe* (1822), pp. 118–22, 190, 232, 304, 313, 340–4, 369, 373, 414–20, 431–2.
45. Ibid., pp. 431, 459–61.

all, logically should have been extended to all ranks in society, and some Unitarians were working-class. Writers such as John Aikin and Anna Barbauld did believe that good government contained a 'levelling principle' to mitigate extremes of poverty and wealth and relieve oppression. Anna Barbauld indignantly castigated those who utilized religion as 'an engine of government against the poor', advising the latter not to 'deem the Lord above like Lords below . . .Nor fear the God whom priests and kings have made'. Aikin recognized the poor as having the same rights as the rich and the same needs for recreation and comfort, a view which put him far in advance of many of his time. When, however, he spoke of raising the self-respect and status of the poor to remove their 'gross ignorance, bad morals and pernicious habits', he gave a foretaste of that paternalism and condescension which infuriated many of the recipients of middle-class advice in the nineteenth century. But at least Aikin castigated the rich in the same way.[46]

Most contemporary Unitarians similarly appeared to have felt respect and sympathy for the poor but did not want to alter the economic structure. They believed that the economic problems of the poor could be solved only by benevolence from those better off and by education, yet fear of possible religious and political tyranny made them wary of a state system of education. Some Unitarian chapels ran charity schools very similar to those run by other religious organizations. Very poor children were taught the three Rs and employed in useful work to fit them for apprenticeship or domestic service without being lifted 'above their station'. In Birmingham, for example, the religious instruction in Unitarian charity schools was very simple, corporal punishment rare and the physical care ample. Pupils were given instruction six hours a day and, once meals or prayers were over, they were free to play – a better option than most working-class children had elsewhere.[47] This was, therefore, a generous version of a class-ridden scheme.

Unitarians positively wished to extend education to the working classes, however, and paternalistic Unitarian industrialists like the Gregs established schools for their workers. The Gregs' Apprentice House is particularly interesting, for, although Samuel Greg established it before he married Hannah Lightbody in 1789, it was

46. Lucy Aikin, *Barbauld*, I, p. 193; *John Aikin*, pp. 121–7; John Aikin, *Letters from a Father to his Son* (1793), pp. 207–19, 293–4.

47. Emily Bushrod, 'The history of Unitarianism in Birmingham from the middle of the eighteenth century to 1893' (MA thesis, Birmingham University, 1954), pp. 155–7, 172.

acknowledged that she was the driving force behind the enlightened welfare and educational provision for the parish apprentices (about 60 girls and 30 boys in 1800). She involved her own children in teaching the apprentices on Sundays, and her daughters particularly came to share the social responsibilities. A Sick Club and Women's Club were established and Hannah ensured proper medical care, clean conditions and fresh food. Music and sewing classes were given as well as a basic education. Although the latter might not always have been welcome on top of a twelve-hour working day, there is evidence that the apprentices were happy and appreciated events such as the annual prize-giving for good scholars.[48] This philanthropic approach revealed the interaction of economic motives and Unitarian social and educational ideas and the mediation of female participation.

Women, indeed, took the educational initiative in some Unitarian chapels. When Mosley Street Chapel was built in 1789 the 'ladies' set up a day school for girls, who learnt the three Rs as well as receiving a moral and vocational education. They were paid to clean their premises – set in one of the most fashionable streets in Manchester – and usually went into service, personally placed by the ladies themselves.[49]

Similarly, Catherine Cappe tried, albeit unsuccessfully, to establish a Sunday school in the 1760s. Unitarians were more appreciative of Sunday schools after Robert Raikes inspired the Sunday school movement of the 1780s. Though orthodox fear of sedition and atheism in the 1790s destroyed their hopes of cooperation with others, they founded early non-denominational Sunday schools at many of their chapels. Here they often gave a much wider education than the simple Bible reading offered in most other Sunday schools and they often wrote books to help the learning.[50] The schools established by William Turner at Hanover Square in Newcastle and those at the Old and New Meetings in Birmingham were only the best examples of many.

The Birmingham schools grew quickly from the late 1780s, attracting many pupils through their emphasis on a broad secular education and democratic organization, both unusual at the time.

48. Mary Rose, *The Gregs of Quarry Bank Mill* (Cambridge, 1986), pp. 28–33; Peter Spencer, *A Portrait of Hannah Greg* (Styal, 1982), pp. 10–13; *A Portrait of Samuel Greg* (Styal, 1989), pp. 15–18.

49. Lester Burney, *Cross Street Chapel Schools, Manchester, 1734–1942* (Didsbury, 1977), pp. 8–9, 12.

50. Cappe, *Memoirs*, pp. 120–22; Bowery, *Turner*, pp. 65–8, 70–5, 85.

Their joint Brotherly Society, established in 1798 to train teachers from among the boy pupils, set up a benefit scheme and allowed the incalculable advantage of fairly independent control by the teachers, who were largely working class. This society had grown out of an older one which not only taught illiterate boys but also gave gratuitous lectures on science and mechanics to factory workers and ran a debating society. Thomas Clark, a member of the 1789 Society, gave scientific lectures in his own home to artisans, some of them foundry workers and so aptly termed the 'cast-iron philosophers'. Hartley's philosophy was certainly discussed, and at least one member, William Matthews, became a Unitarian after hearing Priestley speak at the Society and, to his own astonishment, finding him to be 'placid, modest and courteous' and eagerly prepared to share his great learning with the large number of 'young persons of both sexes, whom . . . he encouraged to ask him questions'. Other Unitarian initiatives for artisans, such as the valuable Artisans Library established through Thomas and Samuel Carpenter, were recalled with great pride by members. They were all for men, as the most spectacular Unitarian educational initiatives were. The Brotherly Society is most remembered for helping to educate men like Thomas Wright Hill and James Luckcock, who became a prominent educational reformer and a prosperous manufacturer respectively, in Birmingham in the nineteenth century. Women, however, were allowed into meetings.[51]

The active part played by women must not be ignored. Many Unitarians had read and debated Catherine Cappe's book, *Thoughts on Charitable Institutions*, for example, as the long correspondence concerning it in the *Monthly Repository* in 1814 illustrated.[52] Other, lesser-known women were also involved in the running of schools. Women of the congregation usually looked after any separate provision for girls although the men ran the general committee. For example, at High Pavement, Nottingham in 1803, the 'ladies' laid on much provision for girls, including evening classes three times a week and an evening class for the teachers of the girls' Sunday school on Thursdays. The male committee, however, curtailed the hours and some of the classes in 1812, but since this was accompanied by a stricture that the girls' room must no longer have a fire all night as this was both extravagant and dangerous, it might well

51. William Matthews, *A Sketch of the Principal Means which have been Employed to Ameliorate the Intellectual and Moral Condition of the Working-Classes in Birmingham* (1830), pp. 6–18, 22–5; James Luckcock, *Moral Culture* (1817), pp. 266–70.

52. *MR* (1814), IX, pp. 424–7, 542–6, 673, 686–8.

be that cost was uppermost in the committee's mind rather than any antipathy to female classes.[53] Mosley Street, Manchester had a girls' Sunday school from 1789 although one for boys was not established until 1808.[54]

These provisions were largely established by one class for another. The activities of the Brotherly Society in Birmingham illustrated a degree of democracy and of fluidity between classes which might indicate that egalitarianism which Unitarian educational philosophy logically promoted. Such a supposition would be too optimistic. Members of the New Meeting were increasingly professional people. A number from both Meetings were small business people, including interestingly one or two women who were businesswomen in their own right, such as Mrs Cantrill the rope-maker. Many of the enterprises proved to be the foundation of famed family businesses, such as the Kenricks, Rylands and Oslers. A disproportionate number of Birmingham patentees appear to have been Unitarians, and even in 1769 so were eleven of the fifty men who had qualified by their wealth to become Birmingham Commissioners.[55] Unitarian congregations of enterprising people consisted of many who were rising in societal status. Birmingham's unique industrial and economic features might have allowed for a truer mixing of social ranks than elsewhere, yet a similar meeting of leading citizens at Hanover Square, Newcastle included owners of small and increasingly large businesses, professional men, teachers and booksellers, all in a largely middle-class, although not uniformly rich, congregation.[56]

Nevertheless, it is important to remember that not all Unitarians were members of the richer middle classes. In Somerset and the south-east there were congregations of tradesmen and artisans. In the early nineteenth century Unitarian working-class congregations of General Baptists in various areas and of Methodists in Lancashire established themselves. In particular, Unitarian converts from the Baptists, William Vidler, Richard Wright and Robert Aspland, made it their mission to take Unitarianism to the humbler ranks of society, ranks from which Vidler and Wright had come themselves. Such converts breathed new life into Unitarianism at a time when political and religious reaction had discouraged growth. On the

53. MSS Nottingham University, HiM, *Minute Books, High Pavement Chapel* (1803, 1812).

54. Burney, *Cross Street*, pp. 8–9.

55. Bushrod, 'Unitarianism in Birmingham', pp. 206–17, 221–3.

56. Bowery, *Turner*, pp. 53–5.

other hand, their stress on emotion and discipline alike shocked the sensibilities of some of the older, more prosperous assemblies who prided themselves on their loose 'catholicity'. Yet some highly respected Unitarians like Catherine Cappe and Charles Wellbeloved supported Aspland's desire to encourage popular preaching, and his gradual success won the eventual approbation of even the more conservative such as Thomas Belsham.[57]

Robert Aspland's career illustrates some Unitarian attitudes on both class and gender. In 1805 he replaced Belsham at the Gravel Pit, Hackney and so held a very respectable position in the Unitarian world. From 1806 he edited the *Monthly Repository*, which he made a central platform for the discussion of rational theology and progressive educational and literary ideas. In the very first number he published translations by Henry Crabb Robinson from Goethe and Herder. At the same time he involved himself in ventures to spread education to the poor and, from 1811, with J.T. Rutt and William Frend, he worked to establish an academy which would give a respectable theological education to those intending to minister to the poorer congregations of Unitarianism. Unusual in being specifically labelled Unitarian, the academy did not gain wide Unitarian support, although the tutors at Manchester College, anxious about their own finances, kept a close and somewhat supercilious eye on the struggles of their humbler rival. The Academy's curriculum and aims were limited but, nevertheless, in its six-year lifespan, it employed very reputable tutors. Aspland himself was principal and encouraged a wide general knowledge and culture. The students were few but achieved much. Thomas Walker Horsfield, for example, became a vigorous and effective preacher, established an excellent mechanics' institute at Lewes, lectured in science, enjoyed landscape painting and wrote about local antiquities. The ex-weaver Benjamin Goodier established a chapel at Oldham before dying young of heart disease.[58]

Undaunted by the short-lived success of Hackney, Aspland continued to try to extend wider education and culture to the less prosperous members of society. Following his gradual conversion to Unitarianism and his marriage to Sara Middleton, he welcomed such education among women. After all, it was encountering the intelligent freedom of enquiry in religion among Unitarian women

57. C. Gordan Bolam, Jeremy Goring, H.L. Short, Roger Thomas, *The English Presbyterians* (1968), pp. 235–9; Robert Brook Aspland, *Memoir of the Life, Works and Correspondence of the Rev. Robert Aspland of Hackney* (1850), pp. 193–7.

58. Ibid., pp. 302–30; MSS MCO, *York Letters 1811*; *CW II* (1814); *JK III* (1816), *passim.*

which had first challenged his old ideas.[59] He worked well with women, and the activities of some of his female friends illustrate the type of work they could do in chapel life. In 1805, for example, as tutor to Samuel Shore's children in Derbyshire, Aspland was particularly struck by the abilities of Elizabeth Shore, who proved to be an apt pupil. She knew the original languages of the scriptures, and later superintended a village school and formed a village library for the poor. Mrs Mary Hughes of Hanwood, Shropshire backed Aspland and Lant Carpenter financially in establishing a non-sectarian Christian Tract Society in 1809 and wrote the first tract for them. Catherine Cappe wrote the third, and Mrs Price, a niece of Mary Hughes, was another early writer. In two years over 52,000 tracts were printed. Mary Hughes herself, along with her mother and sisters, was a convert to Unitarianism. She wrote twenty tracts and with her second sister ran a Sunday school for years. She told Aspland how her family had been isolated Unitarians until she read the *Monthly Repository* in 1807 and the 'Unitarian world opened to my view'.[60]

In these ways Unitarian networks were built up and women played a vital role in them. Education, of both a formal and informal nature, was both the reflection and spearhead of Unitarian beliefs, safeguarding rational religion, disseminating liberal principles and stimulating confident faith in the status and worth of its participants. Yet though this education was for both sexes, efforts in adult education and the most prestigious institutions were reserved for men. How far gendered perceptions affected the role and status of Unitarian women within their more egalitarian educational framework needs further exploration.

59. Aspland, *Robert Aspland*, pp. 22–5, 47, 53–65, 73, 91, 108.
60. Ibid., pp. 166–9, 249–50, 335–40.

CHAPTER FOUR

To 'loose the female mind': Unitarians and women 1760–1815

Unitarian educational philosophy was egalitarian, optimistic and humanistic. Potentially, it should have enabled its participants to take a full part in the emergent culture and power structure of a modern urban, rational and scientific society. Women were included within the educational ventures of the Unitarians, both in theory and practice. They ran schools, wrote on education and were at the heart of educational family life. They were, however, excluded both from the apogee of Unitarian education – the liberal academies – and from the informal societies so often set up and prominently supported by the men in their families. This discrimination raises important questions on how Unitarian educational philosophy interacted with more traditional conceptions of gendered roles. Did it enable Unitarian women to fulfil their familial role in a distinctive way and/or lead them beyond the usual confines of womanhood? Did it affect their ideals of what a 'gentleman' or 'perfect woman' should be? If the men imbibed their political and religious radicalism from seedbeds of subversion such as Hackney and Manchester Colleges, where did the women imbibe theirs? Did they become the influential educators of the future generation in the way their philosophy seemed to demand? At a time when Unitarians were fighting other battles – religious, political and economic – of great import, how far did issues of gender trouble either women or men? Such questions require further discussion.

Unitarian views on womanhood

Their key beliefs enabled Unitarians to hold a much higher conception of womanhood than was generally prevalent. Their rejection of both original sin and the essential depravity of man – the blame for which was usually shifted onto woman's shoulders – gave them a fresh, more generous view of the humanity and possible perfection of all. Their desire for a more rational, enlightened age made them hope that outdated notions might disappear and, since the scriptures were held to be a historical as well as a divine record, this might include scriptural notions about women.[1] Their wish to teach the young of both sexes to understand the principles of rational dissent was, in itself, an assault on female ignorance, but this equality in religious teaching was part of their general assent, along with Priestley, to associationist psychology. Since they believed that it was a careful, rational education, particularly in the early years, which produced the virtuous person, so they agreed that all, regardless of sex or rank, should receive such. They did not accept that women were an inferior species of *man*kind.

John Aikin, for example, preferred to stress the similarities of the two sexes rather than contrast them: 'Virtue, wisdom, presence of mind, patience, vigour, capacity, application are not *sexual* qualities; they belong to mankind.'[2] Using 'mankind' in the larger sense here, Aikin was seeking to refute 'the common notion that women are no better than playthings, designed rather for the amusement of their lords and masters, than for the more serious purposes of life'. He was certain that 'no man ever married a fool without severely repenting it' and that, however much 'infirm and delicate health may interest the feelings', the nervous, timid, rather precious woman 'too much encouraged under the notion of female delicacy' was hardly a desirable marriage partner, especially when one considered 'what exertions of fortitude and self-command are continually required in the course of female duty'. When there was any trouble in the house, he remarked drily, 'the man often runs abroad, the woman must stay at home and face the worst'. Since in the lower ranks of society women often had to do laborious work as well, if they were really 'so weak in temper and constitution as many suppose', Aikin added, then means had not been suited to ends in the way they usually were in nature.[3]

In his *Letters to a Young Lady on a Course of English Poetry*, Aikin was quick to point out and dismiss any scurrilous, despotic or degenerate notions about women held by otherwise worthy poets. He wanted young women to be educated to use their own good sense

1. Margaret Canovan, 'The irony of history: Priestley's rational theology', *The Price-Priestley Newsletter* (1980), 4, pp. 16–25.

2. John Aikin, *Letters from a Father to his Son on Various Topics Relative to Literature and the Conduct of Life* (1793), p. 341.

3. Ibid., pp. 336, 338–40.

and principles to judge literature rather than be denied access to some of it by the false idea that the best guard of innocence is ignorance.[4] Lucy, Aikin's daughter, declared him 'the sincerest friend of the female sex that I have ever known',[5] but other Unitarian daughters could have said the same about their fathers. Gilbert Wakefield, tutor at Warrington and Hackney, believed the female intellect to be equal to the male's, if properly educated. When imprisoned for sedition in 1799, he was distraught over who could continue the classical and literary education of his daughters, which he had personally superintended.[6] Louisa (Potter) Kay's father, a solicitor, gave up his mornings to teach her especially in Latin.[7]

Although such ideas were not unique to Unitarians – Jane Austen for example, concurred with Aikin's ideas on over-emotional women in *Sense and Sensibility* – Unitarians were unusual in displaying them as a group. It is little wonder, therefore, that Mary Wollstonecraft felt at home amongst them. Her arguments that women were so degraded that they almost justified their oppression and that uneducated, irresponsible women were 'flaws in nature', albeit beautiful, exotic ones, echoed the sentiments of Unitarians.[8] They, like her and other radical educationists, utterly opposed Rousseau's sentimental but denigrating and debasing view of females and their intellect.[9] Males like Henry Crabb Robinson and Gilbert Wakefield obviously delighted in the intellectual companionship of women.[10] Friendship of this type could be expected from women like Sophia Frend, for example, whose father took her everywhere with him as soon as she could walk and talk. He gave her a thorough intellectual education including Hebrew and philosophy. Another Unitarian pupil was Annabella Milbanke, who devoured Cicero and Euclid, was brilliant at astronomy and became William Frend's lifelong correspondent, enjoying his affection for much longer than she did that of her later husband, Lord Byron.[11]

4. John Aikin, *Letters to a Young Lady on a Course of English Poetry* (1807), pp. 82 and *passim.*

5. Lucy Aikin, *Memoir of John Aikin MD*, 2 vols (1823), I, p. 168.

6. Gilbert Wakefield, *Memoirs*, 2 vols (1792), II, pp. 172–3.

7. G.M. Ramsden, *A Record of the Kay Family of Bury, Lancashire* (Gift to MCO, 1979), pp. 38–9.

8. Mary Wollstonecraft, *Mary* and *The Wrongs of Woman*, ed. J. Kinsley and G. Kelly (Oxford, 1980), *passim.*

9. e.g. Lucy Aikin (ed.), *The Works of Anna Laetitia Barbauld*, 2 vols (1825), II, pp. 314–15.

10. Thomas Saddler (ed.), *Diary, Reminiscences and Correspondence of Henry Crabb Robinson*, 2 vols (1872), I, pp. 118–267 *passim* (& ff.); Wakefield, *Memoirs*, II, pp. 172–3.

11. Frida Knight, *University Rebel: The Life of William Frend 1757–1841* (1971), pp. 238–40, 243.

Unitarian girls, therefore, often received an excellent education at home and were expected to take full part in the vibrant intellectual life which marked many of these homes. Educationists like Thomas Dix Hincks, Jeremiah Joyce and John Aikin wrote expressly for both sexes.[12] This does not mean, however, that Unitarians believed simply that women and men had the same roles in life and therefore required exactly the same character or education. Sarah (Austin) Taylor's mother, for example, strongly wished her to improve her Italian and French, read English literature as widely and deeply as possible and follow current affairs. She was sure that 'The character of girls must depend upon their reading as much as upon the company they keep. Besides the intrinsic pleasure to be derived from solid knowledge, a woman ought to consider it her best resource against poverty.'[13] At the same time, however, she warned Sarah against her strong expressions and love of contradiction, characteristics which might have been seen as more natural in spirited young Unitarian males.[14]

Anna Barbauld and opportunities for women

The life and writings of Anna Barbauld, Aikin's sister, illustrate well both the excellent, yet gendered, opportunities a Unitarian woman might enjoy. Barbauld too believed that women should wish to sustain the general character of a rational being. In her 'Dialogue of the Dead between Helen and Madame Maintenon', the latter argues that she was greater than Helen because, unlike Helen, who was merely a possession of Menelaus, she inspired a king when old and through personal merit.[15] Barbauld certainly had sufficient personal merit and renown of her own. Debarred from higher education as a woman, she nevertheless was highly educated by her father, Dr John Aikin, mainstay of Warrington Academy for many years, whose inspiring teaching of English deeply affected his children.[16] Through him she became proficient in Latin, French, Italian and English literature and learnt some Greek. This astonishing education for a girl of her time was enhanced further by fifteen

12. Thomas Dix Hincks, *A Syllabus of a Course of Lectures* (Cork, 1803), pp. 1–4; Jeremiah Joyce, *Familiar Introduction to Arts and Sciences for the Use of Schools and Young Persons* (1810), Advertisement; Lucy Aikin, *John Aikin*, I, p. 244.

13. Janet Ross, *Three Generations of Englishwomen* (1888), pp. 15–16.

14. Ibid., pp. 14–15.

15. Anna Laetitia Barbauld, *A Legacy for Young Ladies* (1826), pp. 41, 241–50.

16. William Turner, *Warrington Academy, 1757–86* (Warrington, 1957; first printed in *The Monthly Repository*, 1813–15, vols VIII, IX, X), p. 3.

years of living at Warrington Academy. In 1773 she became a well-known poet, a year before her marriage to the excitable (and eventually insane) Unitarian the Rev. Rochemont Barbauld took her to Palgrave in Suffolk, where they ran an excellent school for boys from 1774 to 1785. Eminent men such as William Taylor, pioneer translator of German, Dr Sayers and Lord Chief Justice Denman remembered her lessons with gratitude. Indeed, Barbauld pioneered reputable writing for infants. The more conservative Anglican writer Sarah Trimmer, for example, publicly acknowledged her debt to Anna Barbauld's *Early Lessons*, which gave 'a new turn to both the composition and mode of printing books for little children'. One of the 'bluestockings', Barbauld continued writing books for children, sometimes with her brother John. She also wrote on education, edited the works of Addison and Steele and, very daringly for a woman of that period, published her views on controversial religious and political matters.[17]

Anna Barbauld's various activities, facilitated by the generous attitudes and educational provision given to females by Unitarians, pushed at the limits of what hitherto women could achieve. At the very least she was establishing a new role model for women. Yet Barbauld was distrustful of any revolutionary change in woman's role. She acclaimed the revolution against despotism in France, attacked the 'sin' of slavery in an impassioned 'Poetical Epistle to William Wilberforce', but refused a proposal from Elizabeth Montague and others in 1774 to run an academy or college for young ladies on the grounds that such seemed 'better calculated to form such characters as the *Precieuses* or the *Femmes scavantes* [*sic*] of Moliere than good wives or agreeable companions'.[18]

Discounting her experience as unusual and therefore no model, Barbauld distinguished between young men, 'who are to display their knowledge to the world', and young ladies, who needed general knowledge only to enable them to be 'agreeable companions to a man of sense' and to give rational amusement to themselves when alone. Since young women were likely to be scorned, she said, if they displayed any erudition, they should seek knowledge quietly within the family and particularly through the conversation and advice of male relatives. On the other hand, whilst Barbauld believed that girls needed knowledge earlier than usually given, certainly before

17. Lucy Aikin, *Barbauld*, I, pp. v–xv, xxv–xxxiii; Grace A. Ellis, *A Memoir of Mrs Anna Laetitia Barbauld* (Boston, 1874), pp. 7–53, 75–81,186–91, 200–1; Gerald Tyson, *Joseph Johnson: A Liberal Publisher* (Iowa, 1979), pp. 84 and *passim*.

18. Ibid., pp. 57, 181–3, 188–91.

the age of fifteen when 'the empire of the passions is coming on', she insisted that mothers were the best educators for girls in their late teens. It was then that they should learn the details of domestic economy and how to behave in 'polished society' and to members of the other sex. She disclaimed any ability to run even a reformed boarding school since she had never been in one herself and was not sufficiently 'well-bred' to direct the upper-class students she assumed would attend.[19]

Barbauld's nineteenth-century biographer regretted the extreme modesty which made her refuse a plan which 'would have formed an era in the history of woman's education'. In the twentieth century Jane McDermid called her 'conservative' and lumped her together with men like Thomas Gisbourne and John Gregory. In some respects Barbauld certainly was akin to these thinkers, but she did not accept their respective assumptions of female inferiority in intellect or feeling, only recognized that women were unlikely either to exceed the inglorious expectations of the education most of them received or become professional workers.[20] She had much in common with the evangelical Hannah More, who was a personal friend, for both wanted a far more rigorous intellectual education for girls while seeing them as essentially domestic creatures. More was much more limited in her approach than Barbauld, however, guarding women from any 'impure' knowledge and hating 'self-complacent heroines' in fiction who sought to rival men rather than please them.[21]

Barbauld, however, although excusing women studies which were needed for a profession and considering Greek took too much time, thought Latin good for girls – an admission which was quite significant. Although she assumed women would not be involved at the frontiers of discovery, she called it 'unpardonable' not to know science in all its forms, an emphasis lacking in More. Conversely, Barbauld lacked the latter's evangelical fervour and generally, as in her remarks on learning history, was willing to allow females to judge morality for themselves from what they studied rather than forbidding them certain knowledge or reading because of its alleged immorality. She did take an instrumental view of education as being 'to fit persons for the station in which they are hereafter

19. Ibid., pp. 57–61.

20. Ibid., p. 61; Jane McDermid, 'Conservative feminism and female education in the eighteenth century', *HofE* (1989), 18, no. 4, pp. 309–22. See e.g. B. Hill, *Eighteenth-Century Women: An Anthology* (1984), pp. 17, 19, 46, 51, 60, 71, 75, 85.

21. Hannah More, *Strictures on the Modern System of Female Education*, 2 vols (1799), I, pp. 30–48, 65–9 and *passim*.

to live', which explains why she considered women both in their domestic role and according to which rank in society they belonged. She thought of male education in the same way, however, and thus reserved professional studies to those men who would need them. She explicitly stated that both young women and men, if they had the opportunities, should study 'everything that makes part of the discourse of rational and well-educated people'. In other words she did not ascribe inferior intellect to women, nor deny them any 'rational' study, but accepted that they would use their time most profitably gaining the best education they could within the limits of their probable role in life.[22]

In this, Barbauld seems less limited than other 'conservatives' of the period, although, in 1790, her brother, indeed, would have liked her to have taken a more public role, using her poetic talents to uphold freedom as she had in former years.[23] Barbauld's youthful admiration of Rousseau's 'nouvelle Heloise', her marriage to a man known to be suffering from hereditary insanity, or perhaps the early lessons of her very decorous and proper mother might have prompted her reserve. This would indeed bear out Barbauld's own dictum that education 'includes the whole process by which a human being is formed' and that the most powerful and lasting education is that of the circumstances which surround the growing child.[24]

Barbauld appeared to pass on some of her own conservatism to those young women who were closely associated with her. Certainly both Lucy Aikin and Sarah Austin in later life disclaimed any assumption of equality with men. Yet both were talented and famed writers who worked hard to ensure greater respect and opportunities for women.[25] Lucy Aikin, a writer and translator from the age of seventeen and later to be a historian and biographer as well as a brilliant conversationalist admired by literary and professional men and politicians, was at least certain that both sexes were equal in talents, potentialities and mental qualities. In *Epistles on Women*, written when she was twenty-nine, she argued that history showed that whenever women had been allowed to share in the best efforts of men 'no talent, no virtue is masculine alone, no fault or folly exclusively

22. Barbauld, *Legacy*, pp. 41–55, 73–9, 121–36; J. Aikin and Mrs Barbauld, *Evenings at Home* (Edinburgh, 1868; 1st edn 1793), pp. 37–42.

23. Ellis, *Barbauld*, pp. 183–4.

24. Anna le Breton, *Memories of Seventy Years* (1883), pp. 118–19; Lucy Aikin, *Barbauld*, II, pp. 305–20.

25. Philip Hemery le Breton (ed.), *Memoirs, Miscellanies and Letters of the Late Lucy Aikin*, pp. xix–xxvii; Sarah Austin, 'Preface' to Lady Holland, *A Memoir and Letters of Sydney Smith*, 2 vols (1855), II, pp. xvi–xviii.

feminine'. The realization of this, she thought, should prevent women being the butt of scorn or malice in the future, or fathers telling daughters they must conceal their wit, learning or even good sense from the jealousy of men. Men and women, indeed, had identical interests and thus the degradation or elevation of one affected the other in the same way. Her poetic trawl of history amply proved her point that humanity at large suffers when tyrannical or foolish man makes woman

> Scorned and caressed, a plaything and a slave,
> Yet taught with spaniel soul to kiss the rod,
> And worship man as delegate of God.[26]

Women should neither suffer the 'Distorted virtue, talent misapplied' of convents nor be corrupted by gallantry but be allowed to realize their natural nobility, intelligence and humanity. By right and in their own interests, therefore, men should

> Be generous then, unbind
> Your barbarous shackles, loose the female mind.[27]

Nevertheless, whilst she delighted both in her own studies and in the general improvement in women's education, Lucy Aikin accepted that since men were physically stronger than women they were able to fulfil many occupations which women could not. Generally, therefore, men had to assume public and active roles in life which conferred authority and implied a certain degree of submission from women.[28] Even more than her aunt, Lucy Aikin preached the intellectual equality of the sexes, but, like her, while stretching the boundaries of what was usually accepted that women could do, she lived at home quietly amongst her family for most of her life.

Some Unitarian women hid their talents even further. Joanna Baillie, a neighbour of Anna Barbauld's at Hampstead, a fellow Unitarian and a great friend of Barbauld and Lucy Aikin, initially kept secret her authorship of the acclaimed *Plays on the Passions* even from her new friends.[29] Could women do otherwise at this time? Those who stepped beyond the limits of 'respectability' lost credibility for their fragile achievements and their opinions, as the examples of Mary Wollstonecraft, Mary Hays and Catherine Graham Macaulay demonstrated. The latter was also castigated for her claims

26. Lucy Aikin, *Epistles on Women* (1810), pp. vi–viii, 17–77.
27. Ibid., pp. 78–81.
28. Ibid., p. v; Philip le Breton, *Lucy Aikin*, pp. 11–131 *passim*.
29. Ibid., pp. xxviii, 7–11; Ellis, *Barbauld*, pp. 230–2.

to scholarship and her open Whig sympathies.[30] She dared to get involved in political questions, but so did Anna Barbauld. In 1790 in her *Address to the Opposers of the Repeal of the Corporation and Test Acts,* for example, the latter upheld the dissenters' *right* to have a share in the state but proudly argued that if this were not permitted then dissenters would make their enforced exclusion an honourable distinction, extracting respect and even emulation of their education. Barbauld claimed that if dissenters' educational institutions excelled, especially in ethos, others would entrust them with the education of their youth. If they enlightened the world by their discoveries, they would earn its involuntary homage. Not least, 'If your restraints operate towards keeping us in that middle rank of life where industry and virtue most abound, we shall have the honour to count ourselves among that class of the community which has ever been the source of manners, of population and of wealth.'[31] In this Anna Barbauld was seen as their champion by the Unitarians, as she was two years later when she defended 'Public or Social Worship' at a time when Unitarians were increasingly under attack for irreligion. Throughout she was sure that it was a time when people had to wake up to change: 'There are periods in which the human mind seems to slumber, but this is not one of them. A keen spirit of research is now abroad, and demands reform.'[32]

Long having celebrated struggles of liberty against the 'proud oppressor's cruel grasp', Anna Barbauld was more interested in such ideals of liberty and the reform of the radical circles in which she moved than in gender issues. Even though she wished domestic tyranny to be abolished,[33] her first concerns were for general causes of rights and liberty not those of gender. Similarly, another Unitarian woman, Ann Jebb, courageously campaigned for a wide range of reforms but not ones concerning gender issues. Writing as 'Priscilla', in the *London Chronicle* from 1772 to 1774, she attacked the universities' imposition of doctrinal subscriptions on undergraduates, a cause over which her husband, Dr John Jebb, resigned from Cambridge in 1775. Supporting her husband further in his fight for constitutional reform, Mrs Jebb welcomed the French Revolution

30. B. Hill, *The Republican Virago: The Life and Times of Catherine Macaulay, Historian* (Oxford, 1992), pp. 130–9, 241–51.

31. Lucy Aikin, *Barbauld,* II, pp. 355–66.

32. Ibid., p. 366; Anna Laetitia Barbauld, *Remarks on Mr Gilbert Wakefield's Inquiry into the Expediency and Propriety of Public or Social Worship* (1829; 1st publ. 1792), pp. 58 and *passim.*

33. Ellis, *Barbauld,* I, pp. 47–9; Lucy Aikin, *Barbauld,* II, p. 375.

and published letters to *John Bull* against the wars with France. She did not write about the rights of women, however, and her obituary in the *Monthly Repository* in 1812 referred to her 'delicacy of mind, which admitted no compromise with that masculine boldness, in which some females, of a highly cultivated intellect, have at times indulged'.[34]

The education of Unitarian women did help them nevertheless to achieve much for women of that time. Anna Barbauld's fame spread beyond Unitarian circles even though some of the most ecstatic reviews contained some barbed comments. William Woodfall in the *Monthly Review*, for example, raved about her poems in 1773 to the point of declaring that Barbauld had 'a justness of thought & vigour of imagination, inferior only to the works of Milton & Shakespeare'. He then, however, regretted that she had tried too much to emulate men rather than following in the 'natural' lines of female genius. This, he declared, was due to her lack of 'proper' education: if she had been more directed by her mother than her father, then 'we should have been as much enchanted by her feminine beauties, as we are now pleased & astonished by the strength of her imagination, the variety of her knowledge, & the goodness of her heart'.[35] Women could never win completely, but literary achievements such as Barbauld's, Lucy Aikin's and later Sarah Austin's did help the gradual acceptance of serious female writing. Another Unitarian, Jane Marcet, for example, introduced Faraday and others to chemistry in her *Conversations on Chemistry, intended more especially for the Female Sex* of 1806. This laid the basis for her even more famous *Conversations on Political Economy* of 1816. Marcet cleverly used fictional dialogue to aid learning by young people, as Aikin and others had done for children.[36]

Other Unitarian women became reputed teachers. Eliza Gould, for instance, having established a thriving Sunday school, ran a successful girls' boarding school until her refusal to give up taking the radical *Cambridge Intelligencer* led to the school's closure.[37] Importantly, teaching was seen by Unitarians as a very respectable career for women if they needed one. Eliza Lawrence, who with her sisters successfully turned to governessing and then school-teaching

34. *MR* (1812), VII, pp. 597–603, 661–72.

35. Betsy Rodgers, *Georgian Chronicle* (1958), pp. 58–60.

36. 'Jane Marcet', *DNB*, XXXVI, pp. 122–3; W. Henderson, 'Jane Marcet's *Conversations on Political Economy*: a new interpretation', *HofE* (1994), 23, no. 4, pp. 423, 427, 433–5.

37. Visiting the journal's editor Benjamin Flower in prison led her to a happy marriage and the birth of two nineteenth-century feminists, Sarah and Eliza Flower: *MR* (Apr. 1810), V, pp. 203–6.

when their father lost his money in 1793, later said: 'no set of females (except perhaps the few who are very happily married) have more substantial happiness than those who enter with all their hearts into the employment of education . . .'.[38] This was unlike Catherine Cappe's Anglican aunts, who dissuaded her from opening a school because they feared it would remove her from the rank of 'gentlewoman'.[39]

Families and female education

Thus, even when Unitarian women did extend the boundaries of female achievement they did so within the limits of writing and teaching. An example of this can be seen in the amazingly successful Aikin family, who set a pattern of mutually supportive, intellectually stimulating and affectionate behaviour. John and Martha Aikin entirely educated their last two children, Lucy and her youngest brother Edmund, and John involved the whole family in his publications, including *Evenings at Home.* Lucy testified to the lively interest the children took in his ideas and the way their reasoning powers were strengthened by their father's genuine encouragement of their eager criticism. Learning much from such enjoyable home teaching, the results were different for the sons than for the daughter. Kind, modest Arthur Aikin became a chemistry lecturer and writer, editor of the *Annual Review,* a founder and later honorary secretary of the Geological Society and secretary of the Society of Arts from 1817 to 1839. Charles, who married Anne, the fascinating, lovely, intelligent daughter of Gilbert Wakefield, became a doctor, and Edmund showed great promise as an architect before his early death in 1819, but clever, effervescent Lucy was to become a successful *amateur* historian and writer.[40]

The Unitarian journal *The Monthly Repository* decried the constraints on female potential in England by printing extracts from Morris Birkbeck. He noted that in France women were naturally deeply and knowledgeably involved in family businesses of all kinds and commended the resulting freedom of action and reliance

38. Dorothy E. de Zouche, *Roedean School 1885–1955* (printed for private circulation, 1955), p. 15.
39. Catherine Cappe, *Memoirs of the Life of the Late Mrs Catherine Cappe* (1822), pp. 196–201.
40. Anna le Breton, *Memories,* pp. v–vi, 1–2, 32–8; Lucy Aikin, *John Aikin,* I, pp. 37–40, 60, 156–9, 165, 201–2; Rodgers, *Georgian Chronicle,* pp. 157–83.

on their own powers in women.[41] Although women were not yet excluded from family businesses in England, their contributions to them were gender-determined and minimal. This was true too of Unitarian industrial families. Archibald Kenrick, in Birmingham, for example, persuaded his father to take some of the money saved for his sisters' inheritance in order to help him set up his buckle business. In later years he had a proper partnership arrangement with his son but settled £300 a year on his daughter, Rebecca, who repaid the family by providing domestic care to whoever needed it, including her sisters-in-law busy producing the next generation. Other relatives were part of the business and wives brought welcome capital into it.[42] This was true of the Gregs of Styal, textile manufacturers. Samuel Greg's wife, Hannah Lightbody, not only brought him a dowry of £10,000 and valuable textile connections, but provided him with twelve children, including sons to carry on his expanding business empire. She and her daughters became responsible for the care of the apprentices but took no part in the running of the business.[43]

Hannah Greg insisted that all her children received the best education obtainable. Thus the girls, as well as the boys, attended the Rev. J.J. Tayler's school in Nottingham. They could not follow to Lant Carpenter's boys' school in Bristol or to Oxford or Edinburgh universities, but they did at least attend scientific lectures in Manchester. Hannah was aware that her upbringing of her daughters was unusual: as she remarked to her eldest daughter's future father-in-law, William Rathbone IV, in the 1790s: 'were I to educate my Daughters as many Mothers are accused of doing, merely with a view to their relation to your sex, my advice and instruction would be far other than what it will be I hope, in the notion of their being individual and rational and immortal beings'.[44]

Nevertheless, despite Hannah's liberal concept of female education, she still expected her daughters to use their accomplishments, the chief of which was 'to be agreeable' at all times, within the home. She saw herself as the ever available servant of the family, its emotional pivot and 'rallying point'. Her 'paramount dread' of her

41. *MR* (1815), X, p. 73.

42. Jane Rendall, *Women in an Industrializing Society: England 1750–1880* (Oxford, 1990), pp. 45, 49–54; Leonore Davidoff and Catherine Hall, *Family Fortunes* (1987), pp. 217, 219, 250, 272–5, 279–89, 301–5, 311.

43. Mary B. Rose, *The Gregs of Quarry Bank Mill* (Cambridge, 1986), pp. 16–18, 28–35; Peter Spencer, *A Portrait of Hannah Greg 1766–1828* (Styal, 1985), pp. 6, 10–13, 29–30.

44. Ibid., p. 20.

home being dull to either husband or children led her to make Quarry Bank at Styal a family society 'where intellect and excellence could rule'. She provided the eager, intellectual and liberal vitality that was to be found in many Unitarian homes, even running a family 'Junior Literary and Philosophical Society' with rules, meetings and officers. Her children were certainly successful, even if they varied somewhat in their liberalism on social matters. They included the brilliant, if hard-headed, businessman Robert Hyde Greg MP, the industrial reformer Samuel Greg, the well-known essayist W.R. Greg, and the best exemplar of Hannah's ideals, the philanthropist and educationist Elizabeth Rathbone.[45]

For her sons, Hannah aimed at producing a 'gentleman to the very core, inside and out'. She was anxious to communicate that 'a good education does not spoil the Man of Business, and a taste for literature, judiciously infused, contributes to form the intelligent merchant as well as the virtuous man'.[46] Some of her more liberal ideas on education, however, were thwarted by the practical concerns of her husband, who was happy for his sons to cultivate a taste for knowledge but not for them to waste time on novels and 'prating books'. It was Hannah who represented the female equivalent of a gentleman, being admired by Elizabeth Fletcher for her 'cultivation of mind, and refinement of manners' even 'in the midst of money-making and somewhat unpolished community of merchants and manufacturers'.[47] The concepts of gentlemen and ladies were obviously integral to this family education but only the men went into business.

Other Unitarian homes bear out this phenomenon. Higher concepts of womanhood than the norm and a wider and deeper education were given to females, but there were still marked gendered differences of role. This was particularly noticeable between brothers and sisters. For example, Susannah Taylor's house in Norwich was known for its central place in the brilliant literary and political society of Norwich and she and her husband produced a stream of distinguished children. She ensured the best education for her daughter Sarah, who became an excellent Latin scholar, a fluent speaker in French, German and Italian and a superb translator. Sarah's successive homes in England and on the Continent, when married to John Austin, were magnets for men and women of scientific and intellectual renown. The boys' lives were to be more varied than their sister's, however: John Taylor was an engineering

45. Ibid., pp. 17–18, 23–5, 29–30. 46. Ibid., pp. 16–22. 47. Ibid., pp. 22, 28.

prodigy; Richard, a renowned printer of European fame, founder of the Taylor and Francis publishing firm; Edward, Gresham Professor of Music; Philip, a first-class inventor and popular shipbuilder in France; and Arthur, printer to the City of London. The Duke of Sussex said of the Taylor family that they reversed the ordinary saying that it took nine tailors to make a man:[48] he would have been more accurate if he had not omitted the part of a woman.

Another brilliant Unitarian family in Norwich, the Martineaus, equally strove to provide their numerous offspring, boys and girls alike, with teachers and schooling. From the age of nine to thirteen its most famous member, Harriet, and her sister Rachel were taught at home by an older brother and sister. Harriet preferred her subsequent education at the mixed school run by the Rev. Issac Perry, who had lost his pulpit and boys' school when he converted to Unitarianism. She welcomed the thoroughness and order usually reserved for boys' education. Through these various means she received a very good grounding in Latin, French, English literature and composition, and through family discussion and reading learnt much history, biography and critical literature. With needlework and music in addition, and much private reading, Harriet certainly had received a wide, thorough education by the time she was sixteen. She later recalled a lack of 'kindly affections' and 'tenderness', but this was to be redeemed in another Unitarian household, that of her relatives, the Carpenters, in 1818.[49]

Harriet was closest in affection and temperament to her brother James, equally 'strangely gifted' but with more career paths open to him. Although younger than her by three years, his more 'systematic studies', first at Norwich Grammar School, whose public-school-type system he found utterly repellent, and then at Dr Carpenter's, enabled him to catch up. Subsequent studies at the epitome of Unitarian education, Manchester College, put James on course for a distinguished career in lecturing and theological writing, or at least as distinguished a career as his disabilities as a Unitarian scholar would allow him. Through opportunism, talents and confidence, Harriet was able to make a name for herself in writing and journalism. The only other avenue open to her talents, teaching, was taken by her sister Rachel.[50]

48. Ross, *Three Generations*, pp. iii–ix, 4–29; *DNB*, LV, pp. 456–9.
49. H. Martineau, *Autobiography*, 3 vols (1877), I, pp. 8–73, 94–5.
50. J. Drummond and C.B. Upton *The Life and Letters of James Martineau*, 2 vols (1902), I, pp. 9, 16–18, 39.

Unitarian networks

Within these Unitarian families women played a huge, if often publicly unacknowledged, role by networking. In Norwich and its neighbourhood the Taylor, Martineau and Aikin families all knew each other. After eight years of living near Norwich the Aikins moved to London in 1792 and then to Stoke Newington in 1797, to which the Barbaulds moved from Hampstead in 1802. Susannah Taylor was a lifelong friend of Anna Barbauld. In London, the Aikin and Barbauld families were part of progressive literary and professional circles which included Maria Edgeworth, Henry Crabb Robinson, William Hazlitt, the brilliant critic and essayist, and Samuel Rogers, the poet. Their Unitarian connections linked them further afield. For example, amongst Lucy Aikin's closest friends were the Unitarian Roscoes of Liverpool. There Lucy enjoyed theatricals and telling ghost stories as well as seeing William Roscoe's natural history collection. Roscoe's 'Renaissance' circle included Thomas Bentley, the great friend of Josiah Wedgwood, a long-standing friend of the Aikins from Warrington days, who agonized as much over his girls' education as he did over his boys'. His daughter Sukey, a devotee of Honora Edgeworth (Richard's muse), learnt from the same tutors as her brothers, attended the best progressive schools and acquired an expensive musical and art education. Her fame was to be the mother of Charles Darwin.[51] William Roscoe's daughter, Mary Anne, long his devoted companion, found her fame in being the mother of the economist William Stanley Jevons. Another daughter, Jane, who married the Rev. F. Hornblower, wrote volumes of verse, as did two sons, Robert and Thomas.[52]

Roscoe's own writings were published by the radical publisher, the Unitarian Joseph Johnson, the connecting link between Unitarians and other liberal thinkers from all over the country, including members of the Lunar Society. His shop and home in St Paul's Churchyard became one of their favourite meeting places. This, therefore, was a particularly important connection for those outstanding women whom he published, including Maria Edgeworth, Mary Hays and Anna Barbauld.[53]

51. Rodgers, *Georgian Chronicle*, pp. 181 and *passim*; S.G. Checkland, 'Economic attitudes in Liverpool', *Economic History Review* (1952), 5, no. 1, pp. 58–75; Julia Wedgwood (ed. C.H. Herford), *The Personal Life of Josiah Wedgwood the Potter* (Manchester, 1915), pp. 27–37, 46, 304–63.

52. George Chandler, *William Roscoe of Liverpool* (1953), pp. xxxii–iv.

53. Tyson, *Joseph Johnson*, pp. 84 and *passim*.

Mary Wollstonecraft

Mary Wollstonecraft too was published by Joseph Johnson. From 1784 to 1785 she resided at Newington Green, where so many Unitarians lived, and attended Richard Price's services. She was much influenced by Price's views on the perfectibility of humankind, by the general Unitarian emphasis on reason and the need for all to develop their mental and moral abilities through education, and by their respect for women's intellectual powers. Her friendship in revolutionary France with Martha and Mary Russell, who were driven into exile there with their father William after the Birmingham Riots of 1791, would have further demonstrated to her how Unitarian families expected women to be interested in political and public issues.[54]

In 1792 in her *Thoughts on the Education of Daughters* Wollstonecraft begged for girls to have a more solid education than was customary, especially since rational parents were needed to develop carefully children's understanding and sympathies. Unfortunately, she added, it does not always happen that both parents are rational, and it was the supposedly weaker, the mother, who had it in her power to do most mischief.[55] Her most famous book, however, then as now, was her *Vindication of the Rights of Women* of 1792, whose basic premise was that God had created all human beings as rational creatures. They therefore had a basic right, irrespective of sex, to develop that rationality through a liberal education and thereby realize their potential as moral, active and useful members of the community. To fulfil this potential and for their own happiness, that of their families, and for the better service of God, she wished to revolutionize the environment and education of females. Indeed, unless women received a proper education instead of their desultory trifling with knowledge, argued Wollstonecraft, they 'will stop the progress of knowledge and virtue' and 'must ever languish like exotics and be reckoned beautiful flaws in nature. Let it also be remembered that they are the only flaw.'[56]

Wollstonecraft also advocated other revolutionary ideas. She supported free public, coeducational schools and considered that

54. Claire Tomalin, *Mary Wollstonecraft* (Harmondsworth, 1974), pp. 45–8, 51–2, 89–109; S.H. Jeyes, *The Russells of Birmingham in the French Revolution and in America 1791–1814* (1911), pp. 116–19, 130, 143.

55. Mary Wollstonecraft, *Thoughts on the Education of Daughters* (Oxford, 1994), p. 12.

56. Mary Wollstonecraft, *Vindication of the Rights of Women* (Harmondsworth, 1975, 1st edn 1792), pp. 86–7, 109, 122.

women could undertake various responsible roles if allowed, such as doctoring, midwifery, politics and diverse business concerns. Much vilified then and for long after for making outrageous claims which would unsex women and emasculate men, she was in fact asking for both to become better people through allowing all equal respect and educational rights. She saw that it was impossible to create a good and just society if one half of it did not have their understanding, taste and judgement properly developed.[57]

In this Wollstonecraft agreed with the ideals and associationist education of Priestley. She shared public hatred with the latter, although in her case this was because of her disordered lifestyle. Since the latter was coupled with demands that shocked traditional gender attitudes, her ideas were generally traduced. Yet many Unitarians adhered to them, two men, George Philips and William Shepherd, publicly supporting female suffrage as early as 1794.[58] Some Unitarians gave an early lead on women's rights. Priestley, for example, tried to circumvent the marriage laws which made all of a wife's property her husband's. He willed annuities to both his daughter Sarah and his daughter-in-law Margaret in such a way that their husbands had no control over them.[59] Other Unitarians did not always go so far, although John Holland gave a sympathetic review of *The Vindication* in the Unitarian journal *The Christian Miscellany.* William Roscoe pressed copies of it on ladies of his circle and William Frend and George Dyer encouraged Mary and Elizabeth Hays, fervent disciples of Wollstonecraft already, to write on women's rights. Joseph Johnson encouraged Mary Hays' *Appeal to the Men of Great Britain on Behalf of the Women* in 1798, but the times were not propitious for such a book, especially as Hays' own lack of propriety in her love life rendered her a target of ridicule. Hays also tried in her book *Emma Courtney* to explain through fiction how difficult it was for women of strong feelings and energies to find an outlet for these, particularly if they were unmarried.[60] Her passionate outpourings were too radical for the times but they were indicative of the willingness of these radicals to explore new, and to many outrageous, ideas.

57. Ibid., pp. 286–7, 261 and *passim.*

58. Raymond V. Holt, *The Unitarian Contribution to Social Progress in England* (1952), p. 152.

59. R.A.M. Dixon, 'Priestley's daughter and her descendants', *TUHS* (1931–34), V, pp. 53–4.

60. H. McLachlan, *The Unitarian Movement in the Religious Life of England* (1934), pp. 172, 17; Tomalin, *Wollstonecraft*, pp. 142–3, 295–8; Mary Hays, *Emma Courtney* (Oxford, 1995), *passim*; Knight, *University Rebel*, pp. 198–213.

Radical ideas and women

Interestingly, Unitarian *men* were sympathetic to Wollstonecraft. Dyer was quite a feminist, partly because he believed that in politics women, provided that they could rise above the 'degrading' customs and education meted out to them, were 'more uniformly on the side of liberty than the other sex'.[61] Frend's daughter Sophie recalled how she was used to meeting literary and political radicals of both sexes with her father. Certainly, growing up in circles where William Godwin, Thomas Holcroft, Francis Burdett and Coleridge (when still a Jacobin) moved was likely to imbue Unitarian females such as her with ideals of liberty. Fanny Holcroft, daughter of the republican Thomas Holcroft, similarly grew up in Unitarian and radical circles. She wrote poetry against slavery – for example, 'The Negro' in 1797, in which a dying slave curses his Christian masters. Such female involvement in the fight to abolish slavery would have pleased the radical Unitarian merchants in Manchester, who, prominent in the campaign against the slave trade, urged women as guardians of morality and compassion to subscribe to the cause.[62]

Anna Barbauld, unlike Hannah More, was inspired by the initial achievements of the French Revolution. Conversely, it was despair at the death of liberty in Europe which led her to write her poem 'Eighteen Hundred and Eleven' in which she hoped that the new United States of America would become the protector of true freedom of thought. It was also the biting anonymous attack (probably by Southey) on this in the *Quarterly Review* which finished her literary career. This virulent denunciation derided her former writing as lacking 'taste or talents' and hoped the nation might be saved without the aid of Mrs Barbauld, regretting she felt the need to 'dash down her shagreen spectacles and her knitting-needles' in some misguided patriotism.[63]

No wonder women otherwise attuned to calls for liberty were disinclined to move too fast on issues concerning their own sex. Lucy Aikin was sure that women like Mary Hays went too far. Referring to the latter's *Female Biography* in 1803, she declared she wanted equal rights for the sexes and recognition of their equal talents:

61. Tomalin, *Wollstonecraft*, p. 143n.

62. Knight, *University Rebel*, pp. 215–16, 236–7, 244, 251; Thomas Holcroft and William Hazlitt, 'Memoirs of the late Thomas Holcroft', in William Hazlitt, *Works*, 21 vols (1830–34), III, pp. 127–268; Clare Midgley, *Women against Slavery* (1992), pp. 1–40.

63. Ellis, *Barbauld*, pp. 272–9.

> but, alas, though I would not so much as whisper this to the pretended lords of creation –
>
> Her arguments directly tend
> Against the cause she would defend.

In showing the excesses of energetic women so much, Hays would make men 'repeat with tenfold energy that women have no business with anything, but nursing children and mending stockings'.[64] Society was not changing so fast that female demands could make too much headway, but Unitarian attitudes and actions were planting the seeds.

This could be seen too in the way that women of energetic mind like Catherine Cappe were drawn to Unitarianism. Born in Yorkshire in 1744 into an Anglican family which positively dissuaded her from intellectual learning of any kind (her mother, granddaughter of a wealthy baronet, had had to teach herself to read and write), Catherine struggled to gain knowledge where and when she could. Visits in her home county to various relatives and friends deepened her dislike of a frivolous life and turned her towards the social and educational work among the poor for which she became famous. In these pursuits she was influenced by Theophilus and Hannah Lindsey, whose conversion to Unitarianism she anticipated. It was among Unitarians that she found the intellectual stimulus and rational theology she craved. She became an ardent Necessarian in Priestleyan mode and she was looked after in Leeds by Mrs Dawson, who, like Mrs Rayner, was an admired friend of Priestley. Mrs Rayner gave needed sponsorship to both Lindsey and Priestley and was among those excellent women who inspired the latter to say that he was sure that there would be more women in heaven than men. He said that Mrs Rayner had 'a cultivated, comprehensive mind, equal to any subject of theology or metaphysics'.[65]

Mary Somerville had a similar battle to gain an intellectual education and, in rejecting the Tory and sternly patriarchal views in which she grew up, turned to liberalism and Unitarianism. Her revolt against oppression and tyranny began with her resentment of 'the injustice of the world in denying all those privileges of education to my sex which were so lavishly bestowed on men'. Her father's discovery of her studies of Euclid made him fear she would end up in a straitjacket, but fortunately her own persistence and

64. Philip le Breton, *Lucy Aikin*, pp. 125–6.

65. Cappe, *Life*, *passim*; Thomas Belsham, *Memoirs of the Late Rev. Theophilus Lindsey, MA* (1873; 1st edn 1812), pp. 76, 294–6; Joseph Priestley, *Autobiography of . . .* (Bath, 1970), p. 116.

eventual second marriage to her liberal cousin, Dr William Somerville, enabled her to develop her talents in geography and astronomy. Her lifelong friend Jane Marcet was equally supported by her husband, Dr Alexander Marcet, and was part of the same Unitarian and radical circles.[66]

By 1815, therefore, within the Unitarian network, there was a strong, active acceptance of women's intellectual capacity which was unusual for the time. Both this acceptance and the educational philosophy which lay behind it were enabling for women, although as yet most wished on principle to enhance traditional roles and seek greater equality within the family rather than reconstruct society. A deep education was promoted as vital to make possible such development. The fact that women naturally played a more equal role in familial and cultural life and that some of them became individually distinguished helped forge new conceptions of womanhood, its potentialities and rights which would be significant in the nineteenth century. Unitarians were fighting for acceptance in other ways, for the men were also struggling for recognition and respect as new leaders in society. Gender issues, however, were an integral part of this. It was within this context of complex change that the seedbed of future feminism was sown.

66. Martha Somerville, *Personal Recollections from Early Life to Old Age of Mary Somerville* (1873), pp. 3–114, 140–1; Henderson, 'Marcet', pp. 424–6.

PART TWO

1816–1860

CHAPTER FIVE

The Unitarian context

The Unitarians continued their concern with gender issues in the first half of the nineteenth century, although with different emphases as the context changed. This was particularly so as they became successful in some of their political and economic campaigns. They were not unique in their attitudes and actions concerning gender but, in this period as earlier, as a group they were usually much in advance of their contemporaries. They often gave the lead in writing and action as to what women were capable of and this stemmed from their educational and religious principles. They equally attempted to posit a new concept of 'gentleman', but both their partial success and failure in this had ambivalent effects on issues concerning women. This chapter will look at changes in Unitarianism and the place of Unitarians in the religious, social, political and intellectual world of the early nineteenth century, examining gender differences within this context.

Unitarianism 1816 to 1860

Although, during the long years of war and political repression at home, the enthusiasm of many Unitarians for radical change was dampened, they remained reformers and throughout the first half of the nineteenth century Unitarians were prominent in movements for parliamentary, municipal, social and educational change. They retained their passionate commitment to individual liberty and justice and an optimistic belief in the capacity of humankind to reach a perfect state in the world if educated correctly. Within this ideal there was a range of views, as might be expected in such an individualistic, non-dogmatic religion. Some Unitarians were becoming very wealthy and wanted an education commensurate with their culture and desired status. Some Unitarian businessmen, indeed, exceeded common expectations by writing learned works. Many Unitarian writers on theology, education and academic topics, however, were ministers. The latter were expected to be erudite and cultured but earned far less than their patrons in industry and commerce. Furthermore, some of their work among the poor gave them a different perspective on social and economic developments which might conflict with those of their co-religionists.

Such differences could be exacerbated in the case of both women and working-class Unitarians, although on general principles they might agree. Contemporary problems of the supply, nature and duration of education and access to certain educational institutions might affect nearly all Unitarians in some measure but how personal those problems might be and at what level they impinged varied according to gender and class. For middle-class women, especially from the wealthier sections, the problem might be how best to use the superior education they had received. Any success in the power, status and culture struggles principally fought by their menfolk might inspire emulation or might have the effect of further demonstrating their comparative inequalities.

Nevertheless, although Unitarians remained in the vanguard on gender issues, they were few in number. In the nineteenth century there were some very strong chapels in the commercial and textile-manufacturing centres of England, but nationally Unitarians only totalled 50,000 in 1851, despite the influx of General Baptists, Methodist Unitarians and dissidents from other denominations.[1] Incomers had some effect on Unitarian doctrine, but for the most part English Unitarianism to the 1830s followed along Priestleyan lines. Thereafter, many were influenced by William Ellery Channing, the ablest defender of Unitarianism in America, who, affected himself by thinkers such as the eighteenth-century Arian Richard Price and the German philosopher Kant, emphasized the power of human reason, biblical scholarship and ethics. Channing believed in the essential dignity of humanity and that people could perfect their own souls through their affections, principles and capacity of 'rising' by their 'own free-will to God'. Such beliefs both appealed to those aspects of extreme individualism, moral improvement and active faith already prevalent in Unitarian philosophy and helped soften

1. A.D. Gilbert, *Religion and Society in Industrial England* (1976), p. 41; R.K. Webb, 'The Unitarian background', in Barbara Smith (ed.), *Truth, Liberty, Religion* (Oxford, 1986), p. 17.

and spiritualize an intellectual religion. Channing's view of Christianity as a constantly unfolding religion, understood by Man's developing reason, similarly both appealed to strands already present in Unitarianism and further reinforced the commitment to an open, developing faith without confining titles or organization. Increasingly from the 1830s, James Martineau and his ministerial friends steered Unitarians towards basing their religion on reason and conscience rather than the Bible.[2]

Within this open-ended religion, however, individual Unitarians throughout the period 1815 to 1860 drew on whichever strands in Unitarianism best suited them. For example, William Johnson Fox's ardent preaching in the 1820s and early 1830s particularly appealed to Unitarians looking for a more spiritual and 'loving' faith, yet he was very much in the intellectual tradition of Unitarianism, finding that orthodox dissent 'does not build up intelligence, does not develop the faculties, does not humanise and raise the entire character, nor shape it for public usefulness; . . . does not tend towards the expansion of our nature in the individual'.[3] For Fox and many others, Unitarianism did precisely this. The new tendencies served only to reinforce the cult of the rational, perpetually self-improving, enquiring, public-spirited individual which epitomized the Unitarian movement.

In nineteenth-century terms this might seem to be a male ideal rather than a female one, and certainly Unitarianism stressed the maleness of God and had neither the Virgin Mary nor the 'gentle' Jesus pray to. On the other hand, some Unitarians, especially those like Lant and Mary Carpenter who were influenced by Evangelicalism, stressed the loving side of Jesus and used this as a model for men as well as their inspiration for their abiding and active compassion for all kinds and conditions of humans.[4] The ideal of homes as places of rational education eulogized by educationists such as John Relly Beard, Lucy Aikin, Harriet Martineau and others similarly expected both men and women to grow in domestic virtues.[5] Michael Watts has suggested that the fault of Unitarianism in being too cold

2. A. Delbanco, *William Ellery Channing* (Harvard, 1981), *passim*; Joseph Estlin Carpenter, *James Martineau* (1905), *passim*.

3. R. and E. Garnett, *The Life of W.J. Fox* (1909), pp. 22–4, 26–7.

4. William Carpenter, *Sketch of the Life and Work of Mary Carpenter of Bristol* (Bristol, 1877), pp. 1–6; Douglas Charles Stange, *British Unitarians against American Slavery, 1833–65* (1984), p. 222.

5. John Relly Beard, *Schools* (1842), pp. 40–1, 43, 46–8; Anna Laetitia le Breton (ed.), *Correspondence of Dr Channing and Lucy Aikin* (1874), pp. 126–423 *passim*; Harriet Martineau, *Household Education* (1870; 1st edn 1848), *passim*.

and intellectual might have been all the more significant with regard to women,[6] but for many females the shifts in emphasis and feeling connected with Channing and Fox appear to have made Unitarianism very palatable. Yet this was also true for many men.

These developments in Unitarianism were important at a time when the influence of Evangelicalism in orthodox Christianity had grown among the middle classes, and this dynamic religion of the heart was very appealing to many women. Its stress on the 'female' virtues of humility, submissiveness, duty, and purity, its profound sense of sin and of a mission to regenerate the world, not least through the examples of 'morally superior' women at home, gave new status to women but within greater limits. For instance, John James, a leading Independent minister, traduced those who would undermine woman's natural instincts and God's law, which both enjoined on her obedience to her menfolk and the power won by 'passive' gentleness, tenderness and self-denial.[7] 'Innocence' seemed best protected at home, where sensitive woman's 'natural' subordination was a Christian example to all. Likewise her reliance on her feelings rendered her unfit for deep or close reasoning.

In Unitarianism, however, females as well as males enjoyed the freedom and responsibility of the individual search for religious truth. In the decades before 1860 when Benjamin Jowett and the Anglican *Broad Church shocked England with their espousal of scriptural criticism, Unitarians, both lay and ministerial, according to Dennis Wigmore-Beddoes, 'contributed not a little to that unsettlement of belief [among non-Unitarians] which occasioned for many the adoption of Broad Church views'. Thomas Belsham, John Kenrick, Francis Newman and Rev. George Vance Smith, for example, were clerical scholars who successively used German, their own critical skills and archaeological discoveries to question the authenticity of the scriptures, put them in historical context and show their composite nature. Lay Unitarians such as Charles Hennell in 1838 and William Greg in 1851 similarly argued reverently but rationalistically and in a scholarly way about the scriptures.[8]

Women Unitarians, for most of this period, were not responsible for writing such influential works of biblical criticism, although

6. Michael R. Watts, *The Dissenters*, 2 vols (Oxford, 1995), II, p. 90.

7. Jane Rendall, *The Origins of Modern Feminism: Women in Britain, France and the USA 1780–1869* (1985), pp. 73–93; Dale A. Johnson, *Women in English Religion 1700–1925* (New York, 1983), pp. 128–32.

8. Dennis G. Wigmore-Beddoes, *Yesterday's Radicals* (1971), pp. 30–9.

some of Harriet Martineau's first public forays were on religious subjects and it was her essay on *Female Writers on Practical Divinity* which prompted her elder brother Thomas to remark: 'Now, dear, leave it to other women to make shirts and darn stockings; and do you devote yourself to this.'[9] Patronizing – but the fact that male Unitarians were comfortable with women presenting their case was illustrated by their journal *The Monthly Repository*'s admiring reception of both her *Traditions of Palestine* and the three separate prize-winning essays she wrote to promote Unitarianism among Roman Catholics, Mohammedans and Jews.[10] Women debated freely with men on theological issues, as illustrated in the correspondence of Lucy Aikin with William Channing and of Anna Swanwick with Frances Newman and James Martineau. Lucy Aikin thanked Channing for his rational religious influence on important women like Joanna Baillie, Mary Somerville and Jane Marcet, since, so she believed, religious women otherwise were prone to become fanatic or bigoted.[11] Francis Newman, too, was warmly admired by several Unitarian women such as Elizabeth Gaskell and Mary Carpenter, but they were sufficiently independent not to accept all his unbelief.[12] Frances Power Cobbe was closer to his thinking and, inspired too by the American Unitarian Theodore Parker, she published anonymously in 1855 her own *Essay on the Theory of Intuitive Morals*, which was criticized for its heresy. Her *theism had considerable influence on Unitarians in later years.[13]

Unitarians and other Christians

No wonder orthodox dissenters cooperated uneasily with Unitarians. Indeed, they increasingly sought both to clip the power that the latter, in the guise of Presbyterians, held in corporate dissenting bodies, and to check Unitarianism altogether by wresting from them the many chapels which the orthodox believed rightfully belonged to them. Such arguments became particularly bitter in the early

9. Harriet Martineau, *Autobiography*, 3 vols (1877), I, pp. 119–20, 146–7.
10. *MR* (1830), NS 4, pp. 521–9; (1832), NS 6, pp. 475–84.
11. Anna le Breton, *Channing and Aikin*, pp. 126–8, *passim*; Mary L. Bruce, *Anna Swanwick: A Memoir and Recollections, 1813–99* (1903), pp. 23, 56–8, 216–17 and *passim*.
12. J.A.V. Chapple and A. Pollard (eds), *The Letters of Mrs Gaskell* (Manchester, 1966), pp. 87–8; Joseph Estlin Carpenter, *The Life and Work of Mary Carpenter* (1879), p. 97.
13. Frances Power Cobbe, *Life of*... (1904), pp. 93–8, 110–34, 524–5; *DNB* (1912), 2nd Supplement, I, pp. 377–9.

nineteenth century, and one long-drawn-out legal dispute was only finally settled in the 1840s.[14]

Partly the fear of Unitarianism was based on a conviction that it led to disbelief in religion altogether. There was some justification for this. The abandonment of some of the central tenets of traditional Christianity, constant questioning of the scriptures, enthusiasm for scientific discovery and a passion for social justice all contributed to readjustments of faith that took some out of Unitarianism into scepticism, agnosticism or even atheism. Arthur Aikin, William Taylor, Harriet Martineau and William Johnson Fox were among prominent Unitarians who, at some time in their lives, journeyed along such paths, although Unitarianism had been a powerful stimulus to their thinking, not least in education.[15]

Conversely, dissatisfied Unitarians who remained Christians tended to turn to Anglicanism rather than other forms of dissent, as the example of Frederick Denison Maurice illustrated, although he never quite discarded the positive tenets of Unitarianism even if he no longer attended its chapels.[16] Generally, however, Unitarians, like other dissenters, were inherently opposed to Church establishment. They attacked vigorously the wealth and privileges of the Church and its failure to use these to benefit the nation at large, particularly in education. The government, fearing the growth of dissent, did react to mounting criticism of the torpor and abuses of the Church, by rectifying some long-standing abuses. Within the Church itself there was some tentative theological research in the 1820s, but its lack of spirituality and the very interference of the state led to the development of the Oxford Movement in the 1830s. This movement, although heartily disliked by more moderate churchmen and attacked as Romanism by dissenters, did stimulate greater spirituality and vigour in Anglicanism. It also strengthened the hierarchical, conservative wing of the Church and helped exacerbate conflict with dissenters, especially over the control of education. The emergence of Christian Socialism in the 1840s and of the Broad Church Movement from the 1850s were developments with which Unitarians such as Frances Power Cobbe and Elizabeth Malleson could sympathize far more comfortably. Octavia Hill was thereby drawn from Unitarianism whilst Catherine Winkworth's theology stayed just outside. Elizabeth Gaskell, on the other hand, was one

14. Watts, *Dissenters*, pp. 92–6. 15. Ibid., pp. 91–2.

16. *DNB*, XXXVII, 98; D. Young, *F.D. Maurice and Unitarianism* (Oxford, 1992), pp. 169–70 and *passim*.

who remained a firm Unitarian yet admired Frederick Maurice and used Anglican churches when a Unitarian chapel was not available.[17]

Even liberal Anglicans such as Thomas Arnold, however, had little room for a group whose leader had avowedly set out to reform 'the corruptions of Christianity'.[18] Unitarianism was abhorred theologically by all orthodox Christians. John Relly Beard bitterly remarked that

> from the parlour as well as from the pulpit the Unitarian is excluded. The very greetings of his orthodox brethren are stiff and cold . . . In the minds of the vulgar especially, there is a certain vague horror of a Socinian which makes them regard such a one as the abstract of evil in religion . . . Tom Paine was once the scarecrow wherewith to frighten the weak; now the Socinian serves the purpose.[19]

There were exceptions to such distrust, but persecution of the Unitarians did not end in 1813 when penalties against anti-Trinitarianism were at last removed. This led some Unitarians, such as Richard Wright and Robert Aspland, former Baptists, and Joseph Cooke, a former Wesleyan, into a more aggressive stance, tighter organization and missionary zeal. Although such activities added a new vitality to the movement and brought in working-class members, this ran counter to the general tendency of the movement against proselytizing or sectarianism. Those half-hearted about 'missionary' work were the wealthy, better-educated Unitarians, the cream of London and provincial dissent, often, like William Smith of Norwich, from successful professional and commercial families. Richard Wright and William Johnson Fox, on the other hand, were also from Norwich but both from much humbler stock. The new organizations they supported specifically went out to the poor and used lay preachers, not necessarily well-educated, a 'methodistical' practice abhorrent to some Unitarians nourished on the learned theological writings and sermons suitable for the highly educated who they believed alone could understand their faith. Since Unitarians believed that salvation depended more on 'disposition of mind and . . . conduct in life' than correct 'opinions', they were less concerned with conversion than other religious groups. This, together with the lack of welcome to newcomers and the intellectualism of the sermons in some of their chapels helped ensure that working-class

17. *MR* (1826), XXI, p. 491; *MR* (1831), NS 5, pp. 627–35, 824–31; Young, *Maurice*, pp. 154–6; Margaret Shaen, *Memorials of Two Sisters: Susanna and Catherine Winkworth* (1908), pp. 20–1, 42–3, 141–9; Jenny Uglow, *Elizabeth Gaskell* (1994), pp. 225, 231, 265, 354, 441, 447–8, 451–2.

18. Thomas Arnold, *Principles of Church Reform* (1833), pp. 31, 35; Joseph Priestley, *A History of the Corruptions of Christianity* (Birmingham, 1782).

19. *MR* (1829), NS 3, p. 696.

membership remained small. There were some solidly working-class congregations in Lancashire such as that in Oldham and isolated pockets elsewhere. There was also a scattering of working-class members in opulent chapels and an important 'Unitarian thread in popular radicalism', but mostly Unitarianism was seen as 'the predilection of the solid, educated, well-heeled bourgeoisie'.[20]

John Seed has argued cogently that 'Unitarianism served specific social and ideological functions for its adherents in early nineteenth century towns'. His thesis stressed the Unitarian chapel as a social and cultural institution and nexus of power relations. He demonstrated that while Unitarianism did not make much impact in many of the new *manufacturing* centres of the north, even industrial Lancashire, most of England's major *commercial* towns did have important Unitarian chapels in the early nineteenth century. These often included among their members 'a substantial elite of merchants, bankers, physicians and solicitors – men of substantial wealth and social influence'. Substantial industrialists could be added since many of the wealthiest – for example, the Gregs, Kennedys and McConnels in Cheshire and Lancashire, the Marshalls in Leeds, the Biggses in Leicester, the Kenricks, Rylands and Nettlefolds in the west midlands and the Strutts in Derbyshire – were Unitarians. Many of these were both interrelated among themselves and with other prominent Unitarian families. The continuing fear of Unitarianism among the orthodox was often a bar to social intimacy and thus stimulated the Unitarians' extraordinary familial networks which gave both financial and cultural support to those within them and to the liberal causes they supported. Interlocking local, regional and national webs of friendship, business and marriage relationships, in which women played a key part, were enriched further by Unitarian adherence to common cultural, social and educational beliefs. These powerful networks made it possible for the Unitarian élite to realize at least partially 'the proper status which their wealth and education merited' and become an important radical influence within the dissenting middle class despite the liability of Unitarianism itself.[21]

20. Watts, *Dissenters*, pp. 83–91, 96–7, 263, 267, 349; R.W. Davies, *Dissent in Politics 1780–1830* (Epworth, 1971), pp. xiv, 196–206; David Gadian, 'Class formation and class action in north west industrial towns, 1830–50', in R.J. Morris (ed.), *Class, Power and Social Structures in British Nineteenth Century Towns* (Leicester, 1986), pp. 24–66; John Seed, 'Theologies of power: Unitarianism and the social relations of religious discourse, 1800–50', ibid., pp. 118–21.

21. Ibid., pp. 109–33; V.A.C. Gatrell, 'Incorporation and the pursuit of Liberal hegemony in Manchester 1790–1839', in Derek Fraser (ed.), *Municipal Reform and the Industrial City* (1982), pp. 16–60; Seed, 'Theologies of power', pp. 108–56.

W.J. Fox, in 1832, confidently expected Unitarians to carry the middle class's 'hitherto neglected mission . . . to conciliate, blend, harmonise and ultimately identify' the higher and lower classes on either side of them.[22] Such a statement both belied the Unitarians' confident élitism against the upper and within the middle classes and the paternalism that assumed that the working classes would follow their 'enlightened' lead. Some Unitarians did sympathize with the 'educational' *Chartists or early cooperative movement, but Unitarians' frequent positing of the working class as a problem to be investigated, educated and nurtured as political fodder met with mixed responses from their 'object'.[23]

Unitarians continued to oppose resolutely the Test and other disabling Acts. William Smith, grandfather of both Barbara Leigh-Smith and Florence Nightingale and, unusually for a Unitarian before 1832, an MP almost continuously from 1784 to 1830, led the dissenting cause in parliament over these. He acted similarly over Roman Catholic Emancipation, which Unitarians supported although evangelical dissenters, often vociferously, did not. The changes, eventually won in 1828 and 1829 respectively, were thus long fought for and hardly represented a sudden collapse of the established order in the 1830s as depicted by Jonathan Clark. It is right, however, that Unitarians were seeking to change the established order of things in government and society. They certainly continued to bear the brunt of unpopularity for such demands for reform in the years of successive, repressive Tory governments, and in 1832 nine of the twelve dissenters elected to parliament were Unitarians.[24] Lucy Aikin commented in 1839 that this surely meant that 'rational religion is silently working its way in society. It is remarkable that the Unitarian sect, confessedly one of the very smallest in the country, has more members of parliament in proportion belonging to it than any other denomination whatsoever.'[25]

Unitarians also played a leading role in many towns, fighting for municipal reform, either to incorporate non-incorporated towns like Manchester and Birmingham, or to reform corrupt or exclusive, self-elected corporations usually monopolized by old-established Tory or Anglican families. This was a struggle for power within the urban middle classes. The change resulting from the Municipal Corporations Act of 1835 was of the men rather than of the system,

22. *MR* (1832), NS 6, 153. 23. Watts, *Dissenters*, pp. 503–5, 513–17, 563–4.

24. Ibid., pp. 417–37; Davies, *Smith*, pp. 203, 216–44; J.C.D. Clark, *English Society 1688–1832* (Cambridge, 1985), *passim* and especially p. 409.

25. Anna le Breton, *Channing and Aikin*, p. 334. See also p. 406.

although local government was ultimately transformed. For Unitarians such change signalled they had arrived in the echelons of local power, for they captured municipal control in many large urban centres. For example, the first seven mayors of the reformed Leicester corporation were from the Great Meeting, the first and nine others of the first 28 mayors of Manchester were from Cross Street, and 23 Unitarian mayors presided over Birmingham from 1841 to 1893.[26]

Unitarians, indeed, continued to pride themselves on their passionate commitment to political and social reform and to individual liberty and justice at home and abroad. Whichever of the theological, political or social groupings of Unitarianism they were in, they were likely to be involved in reform of some kind, especially social and educational change. Above all, their commitment to 'civil and religious liberty the world over' remained their first toast at public gatherings and, as R.V. Holt has said, 'an expression of their deepest faith'.[27]

Asa Briggs has suggested that 'Where Unitarianism was weak in the nineteenth century Liberalism lacked a social cutting edge',[28] but this argument is not straightforward. Energy, drive, economic power, a formidable network and passionate commitment might help cultured Unitarians to local political power, but this did not make them acceptable in religious terms nor secure them in office. The political and social struggles within the middle classes made many suspect the Unitarians' élitist conception of leadership and, indeed, their liberal views were often disliked. The involvement of William and Elizabeth Rathbone and other Liberals in the Liverpool Hibernian scheme in the 1830s and 1840s, whereby Protestant and Catholic children could be educated together, lost William his seat and Liberals their control of this divided town.[29] In education elsewhere, too, the very ideas which empowered Unitarians often proved too contentious to allow others to cooperate with them.[30]

26. Derek Fraser, *Urban Politics in Victorian England* (1979), pp. 40–6, 99–100, 115–75; A.H. Thomas, *A History of the Great Meeting: Leicester and its Congregation* (Leicester, 1908), p. 49; John McLachlan, *Memoir and Proceedings of the Manchester Literary and Philosophical Society* (Feb. 1941), lxxxiv, no. 3, p. 38; Emily Bushrod, 'The history of Unitarianism in Birmingham from the middle of the eighteenth century to 1893' (MA thesis, Birmingham University, 1954), p. 225.

27. R.V. Holt, *The Unitarian Contribution to Social Progress in England* (1952), p. 69.

28. Seed, 'Theologies of power', p. 108.

29. Eleanor F. Rathbone, *William Rathbone* (1908), pp. 48–50.

30. See e.g. A. Temple Patterson, *Radical Leicester* (Leicester, 1975), pp. 242–4.

Political reform – a male concern?

Furthermore, the direct advantage of these public struggles and successes concerned men only. The 1832 and 1835 Acts, natural corollaries of each other, passed by Whig governments, keenly supported by Unitarians, were the first explicitly to exclude women. Joseph Parkes was the secretary of the Royal Commission reporting on municipal corporations in 1835: his daughter Bessie Rayner Parkes fought for even more basic rights for women a generation later. Matthew Davenport Hill stood on a platform for women's suffrage in Hull in 1832, but his family appear to have left the women out of the deliberations which freed Matthew's brother Frederic to fight for the Reform Bill in Birmingham.[31] Although both women and men joined in the wide spectrum of social, health and educational reforms which Unitarians promoted so actively and locally, their participation might be different according to gender. The new literary and scientific societies and exclusive libraries, the very places where the élite of the new middle class proclaimed their distinctive culture, were still for men only. The agitation against slavery in which Unitarians played so large a role amply demonstrated how women's participation differed from that of men, although both the role of women generally and of Unitarians in this sphere have been neglected until recently.[32]

Even so, women were active participants in political culture, whether aiding men in their huge commitment to the Anti-Corn Law League or participating among the early feminists and in the Women's Movement of the 1850s. Unitarian *men* as well as women, indeed, were among the first to stand up publicly for women's rights. For example, as early as 1816 Israel Worsley argued against women having to promise to obey in marriage.[33] Thomas Talfourd's successful support in 1839 of Caroline Norton in her fight for custody of her children marked the beginning of a long line of crucial legislative reforms for married women which other Unitarians such as Barbara Leigh-Smith took further. Not least Unitarians were prominent in the various, often overlapping progressive circles

31. Catherine Hall, *White, Male and Middle-Class* (Oxford, 1992), pp. 161–2, 192–6; Rosamund and Florence Davenport Hill, *The Recorder of Birmingham* (1878), pp. 114–15; Constance Hill (ed.), *Frederic Hill: An Autobiography of Fifty Years in Times of Reform* (1894), pp. 77, 92–9.

32. Clare Midgley, *British Women against Slavery* (1992), *passim* and particularly pp. 18–23, 160–5, 168–9, 173–5, 180–1; Stange, *Unitarians against Slavery*. Even Stange overlooks some of the nuances of the female participation.

33. *MR* vol XI (1816), p. 211.

involving thinkers and reformers such as William Johnson Fox, Clementia and Peter Taylor, John Stuart Mill and Harriet Taylor and George Eliot, where discussion of women's role and rights were the norm.[34] Some Unitarian women also played a very active role in what were normally considered male concerns. Jane Marcet and Harriet Martineau, for instance, became two of the leading popularizers of political economy, that series of ideas drawn from Adam Smith, David Ricardo, Thomas Malthus and Nassau Senior which rationalized so well the actions and aspirations of the new capitalist class that they were sanctified as scientific laws.[35]

Unitarians, in whose ranks were many of the foremost industrialists, merchants and bankers of the day, had close links with political economists. They were also closely connected to the Benthamites, who followed classical political economy although eschewing laissez-faire in other matters. For example, John Bowring, Dr Thomas Southwood Smith, Sarah Austin and the MP for Derby from 1830, Edward Strutt, were Unitarians in Jeremy Bentham's circle. Sarah Austin, always preferring to translate or edit the work of men rather than write as herself, published the work on jurisprudence of her clever but erratic husband, an undemocratic Benthamite.[36]

It is not surprising that Unitarians had links with the Benthamites: their ideas, based on Enlightenment suppositions and much influenced by Scottish thinkers, correlated in many ways. This was especially so once, through the agency of James Mill, the ideas of Bentham and others were fused into the *Utilitarian school. From the late 1830s Utilitarians attacked the economic, political and philosophical abuses and fallacies which they perceived in the landowning, aristocratic, deferent society of their day and advocated practical, 'scientific' reforms based on accurate factual information. These rational principles, not least their assumption of the proper leadership of the able and enterprising in the middle class, stimulated by the free discussion of an educated populace, had much in common with ideas already prevalent in Unitarianism. The very term 'the

34. Kathryn Gleadle, *The Early Feminists: Radical Unitarians and the Emergence of the Women's Rights Movement, 1831–52* (1995), *passim*; Gordon S. Haight, *George Eliot* (Oxford, 1968), *passim*.

35. J.R. Shackleton, 'Jane Marcet and Harriet Martineau: pioneers of economics education', *HofE* (Dec. 1990), 19, no. 4, pp. 283–98.

36. John and Lewin Bowring, *Autobiographical Recollections of Sir John Bowring* (1877), pp. 3–14, 337, 339; *MR* (1832) NS 6, pp. 450–7, 705–13; Janet Ross, *Three Generations of Englishwomen*, 2 vols (1888), *passim*; Strutt remained a subscriber to Manchester College until at least the 1840s but he married Amelia Otter, daughter of the Bishop of Chichester in 1837, so he might have become an Anglican; MSS MCO, *Letter Book . . . 1824–80*, p. 113; *MC Reports* (1840), p. 11; (1847), p. 27; *DNB*, LV, pp. 63–4.

greatest happiness of the greatest number' was one which Bentham acknowledged he borrowed from Priestley.[37]

Furthermore, Utilitarians, like Unitarians, derived their psychology and thus their environmental and educational views from David Hartley, thus sharing a belief in a self-improving society and the perfectibility of humankind. James Mill probably first knew of Hartley's philosophy through the work of Thomas Belsham. On the other hand, the two groups differed in that Unitarians valued Hartley's religious writings as much as the first part of his work. Similarly, they preferred the *Natural Theology* of the influential Dr Paley to his moral philosophy, the somewhat self-centred ethics upheld by Utilitarians. Thus, although they were quoting from Bentham's writings over a decade before they were generally known in England, Unitarians, while close to the Utilitarians, were as a group not of them, deriving their radicalism first from their faith. For example, R.K. Webb has exemplified Harriet Martineau as a Unitarian (in her younger days) who sympathized with much of Benthamite reformism but was less 'rigorous and precise', more utopian and woolly and much more of a radical revolutionary. Harold Perkin depicted the Unitarians' rational religion as the main link between dissent and 'secular dissenters' or 'sceptical utilitarians'. Later they were similarly linked to the agnostic *Positivists, as the career of Harriet Martineau illustrated.[38]

Any association with the Utilitarians, however, hardly won Unitarians any popularity despite the prevalence of a general utilitarian ethic. The Westminster Radicals, as Mill's group became known, were disliked even by the Whigs and won no sympathy at all from either evangelicals or conservative radicals like William Cobbett.[39] Both Utilitarians and Unitarians were attacked as atheistic, politically revolutionary, too analytical, logical and cold. The chief opposition to their ideas came from those like the ex-Unitarian Samuel Taylor Coleridge, who abandoned his beliefs in 'rights', in an atomistic society and of revolutionizing society by political change, for the ideal of an organic society with a spiritual state led, humanized and unified by a clerisy of the learned. Coleridge's developing philosophy

37. Elie Halevy, *The Growth of Philosophic Radicalism* (1972), pp. 153–4, 249–478, 491 (esp. p. 433).

38. Ibid., pp. 433, 437–9; Jeremiah Joyce, *A Full and Complete Analysis of Dr Paley's Natural Theology* (1807); *MR* (1807) II, p. 383; (1811), VI, p. 6, title-page, 279; Robert K. Webb, *Harriet Martineau: A Radical Victorian* (Columbia, 1960), pp. 88–90, 253, 304–9; Harold Perkin, *The Origins of Modern English Society 1780–1880* (1969), pp. 204–5.

39. Holt, *Unitarian Contribution*, pp. 163–4.

heavily influenced the Broad Church, which did have points of contact with Unitarians. His thinking had been transformed by German philosophy and Romanticism and especially by Immanuel Kant, who had also influenced Channing. Kant denied man's ability to plumb ultimate mysteries and such thinking had a conservative effect on Coleridge and others. At the same time Channing found Kant's faith in rationality, human dignity and free will confirmed the reverence for the essential powers of man which he had derived from Richard Price. From the 1830s English Unitarians were influenced by these ideas, and thus the new 'romanticism' which had swept Europe with its emphatic preference for intuitive truth, imagination, lyricism and the mysterious in religion rather than reason, facts and science, did touch on Unitarianism, although its deeper impact was first on Evangelicalism and, in the 1830s, on the Oxford Movement.[40]

The influence of Continental thinkers

Unitarians had spearheaded the introduction of German works into England, and *The Monthly Repository* continued to eclipse other rival religious periodicals in its translations from modern languages, particularly German. Many Unitarians were allured by German biblical criticism, studied German science and attended German universities. Women could not do the latter, yet a number, such as Susanna Winkworth, Sarah Austen and Anna Swanwick, became leading translators and did live in Germany for a time.[41]

Unitarians were among the first to study and adapt the ideas of new educational thinkers on the Continent. From 1815 a small but increasing number of people in England became interested in the work of the Swiss educationist Johann Pestalozzi. First Andrew Bell and Henry Brougham and then, in the 1820s and 1830s, James Pierrepoint Greaves, the Mayos and James Kay attempted with varying degrees of success to establish schools on Pestalozzian lines in England. As early as 1813, however, the Unitarian William Turner read John Bruce's paper on 'Pestalozzi's System of Education' at the Newcastle Literary and Philosophical Society. A number of Unitarian

40. D.A. Stauffer (ed.), *The Selected Poetry and Prose of Samuel Taylor Coleridge* (New York, 1951), pp. 164–89; D.G. Wigmore-Beddoes, *Yesterday's Radicals* (1971), pp. 88–90 and *passim*; William Henry Channing, *The Life of William Ellery Channing* (Boston, 1880), pp. 274–6, 375.

41. *MR*, see e.g. (1825–28, 1830–33), NS 1, 2, 4, 5, 6; Shaen, *Memorials*, pp. 66–73; Ross, *Three Generations*, p. vi; Mary L. Bruce, *Anna Swanwick* (1903), pp. 25, 26–33, 36–41.

educational reformers such as the Hills, Lady Byron, Lant Carpenter and John Beard were all influenced by Pestalozzi. As a pupil, William Herford was so stimulated by Beard's version of Pestalozzian teaching methods that he in turn became a leading exponent of Pestalozzian education in England after establishing the excellent Castle Howell School at Lancaster. Much earlier, in 1818, the keenest interest had been taken in Pestalozzi's writings by the Unitarian periodical *The Monthly Repository*. Such enthusiasm was expressed again from 1827, and with warm conviction once William Johnson Fox had taken over the journal in 1831, especially in the 1834 series of articles on the Pestalozzian school of Caroline Southwood Smith, which Fox described as 'fairyland'. These, indeed, so inspired the East Anglian corn merchant and banker, James Hill, that he met and married Caroline and founded a school on Pestalozzian lines.[42]

In Liverpool, Unitarians were interested in Pestalozzi even before Blanco White, the Spanish intellectual who had been closely involved in the Pestalozzian institute in Madrid, lived among them from 1835 to 1841. William Rathbone VI, for example, was sent to two Pestalozzian schools in turn – one in Cheam followed by another in Everton which other Unitarians such as Thomas Ashton and James Stansfeld attended. Possibly the progressive school in Chorlton-on-Medlock, in which several prominent Manchester Unitarians and others were involved and of which William Hodgson, then a member of Cross Street Chapel, was principal from 1847 to 1851, was Pestalozzian.[43]

Such examples illustrate how eagerly many Unitarians involved themselves in the most progressive educational practice of the period. They believed that many of Pestalozzi's principles were akin to their own. His simple, tolerant yet deep religious beliefs; his insistence that education should be physical and moral as well as intellectual; his basing of teaching on the immediate interests and natural development of the child, on the careful build-up of sense

42. M.M. Bowery, 'William Turner's contribution to educational developments in Newcastle upon Tyne (1782–1841)' (MA thesis, Newcastle upon Tyne University, 1980), p. 187; DWL, James Beard, Duplicate typescript of collection of notes and materials for *Life of John Relly Beard DD* (no date), ref. 1835; *DNB*, 2nd Supplement, II, p. 255; *MR* (1818), XIII, p. 733; (1827), NS 1, pp. 684–5, 842; (1828), NS 2, pp. 43–8, 817–23; (1830), NS 4, p. 829; (1831), NS 5, p. 257; (1833), NS 7, pp. 413–16, 429–33, 839–40; (1834), NS 8, pp. 477–85, 551–61, 687–91, 855–68.

43. Rathbone, *William Rathbone*, pp. 52, 59–61; MSS Liverpool University, *William Rathbone VI*, IX.1.7–9; Sylvia Harrop, 'The place of education in the genesis of the Industrial Revolution with particular reference to Staleybridge, Dukinfield and Hyde' (MA thesis, Manchester University, 1976), p. 152; G.M. Ramsden, *A Record of the Kay Family of Bury, Lancashire* (Gift to MCO, 1979), p. 59; *DNB*, XXVII, p. 73.

impressions and 'things not words'; his fostering of clear, accurate ideas; his focus on the individual child – all these reaffirmed Unitarian educational principles whilst also providing detailed analyses of suitable method. William Frend and the Hill brothers, for example, similarly believed in teaching successively through measuring, drawing and writing.[44]

Mary Carpenter also taught object lessons derived from Pestalozzian method in her crammed night school for working-class youngsters in the 1840s. More importantly, perhaps, her reformatory home for girls at Red Lodge in Bristol was envisaged as a Pestalozzian family educational home. Like other Unitarian educationists, in applying these principles in a school setting she was perhaps truer to Pestalozzi's philosophy than those who associated them chiefly with family, particularly maternal education. The latter interpretation, nevertheless, would also appeal to a group who stressed so much rational education by the mother.[45]

Certainly the importance of women as educators was evinced by the role Unitarian women played in the transmission and application of educational theories – practical application in accordance with individual needs being an axiom of which Pestalozzi would have thoroughly approved.[46] The somewhat paternalistic Lady Byron visited Fellenburg's agricultural school at Hofwyl, for example, and promoted both his and Pestalozzian methods. She also established an agricultural school of her own at Ealing Grove, employing and training an *Owenite and *phrenologist, E.T. Craig, to set it up. This was considered a model of its kind in the 1830s and 1840s, especially for District Schools and workhouse children. Robert Owen and Unitarians like Elizabeth Rathbone and Dr Morrell, for example, were also interested in Fellenberg's work, although the significance of manual labour in general learning was not generally noted at the time. Lady Byron and Elizabeth Rathbone were part of the group supporting Mary Carpenter.[47] In such circles, although different

44. E. Cooke (ed.), *How Gertrude Teaches her Children* (1894), pp. xxv–xxx *passim*; J.H. Pestalozzi, *Letters on Early Education addressed to J.P. Greaves Esq.* (1827), *passim*; W. Frend, *A Plan of Universal Education* (1832), *passim*; Matthew Davenport and Rowland Hill, *Public Education* (1822), p. 143 and *passim*.

45. Jo Manton, *Mary Carpenter and the Children of the Streets* (1976), pp. 88, 100, 126; Michel Soetard, 'Johann Heinrich Pestalozzi', *Prospects: Thinkers on Education*, 4 vols (Geneva, 1994), III, pp. 302, 309 (n. 8).

46. Ibid., pp. 306–8.

47. Stewart and McCann, *Educational Innovators*, pp. 155–69, 216–21; Pollard, *Pioneers*, pp. 202–9, 241–3, 251–2, 254; Joseph Carpenter, *Mary Carpenter*, pp. 121–47, 164–6; MSS Liverpool University, *Elizabeth Rathbone Correspondence*, VI.1.229, 234–VI.1.264 *passim*.

members did not necessarily have the same social background or assumptions, women and men shared ideas, commitment and enthusiasm and eagerly looked to foreign examples which fitted their educational philosophy. Sarah Austin and Frederic Hill, for example, trawled for European and American examples when promoting national education for the working classes.[48] They also looked nearer to home, many Unitarians finding the Scottish George Combe's *Constitution of Man* congenial to their progressive educational aspirations since he too argued that all people were both educable and perfectible and thus should receive a wide, rational and scientific education. William Biggs, for example, lectured on phrenology at Leicester, seeing it, together with Christian principle, as a supreme humanizing force. Although fewer Unitarians fully accepted Combe's pseudo-science of phrenology, its claim to be able to analyse the mind and therefore give scientific guidance on how to develop it had much appeal. So did its advocacy of equal education of boys and girls until fourteen since girls were both 'primary existences' and had an all-important role as rational educators of the young. Such pleadings, coupled with his eagerness to give females a useful education including the laws of physiology and health, drew women to Combe's lectures in droves, although his 'science' found their reflective faculty and thus their power to make decisions smaller than men's.[49]

Women in the educative community

Even if women were part of their educative community both in reality and in ideal, it seemed that reformers at best enhanced their domestic role within the family. The utilitarian Unitarian William Frend exemplified this position. His dream of an egalitarian, democratic community organized around its holistic educational system, for instance, certainly expected the education of both sexes to receive equal attention, even if they would be taught separately except for dancing. In his utopian meritocracy where teachers would be highly valued, all would eventually appreciate that 'the greatest happiness

48. Sarah Austin (trans.), *Report on the State of Public Instruction in Prussia by M. Victor Cousin* (1834); Frederic Hill, *National Education: Its Present State and Prospects*, 2 vols (1836), II, *passim.*

49. George Combe, *On Popular Education* (1893), pp. 57–67 and *passim*; David de Guistino, *Conquest of Mind*, pp. 61, 72–3, 99, 104–6, *passim*; MSS Leicester PRO 5D61, *John and William Biggs' Scrapbooks*, 2 vols (undated), I, p. 281.

of the greatest number – is the foundation of morality, and of virtue, and of religion'. Women would participate in all the advantages of an educative community and have a committee of their own to superintend female concerns, charity and the spiritual instruction of the young. This committee, however, would be elected by the general one directed by men, and female education, though highly regarded, would be 'directed also to objects more peculiar to them'.[50]

Such Unitarian educators thus saw females as able to participate equally in education with males and needing to do so to a high degree in preparation for roles traditionally assigned to them. For example, Unitarians like William Fox and Harriet Martineau believed that well-informed women were more likely to be efficient housekeepers than others, and Emily Shaen, like John Aikin earlier, argued that housekeeping should be professional. The otherwise radical Catherine Barmby even believed she was furthering women's rights by calling the domestic sphere women's 'absolute province', allotted by God and thus inalienable. Such domestic emphasis, nevertheless, was restricting, as many Unitarian women, from Harriet Martineau to Elizabeth Gaskell, acknowledged.[51] It was difficult, however, to get away from the maternal emphasis since marriage was seen as the goal for most women and it was accepted that for a good proportion of her married life a woman would be preoccupied with bearing and rearing children.

Unitarians thus gave a much greater significance to domestic roles but did not envisage women stepping much outside them. In this it would seem that 'rational' reformers were little different from evangelicals who so idealized the mother as the pure, moral guardian of the home, provided she stayed there. Furthermore, through their religious and charitable activities middle-class evangelical women were led indirectly into more public concerns.[52] Despite this and some overlapping rhetoric, there was a difference, however, between the evangelical stress on humility and submissiveness and the Unitarian one of moral equality, based not on instinct and repression but on intellectual parity and rational capability. Such acceptance of active moral and rational worth was emancipating and very unusual.

50. Frend, *A Plan*, pp. 50, 76, 110, *passim*.

51. *MR* (1832), NS 6, p. 640; Martineau, *Household Education*, pp. 221–2; Cobbe, *Life*, pp. 604–6; John Aikin, *Letters from a Father to a Son* (1793), p. 338; *People's Journal* (1847), III, p. 37; Gayle Graham Yates (ed.), *Harriet Martineau on Women* (New Brunswick, 1985), p. 98; Chapple and Pollard, *Gaskell*, pp. 50, 106, 109, 117.

52. Rendall, *Origins*, pp. 93–5.

Even so, radical dissent hardly made its adherents ardent feminists in the twentieth-century sense. The notion of separate spheres for men and women which prevailed in nineteenth-century England affected Unitarian middle-class women too, who tried for the most part to find outlets for their energies compatible with notions of propriety. Elizabeth Gaskell, for example, would only go to lectures ladies commonly attended. Both Harriet Martineau and Mary Carpenter as single ladies deferred to their mothers' wishes until past their twenties. Mary Carpenter for many years had her papers read for her in public; Harriet Martineau, even in cultured Norwich, could not study in the daytime since it was not proper for young ladies to study conspicuously. William Fox was the 'darling' of the Unitarians, and his radical views, including those affecting women, were accepted, until he advocated divorce.[53] On the other hand, Unitarians did not abhor paid work for middle-class women or desist from manual tasks in the home as 'ladies' were characterized as doing. Elizabeth Gaskell, for example, said of the wealthy Mrs Carson in *Mary Barton* that her 'luxury of a headache' would have been cured if she had 'taken the work of one of her own housemaids for a week'.[54]

Unitarians were also prepared to see wider job opportunities for middle-class women, although James Martineau thought that in the end there would be little significant change.[55] Given the fact that most women were expected to marry and spend years rearing children there was some basis for this, but not all nineteenth-century women married. A few were like Florence Nightingale in preferring to resist the conventional pressures to marry, but many had no choice since there were simply not enough men. The 1851 census revealed that there were fewer men than women and of these quite a few remained bachelors – for example, as many as 25.9 per cent at thirty. Others married late while yet others emigrated. Many spinsters were middle-class women with no male relative who could or would support them. However, the only employment considered respectable for such were the over-subscribed, underpaid occupations of teaching and sewing. Through their education and teaching

53. Chapple and Pollard, *Gaskell*, p. 71; Martineau, *Autobiography*, I, pp. 149, 100–1; Joseph Carpenter, *Mary Carpenter*, pp. 126, 146, 184–6, *passim*; Garnett, *Fox*, pp. 159–64.

54. June Purvis, *Hard Lessons* (Oxford, 1989), pp. 60–1; Elizabeth Gaskell, *Mary Barton* (Harmondsworth, 1970), p. 254.

55. Carpenter, *James Martineau*, p. 431.

Unitarians played a part in changing teaching into a profession for women, and some worked actively in the 1850s to extend the range of jobs which women could hold.[56]

Unitarian women, open to fresh ideas and educated not simply beyond women's usual fare but beyond most men's too, were uniquely placed to use their talents to effect both greater opportunities for women and other reforms. Although to late twentieth-century eyes they might appear limited in their aspirations, for the time Unitarians were far in advance of their day. They also grappled with issues of family life and personal fulfilment which remain very pertinent. As a group Unitarians wanted to be the progressive leaders of what they perceived to be a fairer, more egalitarian society. The effects of the working out of such ideals affected their expectations for both men and women. As a whole, although highly individualistic and thus having a range of views among themselves, Unitarians shared a willingness to cut through past traditions and ideas and to introduce new ones. To achieve their aims, they continued to use education.

56. Wanda Neff, *Victorian Working Women* (1929), p. 12; Candida Ann Lacey (ed.), *Barbara Leigh Smith Bodichon and the Langham Place Group* (1987), pp. 10–14, 36–73.

CHAPTER SIX

Schooling for Unitarians

In the post-Napoleonic era Unitarians still believed that their version of a liberal education would enable them to fulfil their rational, religious and political aims. Their educational aims in turn were quickened by their pride in the mercantile, industrial and professional middle class. This was superbly illustrated in novels like *Deerbrook* and *North and South* by Harriet Martineau and Elizabeth Gaskell respectively, where the heroes were the epitome of middle-class provincials , new types of 'gentlemen', honest, upright, scorning feudal 'barbaric' codes of honour. The heroines, likewise, were self-reliant, courageous, intelligent and courteous.[1] They had command over themselves which gave them some control over their lives. Unitarians were deeply convinced that knowledge was power: what knowledge they sought for middle-class children, where they sought it, how they provided it and how far it differed for boys and girls are the questions explored in this chapter.

The need to reform middle-class education

How Unitarians tried to realize their own aspirations for knowledge and power is important. If the sheer amount of involvement in education was the criterion for success then they were very successful indeed. In the first place they set out to attack what they saw as the exclusive, narrow and mind-deadening education pervading the public and grammar schools. Frederic Hill, for instance, called for the public schools to start teaching *real* history, 'not the mere record of court intrigues or antiquarian curiosities', so that their pupils

1. Harriet Martineau, *Deerbrook* (1983; 1st edn 1839), *passim*; Elizabeth Gaskell, *North and South* (Harmondsworth, 1970; 1st publ. 1854–55), *passim*.

might view 'the institutions of their country' more objectively, and to adopt a more modern curriculum leading to 'worthier qualifications . . . than the power of making smart speeches interlarded with trite quotations'. This reflected the stance of those waiting in the wings for power.[2] Unitarians were not the only critics: the Anglican Rev. Sydney Smith was merely one of the most articulate of others when, speaking from bitter experience of Winchester, he slated a system whereby 'every boy is alternately tyrant and slave' and, even more damagingly, toppled the general illusion that England's most illustrious characters in arts and science came from her public schools.[3]

Public schools, often praised for being 'aristocratic and manly' and internally egalitarian, were in fact, or were in the process of becoming, exclusive institutions to which only the rich had access. Surviving endowed grammar schools were also often becoming more exclusive, while any reforms only reinforced classics as the core of the curriculum. Unitarians were not slow to criticize such schools, some of them, like James Martineau, who had suffered Norwich Grammar School for four years, speaking from bitter experience.[4] They keenly felt that educational institutions endowed for the use of everyone had been appropriated by the rich and the established Church for the use of a minority or had been allowed to fall into educational disrepair. In Birmingham, for example, the Unitarian William Matthews pressed such arguments against the local Anglican establishment when fighting successfully, together with the town's powerful and numerous dissenters, against the attempt of the governors of the sagging Free Grammar School to exclude them legally from being governors.[5] John Relly Beard, in attacking waste, exclusiveness and out-dated and bad teaching at Manchester Grammar School, castigated both nationwide alienation of endowments from popular education and the irresponsibility induced by the endowment system itself, accusations reiterated by other educational reformers.[6] Such attacks concerned boys' schools. Only in the 1870s did Unitarians seek for such endowments to be extended to girls.

Eventually, through Lord Brougham's Commission of Enquiry into Charities, 1819–37, some abuses were removed, but generally

2. Frederic Hill, *National Education*, 2 vols (1836), I, pp. 224–8.
3. Sydney Smith, *Selected Writings*, 2 vols (1855), I, pp. 78–91.
4. J. Drummond and C.B. Upton, *James Martineau* (1905), pp. 16–18.
5. William Matthews, *A Sketch of the Principal Means . . . to Ameliorate the Intellectual and Moral Condition of the Working-Classes in Birmingham* (1830), pp. 29–34; *MR* (1831), NS 5, pp. 68–72.
6. John Relly Beard, *The Abuses of Manchester Grammar School* (Manchester, 1837), *passim*.

the middle class, especially nonconformists, turned in despair to private schools. There was no guarantee, however, that these would be any better. They might provide a modern curriculum but not necessarily trained, particularly qualified or even very caring teachers, as Charles Dickens vividly showed in *Nicholas Nickleby*. The extravagant claims of some of these schools were ridiculed in the *Monthly Repository*, Unitarians preferring their own version of a liberal education for the middle classes. Henry Morley, in his satirical *Defence of Ignorance*, depicted most middle-class schools as part of Ignorance's defence, preventing children from developing naturally under gentle discipline or enjoying the excitement either of science, history and other subjects or of a thought-provoking environment and frequent recreation.[7]

It was difficult for Unitarians to agree on a public alternative in middle-class education in the early nineteenth century. William Frend wanted a system run by the entire community, but most Unitarians agreed with William Shepherd on what they saw as the near barbarity of ancient Spartan education and feared that civic regulations would cramp the intellect and fetter the search for truth: 'A man may as well attempt to penetrate the mazes of an entangled wood in fetters, as to investigate the vast variety of intellectual subjects with a mind trammelled by the imperative decisions of human institutions.'[8] For Unitarians the answer seemed to be to provide their own educational establishments.

Unitarian education 1816–1860

In the nineteenth century, Unitarians expanded their educational ideas, whilst always overtly emphasizing freedom of thought and active morality. For both girls and boys, as Harriet Martineau illustrated in her novel *Deerbrook*, it was their total education which mattered most.[9] This included the thorough liberal religious education which continued to be dispensed to the young of both sexes in Unitarian chapels. An excellent example of such teaching was given by Lant Carpenter, whose fervent piety and practical emphasis that

7. Charles Dickens, *Nicholas Nickleby* (1867–68; 1st edn 1838); *MR* (1833), NS 7, pp. 644–52; Henry Morley, 'A defence of ignorance' (1851), in *Early Papers and Some Memories* (1891), pp. 104–17.

8. William Frend, *A Plan of Universal Education* (1832), *passim*; William Shepherd, Jeremiah Joyce and Lant Carpenter, *Systematic Education* (1817), p. 20.

9. Martineau, *Deerbrook*, *passim*.

faith without works was dead seemed to touch the consciences and hearts of all who heard him, rich and poor, male and female alike. His scholars, such as John Bowring, wrote feelingly on his stress on making them think, even sending them to readings and services where his views would be opposed. His impartiality was so respected that he had many Anglicans amongst his pupils.[10] Such vigorous morality rather than mere adherence to precepts suited a group who denied original sin and preferred to concentrate on the good in pupils rather than flog out the bad. Thus there was little corporal punishment in their schools. (One exception to this was James Bransby's school, where the assistant master was a drunk and Bransby himself a kleptomaniac!) Henry Morley's severest punishment was stopping lessons.[11]

The Unitarian alliance of psychology and middle-class aspiration continued to inform their curriculum and teaching methods. Although classics was retained as part of a middle-class education, arguments over how much should be taught still hinged both on what made a 'gentleman' and on how useful classics was to future professional and business men. William Rathbone neatly overcame the difficulty by both opposing his brother Sam, a future businessman, going to the Royal Institute School in Liverpool because 'A lot of Latin and Greek, and only that was crammed down their throats' yet suggesting that he and Sam could study Latin together as 'a gentleman's education is not complete without it'.[12] Eliezer Cogan was a rare Unitarian teacher in offering little but classics. One of his scholars, Samuel Sharpe, became a renowned Egyptologist and one of the four Unitarians involved in the 1870 Revised Version of the Bible. Lady Byron was more typical of Unitarians in wanting a tutor for her grandson 'with more of the living than the dead world in him' and not one of those traditional 'extinguishers of Nature's light'.[13] On the other hand, the self-made Rowland Hill was not so sanguine that a man could earn the status of an educated gentleman, however hard he laboured, if he was not at ease with classical knowledge. His mortification when young on realizing

10. John and Lewin Bowring, *Autobiographical Recollections . . .* (1877), p. 43; Russell Lant Carpenter, *Memoir of the Rev. Lant Carpenter LL.D* (1842), pp. 220–9, 236–42.

11. *DNB*, VI, p. 227; Henry Shaen Solly, *The Life of Henry Morley, LL.D* (1898), pp. 64–5, 81, 129.

12. MSS Liverpool University, *William Rathbone VI*, IX.2.50 (13.11.1839); IX.2.61 (14.4.1839).

13. Henry Solly, *These Eighty Years*, 2 vols (1893), I, pp. 76–7, 81, 93–5, 119, 122; *DNB*, XI, p. 219; LI pp. 425–6; MSS Liverpool University, *Elizabeth Rathbone: Correspondence with Lady Byron 1839–1859*, VI.1.230 (25.2.1840).

the disgrace attached to such ignorance remained a lasting bitter memory.[14]

Would-be gentlemen did have a real problem on the question of classics, therefore. It was not a problem that usually affected would-be 'gentlewomen' since girls, whether rich or not, rarely learnt classics. Yet, as has been shown earlier, Unitarians often differed sharply from contemporary fashion on this. Although some educationists such as Henry Morley and William Turner appear to have omitted classics in girls' education, many Unitarians believed with William Shepherd and John Morell that if classics did exercise the understanding and refine the taste then they were as desirable for one sex as the other. Lady Byron herself 'devoured Cicero' when a pupil of William Frend in the 1800s.[15] That so many Unitarians wanted this 'gentlemen's' subject for women in itself demonstrated how far ahead of others they were in their thinking on women's education. Lucy Aikin, for example, wryly argued that although Englishwomen 'modestly' esteemed themselves above all other woman in knowledge, accomplishments, purity of manners and all the domestic virtues, most were seldom taught to think, reason or comprehend the arguments of others. Consequently, she said, they became prejudiced, narrow, bigoted, frivolous and 'their sentiments grovelling', without any real patriotism or sympathy with public virtue.

> I wish that more women were nurtured in, at least, the Latin classics, because from them they might imbibe *this* elevating sentiment, (i.e. public good first) without which they can never deserve the *friendship* whatever they may obtain of the *love* of noble-minded men.[16]

There are, however, many instances of Unitarian girls being taught Latin or even Greek. The Rev. B. Mardon, for example, hoped girls would be able to read the scriptures in the original. Anna Swanwick studied both Greek and German in Germany. James Martineau taught his own children, both boys and girls, Greek, once they had mastered English grammar.[17]

14. Rowland and George Birkbeck Hill, *The Life of Sir Rowland Hill* (1880), p. 66.

15. H.S. Solly, *Henry Morley*, p. 127; Mary Robberds, 'Recollections of a Long Life', in J.A.V. Chapple and Anita Wilson (eds), *Private Voices* (Keele, 1996), pp. 108–13; Shepherd *et al.*, *Systematic Education*, p. 20; *MR* (1815), X, pp. 242–4; Frida Knight, *University Rebel* (1971), pp. 238–9.

16. Anna le Breton (ed.), *Correspondence of Dr Channing and Lucy Aikin (1826–42)* (1874), pp. 126–8.

17. MSS MCO, Presbyterian Chapels, V, p. 14; Mary L. Bruce, *Anna Swanwick* (1903), pp. 25–31; Joseph Estlin Carpenter, *James Martineau* (1905), pp. 157–8.

The amount of classics taught often depended on the wealth of the consumer, as the Taunton Commission was later to recognize. Lant Carpenter gave a thorough grammatical grounding in classics, but fees at his school were one hundred guineas a year and he taught many Anglicans – although they might, of course, have been equally attracted by his range of modern subjects.[18] A number of those who taught classics – for example, the Hills at Hazelwood, Dr John Morell in Brighton, John Hollings of the Leicester Proprietary School – experimented with new methods of teaching them. Sheer pleasure in the classics was turned to public profit when Richard Taylor, founder of the Taylor and Francis publishing firm, printed many beautiful editions.[19]

Modern languages were increasingly promoted by Unitarians in the nineteenth century. A number of women like Susanna Winkworth studied them at an advanced level. Many young women went abroad to study languages, for example from the Byerley, Aspland, Carpenter and Gaskell families. Miss Wreford spent seven years in Italy, Germany and France to qualify her for establishing a school.[20] French and Italian, at least, were acceptable for girls generally, though Unitarians taught them more thoroughly than was the norm, but they also wished males to learn them too. Dr Morell learnt German on the Hamiltonian system (a system of learning languages quickly, without first learning the grammar), accompanied by a few of his own pupils.[21] New methods, including drama, were introduced into the teaching of modern languages by a number of Unitarian teachers. John Relly Beard, like William Shepherd, recommended learning languages by oral teaching or even better by travel, despite fears of both the cost and immorality abroad! His recommendations were followed by a number of his pupils, including his son Charles, who also helped him compile a Latin dictionary, William Herford and Brooke Herford. Frederic Hill wished to reverse the

18. Russell Carpenter, *Lant Carpenter*, pp. 222–3, 346–8.

19. Matthew Davenport and Rowland Hill, *Public Education of Boys* (1822), pp. 37–43, 126–60; Herbert McLachlan, *The Unitarian Movement in the Religious Life of England* (1934) p. 129; Zena Crook and Brian Simon, 'Private schools in Leicester and the county, 1780–1840', in Brian Simon (ed.), *Education in Leicester, 1540–1940* (1968), p. 126; *DNB*, LI, p. 458.

20. Margaret J. Shaen (ed.), *Memorials of Two Sisters: Susanna and Catherine Winkworth* (1908), p. 22; Phyllis D. Hicks, *A Quest of Ladies* (Birmingham, 1949), p. 65; Robert Brook Aspland, *Memoir of the Life, Works and Correspondence of the Rev. Robert Aspland of Hackney* (1850), p. 503; Russell Carpenter, *Lant Carpenter*, p. 333; J.A.V. Chapple and A. Pollard (eds), *The Letters of Mrs Gaskell* (Manchester, 1966), pp. 894–9; *CR* (1841), opposite 'Contents', Apr.

21. Solly, *Eighty Years*, p. 119.

usual order of middle-class education and teach children their own language first, modern languages next and classics last.[22]

Indeed, in the teaching of English Unitarians became even more enthusiastic, partly in response to the contemporary outburst of English literature and partly through their own love of Shakespeare, Milton and other modern English writers. Some, like the barrister and MP Thomas Noon Talfourd, were intensely interested in the theatre, one of the few sources of emotional expression open to them and seen by some of them as an avenue to the civilization of humanity. Many, like Harriet Martineau and Elizabeth Gaskell, were deeply versed in Shakespeare and Milton, a number of Unitarians sharing in the renaissance of Shakespeare in this period and helping new writers such as Hazlitt, Tennyson and Browning. The discovery and subsequent publication in 1822 and 1825 of *De Doctrina Christiana*, in which Milton revealed his Arian views, was extensively reviewed and discussed by delighted Unitarians.[23] Samuel Rogers, the poet-banker, like many Unitarians was a friend of the poet Thomas Campbell. Because, however, Unitarians both tended to confuse a writer's creative ability and political views and to emphasize strongly the didactic and moral nature of all art, they judged poets and writers by these standards, rather than aesthetically. They thus oscillated over claiming the infamous, amoral Lord Byron, who was married to a Unitarian and apparently agreed with her religious views if nothing else.[24]

The delight shown in the teaching of English was partly the natural corollary to the belief that the ancient civilizations had fostered quick and inventive thinkers who were also men of action because they gloried in their own languages rather than toiling over dead ones. John Beard thus substituted English composition for Latin verses, much to the joy of pupils like William Herford.[25] English here was regarded, therefore, as a very suitable subject for men as well as women.

22. John Relly Beard, *Self-Culture* (3rd edn; 1st edn 1859), pp. 249–55; Shepherd *et al.*, *Systematic Education*, p. 23; *DNB*, XXII, Supplement, p. 154; 'Brooke & William Herford', 2nd Supplement, II, pp. 254, 255; Frederic Hill, *Education*, p. 208.

23. Margaret R. Parnaby, 'William Johnson Fox and the Monthly Repository Circle of 1832 to 1836' (Ph.D. thesis, Australian National University, 1979), pp. 470–7; Harriet Martineau, *Autobiography*, 3 vols (1877), I, p. 72; Angus Easson, *Elizabeth Gaskell* (1979), p. 22; *MR* (1825), XX, pp. 609–13, 687–92, 710–13, 748–50; (1826), XXI, pp. 724–31.

24. A.J. Shirren, *Samuel Rogers* (Stoke Newington, 1963), pp. 21–9; *MR* (1819), XIV, pp. 442–4; (1824), XIX, pp. 200–1, 632; (1827), NS 1, pp. 868–9; (1830), NS 4, pp. 124–8, 605–13.

25. *MR* (1832) NS 6, pp. 557–61; DWL, James Beard, Duplicate typescript of collection of materials for life of John Relly Beard DD (undated), 1835.

Lively history in Priestleyan fashion, using contemporary historians and local records, was the practice of teachers like Morley and Beard, both of whom taught geography in like fashion.[26] Political economy grew in importance in Unitarian teaching, with Unitarians of increasingly national stature (or notoriety) such as Jeremiah Joyce, Jane Marcet and Harriet Martineau providing ample materials for the teachers. This subject comprised those basic tenets of the classical economists which justified capitalism. Although by no means undisputed, these principles generally became very influential in the first half of the nineteenth century. Rather more surprising than the fact that Unitarians were leading popularizers of this worship of the gods of economic individualism and market forces was that two of them were women. Jane Marcet first published her highly successful and readable *Conversations on Political Economy* in 1816, the very year that Cambridge started teaching the subject. Oxford followed in 1825. Her book was praised by economists at home and abroad and used much in both America and the United Kingdom. It was constantly updated through her personal acquaintance with many contemporary economists.[27]

Marcet's lively dialogues between an informed adult and 'an intelligent young person, fluctuating between the impulse of her heart and the progress of her reason', made interesting reading as well as educational sense. Her choice of a female questioner was deliberate, demonstrating that girls regularly but unknowingly dealt with political economy and thus needed to shake off their ignorance and develop into knowledgeable women who could prevent children imbibing 'errors'. Political economy, said Marcet, anticipating Margaret Thatcher in the 1980s, was household economy on a nationwide scale.[28]

Interestingly, a reforming journal like *The Edinburgh Review* allowed women an interest in political economy because of their role in protecting and comforting the poor, an acknowledgment of a public social role for women. It conceded therefore that such knowledge was necessary without this being 'inconsistent with a horror of Amazons in politics'. Equally it rather condescendingly admired the originality and invention of Harriet Martineau, whose fictional

26. Beard, *Self-Culture*, pp. 90–1, 112, 131–5, 237–41; Morley, *Early Papers*, pp. 107–8.

27. Shepherd *et al.*, *Systematic Education*, II, pp. 436–505; Willie Henderson, 'Jane Marcet's *Conversations on Political Economy*: a new interpretation', *HofE* (Dec. 1994), 23, no. 4, pp. 423–37; *DNB*, XXXVI, pp. 122–3; 'Political economy', *The Merchant's Magazine and Commercial Review* (New York, 1840), II, pp. 36, 46–9.

28. Jane Marcet, *Conversations on Political Economy* (1817), pp. viii–ix, 1–13, 17–18.

Illustrations of Political Economy, in monthly volumes from February 1832, became an instant success, at least amongst the middle classes and Whig politicians. But Martineau was not without censure. The *Christian Remembrancer* carped that her economic theories were 'rank poison', her religion tinged with heresy, and generally she was 'like a Mother Carey's chicken, flapping, screaming, screeching, before the coming storm'. 'Much of what she had written was so unfeminine as to be absolutely disgusting', the magazine added in a reference to her tale 'Weal and Woe in Garveloch', in which she illustrated the Malthusian concept of population control when there was a surplus of workers over the means of subsistence. The simple methods advocated were late marriage and sexual abstinence, but the idea of a woman, and an unmarried one at that, discussing such matters in public roused the wrath of those already opposed to her and she had to endure the ribaldry of the *Quarterly Review* for ten years. Interestingly, before publication she had anxiously read the tale to her mother and aunt to ensure it was within the bounds of propriety, but these Unitarian ladies were 'as complacent and easy as they had been interested and attentive'.[29]

Similarly, Unitarian educationists had no problem teaching girls other subjects usually considered masculine if taught at all. Lant Carpenter and Thomas Southwood Smith, the Poor Law Commissioner, particularly urged the teaching of mental philosophy and physical education, the latter remarking scornfully that more attention was given to the health of horses in England than to that of people, who consequently were 'a puny race', unable '[T]o think clearly, to feel generously, and to act vigorously'. Lant Carpenter's present to his eldest daughter Mary on her twenty-first birthday was a copy of Hartley's *Observations on Man* since he, like Priestley, saw mental philosophy or psychology as the best foundation for the highest degrees of intellectual, moral and religious improvement. As such it was a vital study for women both for themselves and for their role as teachers of the young. In his long disquisition on the need for cleanliness, suitable clothing and healthy exercise for children, Carpenter again included girls as well as boys. He thought them less robust than boys but argued that usually too much was made of this 'constitutional difference'. Instead of the usual fear

29. William Empson, Review of 'John Hopkins' Notions of Political Economy' & 'Illustrations of Political Economy', *Edinburgh Review* (Jan.–July 1833), LVII, no. CXV, pp. 1–10; Harriet Martineau, *Illustrations of Political Economy*, 9 vols (1832), I, pp. iii–xvi, 6, 138–40; *Autobiography*, I, pp. 160–239; 'Miss Martineau's tales', *The Christian Remembrancer* (1841), II, pp. 178–9.

for her complexion or becoming a 'romp' keeping a girl from air or exercise so that she became sickly and often capricious or helpless, he advocated that both sexes should enjoy health and animal spirits. Girls, if anything, actually needed to be hardened in constitution and invigorated in body and mind if they were to cope with 'unavoidable evils in life': it was boys, he thought, who sometimes needed to have their mental sensibilities excited. He counteracted common fears that girls might lose their 'purity of imagination and desire' if they took part in physical exercise or knew the facts of life, by arguing that daughters would be safeguarded by their normal 'decent personal reserve' and mother's common judgement and care. Similar sentiments were echoed by other Unitarians such as Henry Morley.[30]

The liberality of Unitarian education was further demonstrated in the way physiology and science were encouraged by leading educators such as Beard, Carpenter and Joyce. Samuel Greg recalled dissecting a sheep's head at Carpenter's school, where science and mathematics were important subjects.[31] Jane Marcet in her *Conversations on Chemistry . . . Natural Philosophy* and . . . *Vegetable Physiology* was again a very popular, innovative writer for both sexes here. Girls were certainly not left out of science. The first volume of Samuel Parkes' world-famous *Chemical Catechism*, for example, was written for his daughter Sarah. Mrs Gaskell portrayed the enthusiasm of a well-educated girl for dynamics in *Cousin Phillis* and Lant Carpenter's scientific teaching was reflected in his daughter Mary's zeal for botany and geology. Catherine Finch, granddaughter of Priestley, taught her pupils astronomy by punching holes in cards for stars and also taught them conchology. The famous examples of Lady Byron and her daughter, Ada, would suggest that mathematics were not neglected either.[32] Anna Swanwick, however, although given the best school education available for girls in Liverpool in the early 1820s, 'often longed to assume the costume of a boy in

30. Lant Carpenter, *Principles*, pp. 145–7; *Westminster Review* (1824), I, pp. 72–3, 76; Russell Carpenter, *Lant Carpenter*, p. 497; Lant Carpenter, *Principles*, pp. 145–7, 202, 329–444 and *passim*; Morley, *Early Papers*, pp. 121, 170.

31. MCO, Samuel Greg, *Letters of . . . 1820–5* (transcribed from shorthand notes by W.S. Coloe, New Jersey, 1963; given by R.K. Webb to MCO 1965), 10 (9.11.1821); John Beard, *Self-Culture*, p. 111; Shepherd *et al.*, *Systematic Education*, I, pp. 454–78; II, pp. 1–243, 506–44, 568–70.

32. Harriet Martineau, *Biographical Sketches* (1870), pp. 388–9; *DNB*, XLIII, p. 307; Elizabeth Gaskell, *Cousin Phillis and other Tales* (Oxford, 1981), p. 289; Joseph Estlin Carpenter, *The Life and Work of Mary Carpenter* (1879), pp. 5, 18–19, 47–8, 89–91; R.A.M. Dixon, 'Priestley's daughter and her descendants', *TUHS* (1931–4), VI, pp. 292–3; Knight, *University Rebel*, pp. 238–9, 300, 304.

order to learn Latin, Greek and mathematics, which were then regarded as essential to a liberal education for boys, but were not thought of for girls'.[33] Swanwick's needs were better met in the next generation when Rachel Martineau's school in Liverpool included both Latin and mathematics in the curriculum.[34]

Unitarians, always eager to turn knowledge outwards, stressed the applied sciences including applied mathematics. They were particularly interested in the new opportunities opening up in chemistry and engineering, as the highly successful careers of John and Philip Taylor of Norwich illustrate. Matthew Hill advocated technical education as early as 1824.[35] Such an emphasis was considered far too radical by many contemporaries – not that this unduly dismayed Unitarians. For example, John Hollings of the Proprietary School, Leicester, faced with the scorn of the *Leicester Journal* at what they called incomprehensible subjects and entertaining tricks, opened his weekly lectures to the public for a small fee, reducing them further for ladies.[36] The latter move was particularly interesting: technical education in its narrowest sense was usually considered a male subject, although sometimes extended to girls as far as domestic subjects were concerned. The books on education written by Unitarians included applied science in the curriculum and were written with both sexes in mind. There was indeed a continuation of publishing a plethora of books, both textbooks and children's books, to suit all ages but always, whether amusing or not, with an emphasis on usefulness, rationality and morality.[37]

Education at home and school

To achieve such an education, some Unitarians chose to educate their children at home either by themselves or by tutors. Wealthy Samuel Darbishire, for example, employed as tutor to his family the scholar James Anthony Froude, whose public religious doubts had alienated him temporarily from his family, Oxford and orthodox Anglicanism.[38] Such an option was not open to all, although Unitarian homes such as those of the Hill family in Birmingham,

33. Bruce, *Swanwick*, pp. 19–20. 34. Shaen, *Winkworth*, p. 58.

35. *DNB*, LV, pp. 456–7; Rosamund and Florence Davenport Hill, *The Recorder of Birmingham* (1878), p. 75.

36. Crook and Simon, 'Leicester', p. 126, n. 51.

37. e.g. Shepherd *et al.*, *Systematic Education*.

38. Jenny Uglow, *Elizabeth Gaskell* (1993), pp. 228–31.

the Carpenter family in Bristol or the Shaen family in Crix, Essex were often centres of learning and eager intellectual and liberal vitality. In this women played a vital part, although the mothers particularly used their understanding for their children's benefit rather than their own. With the exception of Mary Carpenter, the men of these families have been remembered whilst the women have been all but ignored, but the pivotal role of Sarah Hill and Anna Carpenter in both their children's development and their husband's school was deeply felt by their families and others who knew them. Rowland Hill, for example, remembered warmly the cooperative enthusiasm and idealism, though little wealth, of his home so capably run by his mother, 'a woman of strong native talents' but with 'few opportunities of cultivating them'. Emily Winkworth believed her future mother-in-law, Emma Shaen, was the genius of a brilliant household – witty, quoting French and Italian, supporting republicanism, the Chartists and the rights of woman. Her life had been spent successfully rearing nine children and she abhorred making self-development the object of life.[39]

Many Unitarians, especially ministers, ran schools, sometimes just to make up a meagre salary but often with real enthusiasm. These schools were usually small, although some notable ones, such as Standard Hill in Nottingham with five full-time teachers to 80 boys and Hazelwood in Birmingham in the 1820s with 150 pupils, were large for a private establishment. None of these schools was labelled Unitarian and many attracted the children of non-Unitarians of liberal persuasions. From 1813 to 1825, for example, only 30 per cent of William Turner's pupils in Newcastle were Unitarian. Thus these schools had a significance beyond the religious community of their founders. They also often drew from a wider clientele than the locality: Standard Hill, for example, drew from Manchester and London and even France, as well as Nottingham.[40]

Hazelwood was run by the astonishingly talented Hill family. Like other Unitarian educators – for example, Lant Carpenter – the Hills particularly admired Maria Edgeworth and drew on new thinkers such as Pestalozzi. The Hills' seemingly eclectic application of

39. *Inquirer* (13.9.1879), p. 600; Jo Manton, *Mary Carpenter and the Children of the Streets* (1976), pp. 22–8; Shaen, *Memorials*, pp. 29–30; R. Hill, *Rowland Hill*, pp. 19–30, 47, 82, 142, 184–98.

40. Ibid., p. 178; David Wardle, *Education and Society in Nineteenth Century Nottingham* (Cambridge, 1971), pp. 155, 159–61; M.M. Bowery, 'William Turner's contribution to educational developments in Newcastle upon Tyne (1782–1841)' (MA thesis, Newcastle upon Tyne University, 1980), pp. 115–21.

educational ideas, nevertheless, was based in the first place on the direct teaching of Priestley, ardently imbibed by Thomas Wright Hill in Birmingham, applied first at his Hill-Top school and then, from 1819, at its successor Hazelwood, which was developed further by Rowland Hill. This amazingly coherent experiment in useful, pupil-centred education was the result of much thought, trial and experience. Its aim was to equip its scholars with the knowledge, skills and understanding which would allow each to continue self-education through a life 'most useful to society and most happy to himself'. The pupils were placed in sets for subjects according to ability and taught as much as possible through the senses. The wide range of subjects were taught as far as possible through practical activities and with a large amount of pupil participation. The whole school, indeed, including school fund, court and jury system, was run by the boys themselves. An elaborate reward system and a tightly ordered, efficient structure underlay the successful drive towards order, self-discipline, initiative and self-activity. This made Hazelwood a showplace for distinguished visitors who longed for the reform of middle-class schooling on Benthamite lines, that is, inducing useful learning as exemplified in Bentham's rather dry and abstruse *Chrestomathic system.[41] The Unitarian utilitarian Dr Southwood Smith ecstatically hailed Hazelwood as giving the middle classes – 'the strength of the community – the men – who think for the rest of the world' – an education which would enable them to be enlightened, clear, just and influential for good on the classes both below and above them, adding, 'on this admirable system of education the brightest hopes of the human race may anchor'.[42]

This utilitarian middle-class dream, however, was run by the Hill brothers and their father for boys, although the idea for the school was Mrs Hill's and all the eight children, including the two daughters (one of whom was a lifelong invalid), were educated similarly, both morally and intellectually. Caroline Hill did take part in the school's play production, and at Hill-Top at least there were some female pupils, but the thrust of the system was male-orientated and eulogized by its admirers as such. There was nothing similar for girls. Furthermore, although Harry Armytage has termed the

41. M.D. and R. Hill, *Public Education*, pp. viii–ix, *passim*; R. Hill, *Rowland Hill*, pp. 11–13, 30–179; Lant Carpenter, *Principles*, pp. 11, 42–7, 158, 160–5, 249; *The Hazelwood Magazine*, 2 vols (printed and published by the pupils of Hazelwood School, Birmingham, 1822–24), 1, *passim*; Jeremy Bentham, *Chrestomathia* (1816), *passim*.
42. *Westminster Review* (1824), I, pp. 75–9.

Hills' system an 'educational refraction of Priestley's ideas',[43] it was a unique experiment.

Other schools run by Unitarians also appear, from the reports of ex-pupils as well as the teachers, to have had a sense of vitality and interest in those social, political and intellectual questions of the day which so absorbed adult Unitarians. At Lant Carpenter's school, in Bristol, for example, debates were held on such topics as slavery and hanging, Samuel Greg winning the motion that hanging should be abolished for murder at a time when it was still the punishment for about 200 offences; at Hazelwood School the boys carried out their own trials of offenders and debated on how best to administer charity; in Robert Ashdowne's school in Horsham one pupil sealed a letter in 1845 with an inscription praising the arrival of cheap postage but asking also for cheap bread and free trade. Many of them also paid considerable attention to scientific knowledge and experiment: at the Horsham school, for instance, Thomas Saddler was so keen on his electrical machine that he tried electrifying the boys, who in turn electrified Saddler's favourite cat who thereupon burst through the window in hot disapproval. Robert and William Goodacre at Standard Hill in Nottingham owned an observatory as well as scientific apparatus and taught both pharmacy and astronomy.[44]

There is no evidence that similar topics were debated in schools for girls run by Unitarians, although the wide interests evinced by teachers such as Priestley's granddaughter, Catherine Finch, as well as those of their pupils would suggest that they were. Similar stimulation was apparent at the school of Wedgwood's granddaughters, the gifted Byerley sisters. Although they were Anglicans, they retained their Unitarian connections and many Unitarian girls, including Elizabeth Stevenson, the future Mrs Gaskell and Bessie Parkes, a great-granddaughter of Priestley, boarded at their school in Warwickshire. The wry comments on domestic tyrants in the publications of both Fanny and Katherine (later Thomson) and the interests displayed by various of the sisters in medicine, history and domestic economy indicate why Unitarians found their school congenial.[45]

Some Unitarian schools were, indeed, outstanding for their day with a progressive curriculum and enlightened attitudes. Such

43. R. Hill, *Rowland Hill*, pp. 30, 47, 193–5; Colin Hey, *Rowland Hill* (1989), p. 43; W.H.G. Armytage, 'The Lunar Society and its contribution to education', *University of Birmingham Historical Journal* (1967–68), V, p. 67.

44. MCO Greg, *Letters*, 9 (9.11.1821), 12 (1.1.1822); *Inquirer* (1892), Records of Horsham Church, pp. 45, 57–61, in *Presbyterian Chapels: Short Articles 2*; *Hazelwood Magazine*, *passim*; Wardle, *Nottingham*, p. 154.

45. Dixon, 'Priestley's daughter', parts I and II, *passim*; Hicks, *Ladies*, *passim*.

schools appear to have been very highly thought of, at least by the Unitarians themselves and by modern historians such as David Wardle, who estimated that eleven of Nottingham's hosiers of the 1840s were educated at Standard Hill between 1797 and 1825 plus many others outside those dates. He also picked out Catherine Turner's (née Rankin) school in Nottingham as being the exception to the general run of useless, unintellectual girls' schools, the 'singularly able and accomplished' Mrs Turner unusually stressing accuracy, clarity and steady mental application. She was helped by John Taylor of High Pavement School and by visiting masters such as Herbert Spencer's father, who taught science. Her first two pupils, members of the wealthy manufacturing Philips family, like many others of her pupils came from well-known Unitarian families.[46] Lant Carpenter's school in Bristol, from 1817 to 1828, was a small community (about fifteen pupils a year), an extension of his orderly, high-minded household, held together by the superbly efficient management of Mrs Carpenter and the singular moral control of Dr Carpenter himself. John Relly Beard's school, from 1833 to 1849, at Stony Knolls, Salford, was purpose-built with a large playground, gym apparatus and garden plots for the boys. Beard, a well-known radical in Manchester, took in many Jewish as well as Unitarian boys. Like the Hills, Beard well rewarded voluntary work, especially practical work, with marks. Both Carpenter and Beard educated their own daughters at their schools. Beard's wife Mary (Barnes), another key figure in a vigorous, educational household, had been educated at Ruth Jeffrey's school in Horsham alongside other Unitarians such as Louisa Jeffrey, the future wife of James Riddell McKee, tutor at Beard's school for ten years.[47]

These connections are symptomatic, for although these schools were very individualistic, it was the vital familial and religious link of Unitarianism which sustained a liberal, rational outlook in them. Many of the male teachers had attended the same dissenting academies and sent pupils on to them, Manchester College becoming particularly important in this respect in the nineteenth century. Some of them attended Glasgow university too. Teachers moved schools and learnt from each other and many of them, both women and men, were related, so that the web was ever more tightly spun.

46. Wardle, *Nottingham*, pp. 159–62; *Inquirer* (5.5.1894), p. 179; (12.5.1894), p. 297; (19.5.1894), p. 319; (26.5.1894), p. 337.

47. Russell Carpenter, *Lant Carpenter*, pp. 342–5; Joseph Carpenter, *Mary Carpenter*, pp. 5–7; James Beard, *Beard*, 1833, 1835, 1843, *passim*, Memorandum concerning Mary Barnes.

Just one educational chain may be used as an illustration: the Wreford sisters were nieces of Dr John Morell, the success of whose school at Hove, Brighton was maintained by John Malleson from 1828. One of Malleson's pupils was Peter Taylor whose cousin was Louisa Jeffrey, Harriet Martineau's companion to America. Harriet never stopped teaching in her voluminous writings and was sister of Rachel and James Martineau, who were teachers, as were James's relatives by marriage, Edward Higginson and Samuel Bache.[48]

From the schools of these Unitarians came a disproportionate number of future progressive educationists, professional and business men, industrialists, scientists, public figures and reformers. Professor Thomas Solly, Henry Solly, C.P. Scott of the *Manchester Guardian* and Isambard Kingdom Brunel were pupils of Morell, Peter Taylor MP and William Shaen were two of Malleson's. Taylor became a partner in Courtauld and Company (his mother's family), a radical politician and, with his wife Clementia, keen supporter of the Women's Movement, as were Malleson's sons and Shaen. The Hills' schools produced an impressive array of inventors, scientists, liberal politicians and local leaders, including Follet Osler FRS, the first person to produce sheets of glass up to 20 feet high, and a number of the twenty-three Unitarian mayors of Birmingham between 1841 and 1893.[49] Charles Berry in Leicester educated many future professional men and important leaders of commerce and industry, apart from ministering to a congregation which produced four MPs and six mayors of Leicester in uninterrupted succession.[50]

Another such example was Lant Carpenter's school: Robert Needham Philips MP, merchant and manufacturer, for example, claimed that in 1857 there were more Members of Parliament from this small school than from Rugby. Amongst Carpenter's former pupils were James Martineau, a radical and renowned philosopher, Sir John Potter, thrice mayor of Manchester, Thomas Potter MP and James Heywood FRS, university reformer and benefactor, a founder of the Manchester Athenaeum, prominent in the Royal

48. *CR* (May 1840), pp. 348–50; *Inquirer* (3.4.1869), p. 222; (1.9.1883), p. 555; (17.9.1887), p. 607.

49. *Inquirer* (17.9.1887), p. 607; *DNB*, LV, pp. 455–6; Solly, *Eighty Years*, I, pp. 84–122; Elizabeth Malleson, *Autobiographical Notes and Letters* (privately circulated, 1926), *passim*; Colin C. Hey, 'The history of Hazelwood School, Birmingham, and its influence on educational developments in the nineteenth century' (MA thesis, Swansea University, 1954), pp. 250–76.

50. J.C., *In Loving Remembrance of the Rev. Charles Berry* (Leicester, 1877), pp. 1–7; I am grateful to Dr David Wykes for details on Berry's pupils.

Historical Society and Statistical Society, Liberal MP, fighter for popular and women's education and pioneer in liberal theology. Other pupils included Carpenter's own children, three of whom achieved sufficient fame to be included in the *Dictionary of National Biography*. Martineau's praise of Dr Carpenter was echoed by Samuel Greg, who said that under him he had had 'every advantage for improvement . . . every means of knowledge . . . opened to me'.[51] From John Relly Beard's school came Thomas Worthington, Gothic architect, John Ashton Nicholls, cotton spinner, philanthropist and educationist, William Herford, pioneer of *Froebelian education in England and Beard's son Charles, Unitarian minister and supporter of popular education and higher education for women. Testimony was given to the excellence of their schools by former pupils: Herford put Beard on a par with Arnold as an educational reformer, and although he had previously attended both Shrewsbury and Manchester Grammar felt that it was Beard who had first opened up his mind.[52]

Herford himself is an example of the way that Unitarian teaching dynasties were established. His accomplished, artistic mother ran a school, an example he followed in 1850 when he established Castle Howell at Lancaster. This school, run on Pestalozzian principles, had an excellent academic record. Herford pioneered Froebelian education in England and later established a successful coeducational school, Ladybarn, in Manchester, where John Beard's granddaughter, Mary Shipman Beard, and Herford's daughter, Caroline, were successive headmistresses.[53]

There were many good women teachers, indeed, although of course none of them had had higher education and their pupils, similarly from leading Unitarian families, did not have the career opportunities of the boys. The school run by Mrs Carpenter and her daughters had Mary Carpenter as an especially brilliant teacher, and Rachel Martineau's school in Liverpool was highly praised by both Sarah Dendy (née Beard) and Susanna Winkworth for its thorough intellectual education and wise care of health. James Herman, leader of the Liverpool concerts, taught music at the latter school; James Martineau taught Latin, mathematics, history, botany

51. McLachlan, *Unitarian Movement*, pp. 131–2; Richard Wade, *The Rise of Nonconformity in Manchester* (1880), pp. 60–1; *Inquirer* (23.10.1897), pp. 689–90; *DNB*, IX, pp. 159–63, 166–8; MCO Greg, *Letters*, 32 (8.4.1822).

52. James Beard, *Beard*, 1833, 1835; Leonard Smith, 'Unitarians and the Gothic Revival', *TUHS* (July 1980), XVII, no. 2, p. 85; *DNB*, 2nd Supplement, II, p. 255.

53. Ibid.; Herbert McLachlan, *Records of a Family* (Manchester, 1935), p. 98.

and the New Testament, to the intellectual delight of pupils like Julia Wedgwood. Some of Martineau's children attended the school, as did Meta Gaskell.[54]

Unitarian schools, therefore, may not have educated a large proportion of the English population but they contributed much by their example and by the type of people they sent forth. Yet although Unitarians could own to an astonishing number of schools of high quality for such a small group of people, they often only lasted as long as the teaching life of their founders, were inaccessible to many before the railways were built up and were very expensive, many of them charging between 40 and 70 guineas a year.[55] Some were cheaper but, considering the size of many families, there was a need, even amongst the wealthier, for these to be on a wider scale. Not all Unitarian teachers were brilliant: Elizabeth Malleson, for example, believed she learnt far more in the homes of her family and friends than at the Misses Woods' school in Clapton.[56] Nor was it possible that one small group, highly unpopular in religion, particularly with evangelicals, could provide education for the middle classes as a whole.

Unitarians and the reform of middle-class education

Unitarians began turning to other solutions. Frederic Hill was one of the first English educationists to advocate a national system of education. He had helped run the family school at Hazelwood, but found, despite the admiration of Utilitarians, that the middle class was largely unappreciative of schoolboys land-surveying, making astronomical observations, marching to lessons to band music or earning marks to pay fines for wrongdoing. Once pupils from further afield were admitted in large numbers, the political liberalism and undogmatic religion of Hazelwood's owners became suspect. Although a more traditional, Anglican version at Bruce Castle in London continued to inspire liberal educationists, Hazelwood could hardly become the basis of a national system as its chief progenitor, Rowland Hill, wished.[57]

54. Ibid., p. 117; Manton, *Mary Carpenter*, pp. 38–9; Joseph Carpenter, *James Martineau*, pp. 158, 271–2; Shaen, *Winkworth*, p. 58; Chapple and Pollard, *Gaskell*, pp. 214, 259–60.

55. e.g. *CR* (1834) 5 Jan., 7 Aug.; (1841) 7 Feb., 7 Apr.

56. Malleson, *Autobiography*, pp. 35–9.

57. P.W.J. Bartrip, 'A thoroughly good school', *BJES* (1980), XXVIII, pp. 49–59.

As rational dissenters had already found in their dissenting academies in the eighteenth century, more long-term progressive educational establishments might be possible through setting up joint-stock companies whose committee would determine the curriculum, appoint the teachers and, hopefully, raise greater resources. Such ventures in middle-class schooling, called proprietary schools, were pioneered by Unitarians and their friends, the Utilitarians. The model for these was University College School, established in 1829 by Thomas Campbell, James Mill, Henry Brougham and others after they had founded London University. In turn, this school was much influenced by Hazelwood.[58]

Frederic Hill, from bitter experience, saw the major advantage of proprietary schools in a respected board of governors being better able than a private schoolteacher to stand up to ignorant parents and insist on prioritizing moral feelings, discipline and the development of the reasoning powers before mere instruction. Only in public education, said Hill, would it be possible to secure schools able to adapt the advances which were slowly being made in the 'science and art of education' and to educate pupils according to their individual needs and talents, which might well be better served by subjects not commonly taught previously. Hill applied his general thesis to middle-class girls too, finding their education not so much inferior to that of boys as equally limited, narrow, unprofitable, uninteresting and irksome. He was sanguine that 'enlightened' views were making progress and 'a silly admiration for Oriental ignorance and mental torpor among females, will soon give way to just appreciation of the superior beauty of a vigorous intellect and a cultivated mind'.[59]

Unitarians were closely involved in establishing a number of proprietary institutions, the Liverpool Institute schools of 1835 and the high schools of 1838 and 1844, the Leicester Proprietary School of 1837 and the Edgbaston Proprietary School in Birmingham in 1838. Despite great initial optimism, however, none of these, apart from the Liverpool commercial (lower) school and the Liverpool Girls' High School, fulfilled the original expectations of their founders. In each case a liberal, modern scheme of education, eagerly promoted by Unitarians, failed to win the support of the commercial middle classes. In Liverpool, the drive and munificence of James Mullineux and Richard Vaughan Yates, in Leicester, the gifted

58. Hey, *Hazelwood*, pp. 181, 315, 317.
59. Frederic Hill, *National Education*, 2 vols (1836), I, pp. 204–14.

teaching of J.F. Hollings backed by a 'roll-call of Leicester Radicals' and in Birmingham, the active support of ex-Hazelwood pupils such as William Sargant was not enough – or perhaps was too much – to win widespread allegiance. The Liverpool High School was spectacularly successful later in the century and Edgbaston continued on traditional lines, but the proprietors of Leicester were unable to maintain its viability in the face of their own overspending and the rivalry of an Anglican proprietary school.[60]

It is interesting that of all these ventures in which a number of Unitarians invested considerable time, effort and money, the one success in this period was a girls' high school, an early forerunner in some ways of those new endowed and proprietary schools which were to breathe new life into middle-class female education in the late nineteenth century. It was the Unitarian merchant George Holt who supplied Blackburne House for Liverpool Girls High School and gave it his unstinting support. The curriculum was an intriguing mix of traditional and radical, including drawing, singing and needlework but also science, in which it earned a good reputation. It also included callisthenics, a very early recognition of the need for girls to have proper physical exercise. The training of teachers was another pioneering venture of the school and twelve such trainees were there in 1846, both aiding in the classroom and receiving lectures on the 'the principles of tuition' from Dr Hodgson, the headmaster of the boys' school from 1845 to 1847. The school did so well it had to be limited to 300 pupils in 1859.[61]

With such immediate and growing success it was surprising that Unitarians elsewhere did not copy the Liverpool venture. It was not until the 1870s that Unitarians of Birmingham were stirred to play a significant part in the establishment of the Edgbaston High School for Girls, for example.[62] Perhaps their energies were too absorbed by their struggles to reform education generally. Proprietary schools did flourish in the nineteenth century, but as a cooperative venture they had to appeal to a fairly wide section of the community, which usually meant allowing Anglican control. Similarly, newly established boarding schools for the middle classes such as the Woodard schools were Anglican and had a traditional curriculum. However much

60. M. Greenwood, 'Education and politics in Leicester 1828–50' (M.Ed. thesis, Leicester University, 1973), pp. 59–61, 278, 288–9; Hey, *Hazelwood*, pp. 267–8; H.J. Tiffin, *A History of the Liverpool Institute Schools 1825 to 1935* (Liverpool, 1935), pp. 26–31, 63–7, 73–87, 103–7.

61. Ibid., pp. 76, 103–6.

62. Janet Whitcut, *Edgbaston High School* (Birmingham, 1976), pp. 1–67.

Unitarians bemoaned this,[63] the fact was that their radical, liberal education ideal was simply not universally accepted by the middle classes. Buffeted between those who wanted a traditional education, albeit somewhat reformed, and those who were content with a basic, commercial education, the Unitarian ideal did not attract more than a minority of like-minded liberals. There was a need for a reform and an extension of 'public' education but it was not until the 1860s that the investigations of public commissions led to these, although even then classical literature remained the staple of middle- and upper-class male education.

Reform of the public school ethos began earlier with Thomas Arnold's attempts to make Rugby 'a place of Christian education'. Like the Hills he tried to develop his pupils morally and spiritually through a wisely ordered corporate life, but his system was hierarchical not republican. He might, like Unitarians, deplore many aristocratic and feudal notions, but he was not upholding the same gentlemanly culture as they were. He reformed the classical syllabus and, with difficulty, introduced modern languages and mathematics (but not science) into the curriculum . He deplored attacks on corporal punishment as 'Jacobinism' and found Unitarian tenets irreconcilable with essential Christianity.[64]

It was only gradually that even Arnold's ideals took hold in more establishment circles, but Rugby's growing success, followed by that of Uppingham under Edward Thring, coupled with the establishment of new public schools, increasingly viable because of the railways, meant that by mid-century the image of public school education was being transformed from within. In the following decades these schools subtly and efficiently excluded sons of tradesmen to concentrate on the education of 'gentlemen' – a concept which was to change from Arnold's Christian manliness to muscular Christianity. The reformed endowed schools were to follow suit. As such, all of these were to have great appeal to those who had risen to wealth through industry and commerce and now yearned for the social and cultural status commensurate with their riches. Such people believed they needed a traditional, albeit revitalized and modified, classical education, the civilizing culture which, according to Matthew Arnold, would remove the taint of philistinism.[65]

63. See e.g. *CR* (1841), pp. 227–8.

64. A. Percival, 'Dr Arnold: man and myth', *Times Educational Supplement* (29.12.1972), pp. 18–19; Bartrip, 'A thoroughly good school', pp. 56–7; A.P. Stanley, *Life of Thomas Arnold, DD* (1904), *passim*.

65. Matthew Arnold, *Culture and Anarchy* (1938), *passim*.

In these ways the bitter attacks on the corruptions, exclusiveness and anachronisms of the old educational system, in which Unitarians had played a vital part, helped to lead to changes which gave it new life and attracted many of the middle classes, including some Unitarians themselves. These thus turned away from the more radical ideals once professed so ardently. The endowed public school system, however inept or corrupt it had been, illustrated its capacity to prevail over private institutions, however brilliant or worthy. Furthermore, such changes seemed to re-emphasize traits, attitudes and curricula deemed 'masculine'. At the same time the growing opportunities for middle-class males in the professions, business, industry and politics made the disparity between them and their sisters more acutely obvious.

The most significant step forward in educational provision for girls before 1860 was the establishment of the North London Collegiate School by Frances Buss and her mother in 1850. This liberal, tolerant school was to become a model for the girls' high schools of the later nineteenth century in its management, ethos and emphasis on an academic curriculum, intellectual rigour yet at the same time traditional feminine qualities. Before 1860 there was little emulation of this pioneering school, however, and its equivalent in public boarding schools, Cheltenham Ladies' College, was hardly yet established.[66] There were some excellent pioneering private schools run by other nonconformists, but only a few.[67] In the period 1815 to 1860, therefore, the attitudes and achievements of Unitarians in girls' education were progressive and important. At this level, indeed, many Unitarian girls might not have seen a significant difference between their education and that of their brothers. It was in higher education that gender differences amongst Unitarians were most marked, yet even there they proved to be pioneers.

66. June Purvis, *A History of Women's Education in England* (Milton Keynes, 1991), pp. 73–81, 84.

67. Clyde Binfield, *Belmont's Portias: Victorian Nonconformists and Middle-Class Education for Girls* (1981), *passim.*

CHAPTER SEVEN

Knowledge is power: gentlemen of England

> What in the world do manufacturers want with the classics, or literature, or the accomplishments of a gentleman?[1]

In higher education gender differences were much more marked though this, perhaps, was the most keenly contested ground between Unitarians and traditional educationists. The struggle to reform and expand admission to the universities was the educational aspect of the struggle for power between the upper and middle classes and among the middle classes themselves. Fundamental to the contest was the desire to keep or wrest control of higher education and through this to define the concept of a 'gentleman' – a key element of Unitarian higher and further education for males. Higher education for females was a secondary consideration albeit Unitarians did take some important initiatives in this area. Both this and the significance of the conflict over male higher education in a changing society will be discussed in the following pages.

Reform of higher education

The first battle was over admission to higher education, Unitarian scholars like John Kenrick being bitterly aware of the 'lock' on knowledge imposed by the requirement for subscription to the Thirty-nine Articles at Oxford and Cambridge. Unitarians fought long and hard to get subscription abolished, but George Dyer was as unsuccessful at Cambridge in 1824 as George Wood was in Parliament in 1834.[2] In 1850, however, it was the Unitarian James

1. Elizabeth Gaskell, *North and South* (Harmondsworth, 1970; 1st edn 1854–55), p. 72.
2. MSS MCO *JK IV* (17.3.1834–7.7.1834), Letters to GWW; James Yates, *Thoughts on the Advancement of Academical Education in England* (1827), pp. 5–7.

Heywood MP, grandson of Thomas Percival, son-in-law of the Manchester industrialist John Kennedy, and a former pupil of Lant Carpenter's, who won a Royal Commission to enquire into the universities of Cambridge, Oxford and Dublin. He too successfully moved the abolition of religious tests on matriculation and bachelor degrees in 1854, a limited but significant gain.[3] The door had been opened – as conservatives feared.

But it was not just restricted admission to the ancient universities that annoyed Unitarians; there was a deeply felt rejection of the ethos of the universities and their narrow curriculum. As John Relly Beard asked scornfully, how often was 'the receipt of . . . rich endowments' the 'only labour' universities performed and how much was their teaching 'useless' and 'injurious' rather than what was needed. Thus, he argued, 'wrapped in' an entirely classical education, 'the universities . . . stand not as beacons bearing the torch before advancing civilisation, but as monuments of the antique, the obsolete, the disallowed, the effete'.[4]

The conflict was still between traditional and 'modern' views of what a liberal education was, who should receive it and what was needed in a new scientific and industrial age. Both English universities continued to stress their aim of developing reasoning powers, preferring their own 'active' tutorial methods to 'mountebank lecturers . . . superficially descanting on some popular topic, to . . . a gazing [passive] audience of beggarly boys'[5] – a caricature of Unitarian teaching. They neglected contemporary scientific advances which were revolutionizing medical and many industrial processes. They saw little connection between themselves and the commercial and industrial world and generally had no mind to encourage change in ethos, curriculum or type of student. They remained dominated in both government and teaching by Anglican clerics, not necessarily chosen for their intellectual brilliance and comfortably housed in wealthy and indolent colleges. That mattered little to the sizeable, albeit decreasing, proportion of students who had no intention of becoming great scholars and accepted the easy-going aristocratic system as a natural part of becoming a gentleman. Well-balanced, polite, high-minded public servants in the classical tradition were at a premium and reforms to bring in a more vigorous examination system interjected an alarming alternative. Although the already prestigious Cambridge Tripos was progressively reformed,

3. *Inquirer* (23.10.1897), pp. 689–90. 4. *MR* (1831), NS 5, pp. 830–1.
5. *Apologia Academia* (Oxford, 1831), p. 28 and *passim*.

at Oxford classics remained pivotal and the little interest shown in science quickly evaporated in the 1830s during the consuming wrangles of the *Tractarian Movement. Even so, Oxford's interminable wrangles about theology largely ignored German advances in the historical criticism and philology of the Bible. The English leadership in biblical criticism and rational theology came from Unitarians, especially the run of outstanding scholars at Manchester College including John Kenrick, John James Tayler, George Vance Smith and James Martineau, who had all studied for a time in Germany. Similarly, it was Unitarian scholars who developed further the study of modern history in higher education, John Kenrick deploring the neglect of such at Oxford and Cambridge as another instance of their unaccountability to the public. The few who did seek reform, such as Thomas Arnold in the 1840s, were fairly moderate in their demands. Those Oxbridge men who did study modern subjects such as geology or natural history tended to turn from orthodox religion, Sir Charles Lyell, the renowned geologist and prominent university reformer, being a prime example.[6]

By 1856 James Martineau was predicting that if Christian theology continued to abdicate its intellectual function of reconciling human pursuits, science would take the retribution of remaining outside religion. The Unitarian synthesis of the two, however, allowed Unitarians to take scientific developments in their stride. Both Charles Lyell and Charles Darwin, grandson of Josiah Wedgwood, were closely involved in Unitarian circles, where there was a general welcome acceptance of evolutionary theory as a rational account of humankind. Whewell at Oxford and Adam Sedgwick at Cambridge, on the other hand, were scientists who challenged such ideas.[7] Unitarian commitment to science as a necessary part of a liberal education, therefore, was a deeply founded principle.

Such commitment was reiterated by others in the liberal camp. Writers to the *Edinburgh Review*, especially the brilliant Rev. Sydney Smith, found Oxford and Cambridge lamentably deficient even in scholarship. The Utilitarians Jeremy Bentham and James Mill likewise found the ancient universities 'useless', stifling and 'preposterous',

6. Dennis Wigmore-Beddoes, *Yesterday's Radicals* (1971), pp. 34–40, 55–9, 70, *passim*; MCO, JK, 'History', *MNC Introductory Lectures* (1840), p. 4; Ben Knights, *The Idea of the Clerisy in the Nineteenth Century* (1978), pp. 10, 21–6, 81, 117–18, *passim*; Martha McMackin Garland, *Cambridge Before Darwin: The Ideal of a Liberal Education 1800–1860* (Cambridge, 1980), pp. 3, 18–24, *passim*.

7. James Martineau, 'A plea for philosophical studies' (1854), *Essays, Reviews and Addresses*, 4 vols (1891), IV, pp. 24–33; Coral Lansbury, *Elizabeth Gaskell: The Novel of Social Crisis* (1975), pp. 194–5; Garland, *Cambridge*, pp. 96 ff.

the latter deciding it would be better to be ruled by the 'rational', 'judicious' middle classes in any practical matter engaging a statesman or leader in a commercial country.[8]

The universities did not remain quiescent under demands for reform. The most famous contemporary defence of a liberal education based on the classics, John Henry Newman's, would have had more appeal to reformers such as Unitarians, however, had not his ultimate aim for a Catholic Irish university justified their own fears of sectarian university education where ultimately liberal studies were checked by the power of the religious establishment.[9] Other university reformers of the mid century, although wishing to draw in those of the middle classes who were rising in wealth and power, nevertheless retained élitist and esoteric aims. Therefore, particularly before the 1850s, when reforms imposed by Acts of Parliament helped middle-class access, dissenters continued to go elsewhere.[10]

Alternative higher education

Thus Unitarians continued to use the Scottish universities in the early part of the century. It is hardly surprising therefore that the Unitarian James Yates, who had attended Glasgow, advocated that the religious openness, general democratic tenor, diversity of subjects and structural character of Scottish university life should be copied in England. The chance of achieving this came in the late 1820s with the foundation of the University of London, by a group of Benthamites, men from the Scottish universities and Issac Goldsmid, a wealthy Jewish merchant. No Unitarians served on the first committee, but thereafter a number of them made outstanding contributions in expertise, time and substantial bequests to what became University College London.[11]

In its early years the new institution faced many problems. Opposition from the ancient universities and other conservative bodies perceiving a threat to the interests of both the upper classes and

8. Sydney Smith, *Selections from the Writings of*... 2 vols (1855), I, pp. 19–41; *Edinburgh Review* (Jan. 1808), XI, no. XXII, p. 378; (July 1809), XIV, no. XXVIII, pp. 429–41; (Apr. 1810), XVI, no. XXXI, pp. 158–87; Brian Simon, *The Two Nations and the Educational Structure 1780–1870* (1974), pp. 90–1.

9. John Henry Newman, *The Idea of a University* (New York, 1959; first publ. 1873), *passim*; P.A. Dale, 'Newman's idea of a university! The dangers of a university education', *Victorian Studies* (1972), XVI, no. 1, pp. 5–36.

10. Knights, *Clerisy*, *passim*.

11. Yates, *Academical Education*, *passim*; H.H. Bellot, *University College, London, 1826–1926* (1929), *passim*.

the Anglican Church was compounded by the indifference of the middle classes and thus a lack of funds. Religious problems were complex, as Unitarians ruefully discovered. On the one hand, some orthodox dissenters and evangelicals such as Wilberforce refused to stay in what they perceived would be an 'ungodly' university, on the other, the Unitarians Thomas Southwood Smith and John Bowring were denied chairs because of their unorthodoxy. Anglican opposition soon led to the establishment in 1828 of the rival King's College, backed by royal, governmental and parliamentary support. Despite close, sympathetic ties with University College and the new London University of 1836, before the 1850s, therefore, Unitarians mostly turned to their own Manchester College as the chief institution of higher education.[12]

From 1805 Manchester College was the one remaining liberal dissenting college. It remained in York until 1849, when it moved back to Manchester in a great, although unsuccessful, effort to establish it as a university of the north. The college remained proudly true to its principles of non-subscription and free enquiry and to its aspirations of developing highly and widely educated ministers and laymen who would thence disseminate the liberal and scientific ideals which they had imbibed. Tutored by some excellent scholars, many influential and powerful industrial, professional and political men were educated there. Yet the college had a shaky history, culminating in its translation to London as a theological college working with the new Unitarian foundation of University Hall in 1853, thus living alongside University College rather than trying to rival it in the north. Despite exceedingly generous contributions from some of its wealthier supporters, the college regularly found itself in financial difficulties. At the same time ex-students such as James Yates lauded its virtues as the best 'seminary in England' in both arts and sciences.[13] Both its success and failure can suggest much about the position of Unitarians in nineteenth-century society and how far their educational and social ideals commanded support.

Manchester College received much of its patronage from the principal congregations of Unitarianism, drawn from the élite of dissent socially, economically and culturally. It catered for their desire for learned ministers and laymen able to perpetuate rational dissent and thereby help the civil liberties of their country and the 'true' interests of religion. At both York, where over half its scholars

12. Ibid.; *MR* (1828), NS 2, pp. 411, 632, 771–7, 786; (1829), NS 3, pp. 129–3; (1830), NS 4, pp. 53–4, 151; Yates, *Academical Education*, pp. vi, 164–8.

13. Ibid., p. 57.

took the divinity course, and in Manchester, the basic three-year course for laymen and five years for divinity students remained deliberately broad, intended to enable its participants to develop mental acuity and lay a basis for future studies. It remained educationally innovative: a chair in civil engineering was liberally pioneered by James Heywood from 1842 to 1845; the chair of ecclesiastical history in 1840 was the first such in a nonconformist college; and in 1846 'belles-lettres' was translated into a new course in English literature and language. High standards were maintained in the scholarship of the tutors, some outstanding ones such as William Gaskell, John James Tayler, 'the English Schleiermacher', and James Martineau being ex-students. Throughout the period from 1810 to 1853 John Kenrick towered above them all, a stimulating classicist and an objective and absorbing historian and scholar who even earned fame at the ancient universities despite being a 'heretic'.[14]

Yet with all this talent Manchester College still struggled hard to survive. Some of its problems were intrinsic. The extensive curriculum caused many headaches for students and tutors alike, the latter being further wearied by periodic disciplinary and financial crises. The sons of the 'cream of dissent' were not always predisposed to follow scholarship in monkish virtue, yet attracting lay students was obviously vital for the viability of the college since most of the divinity students, often of poorer parentage anyway, had their education paid for by the foundation. Only 235 students altogether were educated from 1803 to 1839, and only 50 full-timers from 1840 to 1853, of whom 113 and 32 respectively were lay students.[15] This hardly purported massive support for a college with such high perceptions of its role and mission. When in the 1840s, free from the shadow of York Minster, the college found it hard to survive even in Manchester, the stronghold of Unitarianism, it became obvious that, despite the generosity of some individuals and congregations, its resources were too slender to sustain its high ambitions.

The majority of those who did attend came from the great manufacturing and commercial centres of the mid nineteenth century, but even from these areas there was an obvious lack of interest in

14. MCO, *MCY Reports* and *MNC Reports* 1817 ff. especially 1834, 1840, 1842, 1847; *CR* (1836), III, p. 198; *DNB*, LV, 'John James Tayler', pp. 399–400; XXXI, 'John Kenrick', pp. 14–16.

15. DWL 24. 102 (1) *J.J. Tayler to cousin* (5.11.1814); MSS MCO *CW II* (30.11.1807) and *passim*; *York Letters* (1.4.1817) and *passim*; *JK III* (18.1.1817, 2.4.1819); IV (21.11.1827); William Rayner Wood, *Correspondence . . . to his Parents* (1830–31), *passim*; MCO *College Roll*, 1803–53.

such a college. The high cost of the fees, at 80–100 guineas a gear at York, made the college prohibitive, even to many Unitarians. Other dissenters would not overcome their religious prejudices to use the college or allow grants from dissenters' funds to assist those who did. Increasingly it was recognized that a small denominational college could not provide a complete liberal education on its own, especially considering the 'comparative apathy and indifference of the very classes' for whom it was intended. Those relatively few of the commercial and industrial middle class who were persuaded of the need for higher education for their sons used German or Scottish universities or, from the 1830s, were increasingly attracted by the University of London. Such considerations, exacerbated by the opening of Owens College in Manchester on the same principles but with richer and wider resources, helped to effect the move of Manchester College in 1853 to University Hall, London. Here, as their new Principal, John James Tayler, said, it was hoped that an education appropriate to 'a more advanced age' would benefit the class which held 'so much of the freedom and vigour of our national mind', unlike the old universities, which 'represent the interests of the Church and Aristocracy'.[16]

In spurning Manchester College, even when it was in Manchester and charging reasonable fees, the middle classes were rejecting the kind of culture offered by the élite of Unitarianism. Owens College, in which some Unitarians were also involved, although happy in John Owens' bequest of £100,000, had a similar shaky time in the 1850s, only beginning to revive in the 1860s, chiefly through the work of the Unitarians Henry Enfield Roscoe and Thomas Ashton. It did seem that Manchester and higher learning were incompatible. Businessmen still preferred their sons to enter the firm at fourteen at the latest, in order, as Elizabeth Gaskell explained, to catch 'a lad . . . young, and acclimated to the life of the mill, or office, or warehouse'. Universities, they thought, only 'unsettled' young men 'for commercial pursuits'.[17]

These factors had made all the more vital and significant the earlier enthusiastic backing of Manchester College by a number of wealthy, commercial and industrial Unitarian families particularly

16. MSS MCO, *York Letters*, 25.5.1816; *Letterbook 1824–80*, p. 17; *MNC Proceedings 1853*, Petition 26–37, Report on Proceedings in Chancery; *MNC Addresses 1853–81*; *MNC Report of a Special Committee*, (4.5.1853); MCO, John James Tayler, 'Inaugural Address 1853'.

17. Henry Roscoe, *The Life and Experiences of* . . . (1906), pp. 102–12, 127, 148, 244–7; Gaskell, *North and South*, p. 107.

of the north and midlands. Such included industrial giants like Fielden, Ashton, Marsland, Houldsworth, McConnel and William Strutt, who sought to tap the knowledge of his son Edward's tutor, William Turner junior, for his own inventions. This helped the continuation of cultured Unitarian industrialists and equally professional men who could provide vital support services for the often crowded family business. Over a quarter of the lay students at York went into the law, a number becoming Queen's Counsels and two, colonial Chief Justices.[18]

The keen support of wealthy families and the uses to which they put their education are clear indications of what they wanted from the college. They were a small group linked by religion and family ties – over a third of the lay students at York were brothers, a fifth were cousins. Many had attended schools run by Unitarians who themselves had often attended the college. Even though some laymen only stayed for part of the course and some congregations neither wanted nor could afford the highly educated ministers who emerged, supporters had the satisfaction of knowing that the college in all its phases helped to produce the élite of dissent they craved, men who were liberal Christians, scholars and gentlemen.[19]

The proof of this assertion can be seen in the number and types of successful men who emerged from a college with such a small intake. Not only were its results in the London examinations and prizes excellent but it produced a stream of notable men, including James Yates in antiquities, and William and Thomas Hincks in science; Samuel Robinson the industrialist; Russell Scott Tayler and Richard Holt Hutton, the editors of the *Manchester Guardian* and the *Spectator* respectively; Edward Strutt and Mark Philips, amongst the first nonconformist MPs to be elected in the 1830s; William Enfield, the solicitor and town clerk of Nottingham who supported and championed the mechanics' institute, the School of Art, decent homes for the poor, healthful places of recreation, the Institute for the Blind, the lunatic asylum and the Town and Country Hospital; and Henry Crosskey, minister of the Church of the Messiah in Birmingham from 1869 and an outstanding promoter of both popular education and a new civic gospel. Samuel Fielden upheld his father's eager fight for factory reform, although this was not so

18. MSS BL 24, 442, Joseph Hunter, *Collectanea Hunteriana*, VIII, 'Memoirs to serve for a history of Protestant Dissenters'; *Roll, passim*; R.S. Fitton and A.P. Wadsworth, *The Strutts and the Arkwrights 1758–1830* (Manchester, 1958), pp. 171–3, 189; David Wykes, 'Sons and subscribers', in Smith, *Truth*, pp. 58–64.

19. Ibid., pp. 62–9; MCO, Tayler, 'Inaugural Address'.

typical of Unitarians. Not least among ex-students were the many who worked tirelessly in education, such as John Relly Beard, William Gaskell and Travers Madge, the first editor of the *Sunday School Magazine* in 1848 and the enthusiastic teacher at Mosley Street Sunday school who taught young male factory workers as early as four or five in the morning. Other ex-students campaigned for state education and/or founded, supported or taught at mechanics' institutes.[20]

The college also became a centre of intellectual and social activity. In London perhaps this was less obvious, but A.D. Orange has attributed to Manchester College's presence in York until 1840 the major reason for the city's intellectual pre-eminence at that time. Charles Wellbeloved's enthusiastic efforts to preserve antiquities, especially the remains of St Mary's Abbey, and William Hincks' lectures at the medical school and curatorship of botany at the Yorkshire Philosophical Society, where Wellbeloved, Kenrick and William Turner junior were also prominent, are instances of this. Through this society the newly formed British Association for the Advancement of Science (BAAS) was encouraged in 1831 to hold its first meeting in York. The conservatism shown by the Dean of York in the British Association's 'Genesis and Geneaology' controversy was most radically answered in York by John Kenrick's *Essay on Primeval History* in 1844.[21]

Unitarians in urban culture

In Manchester too the college provided a strong intellectual centre. Yet Manchester was already *the* centre for Unitarianism and a prime example of its activities, a fact which made the failure of Manchester College to attract a large number of students there particularly significant. Unitarian involvement in a range of cultural and educational activities, from the Portico Library to the mechanics' institute, exemplifies the wide intellectual and social interests both of those associated with Manchester College and with the social élite who attended Unitarian chapels. Wealthy merchants, key local professional men, some of the leading bankers such as the Heywoods and

20. MCO *Roll*, 1835–55; *MC Report* (1854), 25, p. 6; Richard Armstrong, *In Memorian William Enfield* (privately printed, London, 1873); Asa Briggs, *Victorian Cities* (Harmondsworth, 1968), pp. 135, 198, 202, 206; Lester Burney, *Cross Street Chapel Schools, Manchester, 1734–1942* (Didsbury, 1977), pp. 40–1, 46–7.

21. A.D. Orange, *Philosophers and Provincials: The Yorkshire Philosophical Society from 1822 to 1844* (Yorkshire, 1973), pp. 23–4, 41, 51, 54–5, 59–63.

rising capitalists such as the Potters sat in the Cross Street pews. The nearby Mosley Street Chapel, which transferred to Brooke Street in 1839, was similar. With the scholarly John James Tayler as minister from 1820 to 1853 and members including the largest cotton spinners in town, such as McConnel, Kennedy, Peter Ewart, the Gregs, the Murrays and George Augustus Lee, it too brought together wealth, learning and the interests of industrial England. Its members, likewise, were prominent in a host of public cultural ventures which both proved their commitment to public service and earned them prestige, authority and status.[22] R.J.W. Selleck said, for example, of the members of the early Manchester Statistical Society that most shared 'Unitarianism, the occupations of the cotton trade and banking, and membership of so many committees that on occasions they might have wondered which one it was that they were attending'.[23] As Susanna Winkworth testified, 'The Unitarians in Manchester were, as a body, far away superior to any other in intellect, culture and refinement of manners, and certainly did not come behind any other in active philanthropy and earnest efforts for the social improvement of those among them.'[24] Unitarians provided four of the six presidents of the Manchester Literary and Philosophical Society between 1790 and 1842, for example, and gave the society 'its tone, its energy and its orientation'.[25]

Other major English commercial towns similarly had one or more substantial Unitarian chapels with a significant élite of the mercantile, banking, medical and legal men of the area who were prominent in establishing a whole range of informal agencies of middle-class education. This was true of Leeds, Leicester, Liverpool and Newcastle, for example, and even of Bristol where both Anglicanism and orthodox dissent were strong. The societies such men established, often small, usually middle-class, were essentially for 'gentlemen' (and only to a limited extent their 'ladies') to demonstrate or gain culture and science and generally facilitate communication of advances in knowledge. Ian Inkster and Jack Morrell have

22. John Seed, 'Unitarianism, political economy and the antinomies of liberal culture in Manchester, 1830–50', *Social History* (Jan. 1982), 7, no. 1, pp. 4–7.

23. R.J.W. Selleck, *James Kay Shuttleworth: Journey of an Outsider* (Ilford, 1994), p. 82.

24. Margaret J. Shaen (ed.), *Memorials of Two Sisters: Susanna and Catherine Winkworth* (1908), p. 26.

25. F. Nicholson, 'The Literary and Philosophical Society 1781–1851', *Memoirs and Proceedings of the Manchester Literary and Philosophical Society* (1923–4), lxviii, no. 9, pp. 98–143; Arnold Thackray, 'Natural knowledge in cultural context: the Manchester model', *American Historical Review* (Feb. 1974), 79, no. 1, pp. 694–709.

depicted scientific societies in this period as being used to distinguish marginal groups outside the mainstream of the middle class. Arnold Thackray argued more narrowly that they were used as the 'social legitimisation of marginal men', often Unitarian and to a lesser extent Quaker, in order to gain status in their rise to power, but then left once they were successful and hankered after more traditional prizes. Amongst Unitarians, however, this was only true of those like John Kennedy's son, who left Unitarianism too. From the late 1840s a greater specialism did creep in, for example in the Manchester Literary and Philosophical Society when William Fairbain and Eaton Hodgkinson, both Unitarians and engineers, presided, and this could detach science from being a necessary part of a gentleman's culture. Before 1850, however, the general concept of science in these societies, even if rather amateurish, was important if a scientific community was to be created, and owed much to the presence of Unitarians.[26]

Unitarians, therefore, were consistently members and often leaders of reforming groups, particularly in education. But this was always contested. The education, power and wealth of their leading members did make them, with the Quakers, the élite of dissent and of provincial commercial and industrial life, but their religion kept them out of prestigious educational institutions and society whilst their reforming zeal was too advanced for many of the middle class and they fought with other dissenters over chapel ownership. Even in Manchester their political and cultural ambitions were suspect, as James Kay (later Kay-Shuttleworth) bitterly discovered when he associated with them. There was such active hostility to the Unitarians, indeed, that James Heywood was nearly removed from the presidency of the Athenaeum which he had done so much to found, and wealthy industrialists were anxiously watching the rise of smaller cotton masters unsympathetic to both their economic and cultural leadership. The intellectual aspirations of the 1830s and 1840s were far too ambitious for their circumstances.[27]

Furthermore, the societies mentioned above were local and often very small, although this in itself could emphasize élitism when the members were prominent citizens. Some, however, purposely stressed their aim of supplying to middle-class youth 'the deficiencies of an

26. Ibid., pp. 678–81, 698–709; Ian Inkster and Jack Morrell (eds), *Metropolis and Province: Science in British Culture, 1780–1850* (1983), pp. 39–42; Robert H. Kargon, *Science in Victorian Manchester* (Manchester, 1977), *passim.*

27. Selleck, *Kay-Shuttleworth*, pp. 95, 102–3; Seed, 'Antinomies of liberal culture', p. 10.

imperfect education' and refined rather than 'destructive and debasing amusements'.[28] Nevertheless, they offered sufficient threat to the hegemony of the ruling élite for more liberal members of the latter to establish the British Association for the Advancement of Science as a way of bringing together a 'gentlemanly' coalition focused on the natural sciences. By contrast to the provincial societies, the BAAS was led by 'Gentlemen of Science', minor gentry and leisured upper-class men of secure income and traditional education. For the most part Anglicans of Whig or Peelite sympathies, they did admit others who matched their undogmatic or natural theology – Unitarians and Quakers but not Roman Catholics, Jews or other sectarians, nor, indeed, socialists or the working class. Originally scorned by major Oxbridge scientists, the Association nevertheless remained élitist in personnel and ideology and, before the 1850s, firmly metropolitan and academic in outlook, aspects which estranged some Unitarians like James Yates. Others remained keen supporters and anxious to be recognized by the BAAS. Lant Carpenter, for example, saw his attendance at the meeting at Bristol in 1836 as a chance to be regarded as the equal he knew he was, since he was acutely aware that, despite all he had done to diffuse science wherever he had lived, generally his influence and 'wishes were thwarted, and his motives misinterpreted, by those who felt a bitter prejudice against his opinions'.[29]

Women in urban culture and higher education

Carpenter's daughter Mary had reason to feel even more bitter since, as a woman, she was excluded altogether from the sections of the BAAS where the real work took place. Her solace had to be that many of the scientists attending visited her father. Pressure from ladies to attend the increasingly prestigious itinerant annual meetings triumphed over the fear of the charge of dilettantism as the financial benefits of allowing this were realized, and by 1838 Harriet Martineau was complaining that the Newcastle meeting was sadly spoiled not only by coxcombs, third-rate men and tiresome 'one-ideal men' but also by the inattentive, silly women who either quizzed or sketched the 'savons' and should have stayed at home. It was because of women's lack of education that she made this objection:

28. *Manchester Guardian* (5.10.1844).

29. Jack Morrell and Arnold Thackray, *Gentlemen of Science* (Oxford, 1981), *passim*; Russell Carpenter, *Memoir of the Revd. Lant Carpenter LL.D* (1842), p. 401.

she was hardly averse to learned women and publicly eulogized Mary Somerville, who had diplomatically stayed away from the 1832 meeting in Oxford. The latter was honoured at home and abroad for her excellent scientific writings yet ordinary membership of most scientific societies was closed to her.[30] Indeed, the scientific and literary societies so much promoted by Unitarians were, for the most part, exclusively for men. Women could attend as guests on selected occasions and even take part in some activities in some societies, but at best they were only second-class members. They might subscribe to such a cultural institution as the Manchester Athenaeum, as twenty-five women did in 1844, but the 1,721 members were men, almost exclusively middle-class and mostly young. Anna Swanwick was elected to be one of the first lady members of the Royal Institution in 1858,[31] but as late as 1859 Elizabeth Gaskell complained: 'With a struggle and a fight I can see all the Quarterlies three months after they are published; till then they lie on the Portico table, for gentlemen to see. I think I will go in for Women's Rights.'[32] Gaskell's interest in culture and science was comparable with her husband William's but their opportunities to exercise this differed. This was important because at the point when males went into higher education, the females of the family had to rely on informal agencies of education. The evidence explored indicates that Unitarian women used the latter extensively when they could. Caroline Thornley recorded in her Journal of the 1840s and 1850s, for example, visits to the Liverpool mechanics' institute, Anti-Slavery meetings, the Philharmonic Hall and Renshaw Street Book Club. In chapel and in private houses she mixed freely with some of the leading citizens of the liberal and radical middle class. In 1856 she was engaged in petitioning the Houses of Parliament to allow married women some control over their own earnings.[33] But she had no career or higher education and even women like *her* could not belong as of right to the various institutions she visited.

Having no access to higher education was a vacuum all the more keenly felt by some Unitarian women who, to that point, had been

30. Joseph Estlin Carpenter, *The Life and Work of Mary Carpenter* (1879), pp. 48–9; Harriet Martineau, *Autobiography*, 3 vols (1877), II, p. 137; Gayle Graham Yates, *Harriet Martineau on Women* (New Brunswick, 1985), p. 95; Martha Somerville (ed.), *Personal Recollections from Early Life to Old Age of Mary Somerville* (1873), pp. 173–6.

31. *Manchester Guardian* (5.10.1844); Mary L. Bruce, *Anna Swanwick* (1903), p. 81.

32. J.A.V. Chapple and A. Pollard (eds), *The Letters of Mrs Gaskell* (Manchester, 1966), p. 567.

33. Herbert McLachlan, 'A Liverpool ladies journal a century ago', *TUHS* (Oct. 1955), XI, no. 1, pp. 1–28.

educated almost equally to their brothers. At the most they might have private tutors or, like Marianne Gaskell, go to schools which took females beyond the age of sixteen.[34] As Frederic Hill said, 'it is in the time immediately following the period passed at school that the disparity is greatest'. For then a young man had all the inducement of qualifying for an 'occupation for life' to spur him on in study, whilst young women saw no reason to cultivate their minds and so fell into frivolous, unintellectual habits which lead to 'mental slavery' to men.[35]

The young Harriet Martineau, writing 'On Female Education' for the *Monthly Repository*, argued similarly, noting that male and female achievements were equal for as long as they were educated the same. Once having obtained 'the rudiments of knowledge', however, the boy from the 'cultivated' middle class concentrated on increasing his knowledge and exercising his mind, while the girl usually was 'confined to low pursuits' and taught that aspirations after knowledge were unfeminine, 'and thus before she is sensible of her powers, they are checked in their growth; chained down to mean objects, to rise no more; and when the natural consequences of this mode of treatment arise, all mankind agree that the abilities of women are far inferior to those of men'.[36]

Martineau argued not so much for women to gain 'great stores of information' as to have as much care taken in 'the formation of their minds'. Not only could the 'appropriate duties and peculiar employments' of women be done better by those with active minds and 'noble' interests, she contended, no one with an 'uncultivated' mind could be a true friend to her husband or suitable teacher of children. Twenty-five years later she was able to urge her case even more cogently, ridiculing the argument that females were denied certain subjects because they would not enter professional life since males supposedly studied to 'improve the quality of their minds'. She also urged forcefully from personal experience that, since so many women had to fend for themselves, it was only just that their intellect be developed and their educational resources be as great as possible. Besides, 'every human being is to be made as perfect as possible . . . this must be done through the most complete development of all the faculties'.[37]

34. Jenny Uglow, *Elizabeth Gaskell* (1993), pp. 226–7.
35. Frederic Hill, *National Education*, 2 vols (1836), I, pp. 215–16.
36. *MR* (Jan. 1822), XVIII, p. 77.
37. Harriet Martineau, *Household Education* (1870; 1st edn 1848), pp. 221–6.

Although by the late 1840s Martineau was abandoning Unitarianism as such, she thus remained true to her Hartleyan education. Such arguments had been similarly advanced by the Reverends William Shepherd, Jeremiah Joyce and Lant Carpenter in 1817 in *Systematic Education*. They had added that if men despised learned females it was no matter for such men were 'fools and coxcombs' and there was no worth in suppressing female talent to please such – 'a lovely woman cannot be rendered less lovely by the high cultivation of her talents'.[38] Martineau's mature feminism led her in 1861 to state drily, 'Girls will never make a single effort . . . for such an object as being companions to men, and mothers of heroes.'[39] This was in contrast to the more conservative Sarah Taylor, who worked systematically through a reading list to fit her for marriage to John Austin.[40]

For whatever reasons Unitarian women studied, such an education as they could gain in their knowledge-thirsty environment might enable women to go far. Similarly, the delight of Elizabeth Whitehead (later Malleson) of attending almost every speech in London on free trade in the early 1840s shows a real education in religious and political issues which could be used in a wider sphere. This was not always the result: the Shaen sisters, for example, spent hours arguing over political and social issues but it was their brother William who publicly fought for these, including women's rights.[41] Although many Unitarians did use their education to good effect as social reformers, teachers, educationists, translators and writers, nevertheless, even those in an enlightened Unitarian household, and aware of their intellectual needs, might find serious study on their own neither fully satisfying nor easy. In no way did Unitarian women have the same opportunities as men, even in education where an egalitarian ideal was upheld and where the men themselves were fighting for reform and extension. No woman could go to Cambridge, as James Heywood had done even though for long denied his degree. Nor could they attend Manchester College, into which Unitarians like Heywood and William Gaskell poured so much of their resources and energy.

38. William Shepherd, Jeremiah Joyce and Lant Carpenter, *Systematic Education* (1817), pp. 18–20.
39. Yates, *Martineau on Women*, p. 98.
40. Janet Ross, *Three Generations of Englishwomen* (1888), pp. 130–1.
41. Elizabeth Malleson, *Autobiography* (private circulation, 1926), p. 39; Uglow, *Gaskell*, pp. 166–7.

On the other hand, Unitarians were pioneers of higher education for women in this period. John Relly Beard, for example, saw no reason why women should not experience the highest university learning.[42] In 1831 Lant Carpenter's course of lectures in Manchester led William Wood to write home from Manchester College, hoping that Dr Carpenter 'may succeed in making Mental Philosophy more popular with the ladies of Manchester than it is with the students of York College'.[43]

James Martineau was also amongst the first to give formal higher education to women. In the 1830s he lectured to both sexes in Liverpool whilst in 1846 his lectures on mental and moral philosophy in Manchester foreshadowed later University Extension lectures and gave a welcome mental stimulus to such talented students as Anna Swanwick, Julia Wedgwood, Susanna and Catherine Winkworth, and Frances Grundy. The latter three all testified to the immense intellectual change this made to their lives. Anna Swanwick, already having translated Goethe's *Iphigenia*, subsequently went to Berlin with two other Unitarians, Misses Zumpt and Lupton, for eight months' intensive study of German and Greek philosophy, language and literature and returned to become an even more acclaimed translator. She also intensely enjoyed mathematics and learnt Hebrew with Miss Lupton. Her studies enabled her to become a well-known translator of both German and Greek, highly respected by her former tutor, Martineau, and recognized by an honorary LL D from the University of Aberdeen. William Gaskell, a gifted colleague of James Martineau's at Manchester New College, provided private advanced studies to females, including the gifted Winkworth sisters, Catherine and Susanna, who became renowned translators of German. Catherine Winkworth attributed her knowledge of English literature and appreciation of style to him.[44]

Julia Wedgwood, a student of Martineau's, was related to Fanny Wedgwood, one of the first of the Council of Bedford College, the second college in England founded for women and the first to become a constituent part of the University of London. Bedford was founded by a Unitarian, Elizabeth Reid, a friend of the Aikin family, Lady Byron and Harriet Martineau, and had strong Unitarian support – a factor which might have substantially increased its

42. John Relly Beard, *Self-Culture* (3rd edn; 1st edn 1859), p. 256.
43. MSS MCO, Wood, *Correspondence*, 39 (16.1.1831).
44. Joseph Carpenter, *Martineau*, pp. 160, 271–4, 527; Shaen, *Two Sisters*, pp. 18–23, 73, 85, 93–4, 103; Mary L. Bruce, *Anna Swanwick* (1903), pp. 25–33, 36–43, 202, 220–2; Chapple and Pollard, *Gaskell*, p. 190; *DNB*, LXI, pp. 665–6.

difficulties in its early years.[45] Although in this field too Unitarians were amongst the foremost pioneers of change, they did not establish the first college in England for women. That was done in 1848 by F.D. Maurice, Christian Socialist and ex-Unitarian. Maurice led a group of lecturers and professors from King's College, London in establishing Queen's College, the first institution in England where a young woman could receive advanced education and from first-class minds. The College was set up with governesses and teachers in mind in the hope that better qualifications would bring higher status and pay. However, all 'ladies' over twelve could attend, since reality taught that any middle-class lady might suddenly find herself teaching – the only 'respectable' work, apart from sewing, for ladies. Maurice had long denounced the rote learning, inferior books and lack of imaginative training in female education, all designed to inculcate submissiveness. Thus, at Queen's the emphasis was on raising the mental culture of girls especially through offering a wide range of subjects including mathematics, mechanics, natural philosophy and pedagogy as well as languages, history, geography and music. Queen's, indeed, was to become a unique educational establishment, a cross between a school and college, which educated many pioneers in female education, for example Miss Buss and Miss Beale.[46]

Yet, although teaching women to think might be revolutionary, Queen's was conservative in keeping the government and teaching of the college firmly under the control of men, Maurice initially being against women taking degrees or entering professions.[47] Bedford, established only one year after Queen's and the only comparable college for many years, was markedly different. It offered the same full and liberal higher education together with an art school, the only one in England in which women could work from life. An ex-student, the Unitarian Laura Herford, was the first woman artist to be admitted to the Royal Academy School. Unlike Queen's, however, Bedford was aimed at all middle-class women from the start. It had both women and men in a single governing body and, later, the 1860 Reid Trust was controlled by three women trustees. Trustees were to be women to ensure that Bedford remained a college not a school, and to be unmarried so that no husband could assert a right to control the money or property. Two of the first trustees,

45. M.J. Tuke, *A History of Bedford College for Women, 1849–1937* (1939), *passim.*

46. Elaine Kaye, *A History of Queen's College, London, 1848–1972* (1972) pp. 16–27, 38–55, *passim.*

47. Ibid., p. 87.

Eliza Bostock and Jane Martineau, were Unitarians, as were many of the students, lady visitors and staff in the early years. A number of prominent women from Unitarian families – Barbara Leigh-Smith, Anna Swanwick, Sarah Austin – attended as mature students. Indeed, Mary-Anne Busk recalled whole families, or at least the female members of them, attending: not only her own interrelated le Breton, Busk and Aikin families, but the Martineaus, Cromptons and Swanwicks, among others. William Shaen, husband of Emily Winkworth, was a fervent supporter and, in later years, Samuel Courtauld, Samuel Sharpe and Henry Tate and his wife were major benefactors. Unitarians and those of Unitarian descent, such as Hensleigh Wedgwood and his wife Fanny (née Mackintosh), and Julia Smith, aunt of both Barbara Leigh-Smith and Florence Nightingale, were closely involved in the founding and running of the college. In the early days Francis Newman, William Carpenter and Augustus de Morgan, all professors at University College, taught at Bedford.[48]

Bedford's links with secularist and radical educationists, unlike Queen's royal and upper-class support, probably was a factor in its initial difficulties. Nevertheless, the college, and its school, founded in 1853, eventually flourished, and, again unlike Queen's, from 1878, when London opened its degrees to women, became a university college. Subsequently in 1900 it became a constituent part of the University of London. In this progress many Unitarians were prominent, not least William Shaen, aided by Henrietta and Edward Busk, and James Heywood, so actively involved in the whole struggle to reform and open up liberal higher education for males.[49]

The comparative generosity of Unitarian patronage later in the nineteenth century to the fledgling women's colleges at Cambridge and Oxford – Girton, Newnham and Somerville – has been acknowledged by historians.[50] Yet even among the Unitarians the question of support for higher education for women was not without problems. Some were far less keen on higher education for women than for men: for example, Henry Crabb Robinson reluctantly gave £50

48. Tuke, *Bedford, passim*; Ruth Young, *The Life of an Educational Worker: Henrietta Busk* (1934), pp. xxii–xxiii, 3–6, 14–34, *passim.*

49. Ibid., pp. 43, 47–8; Tuke, *Bedford*, pp. 78–134; *Inquirer* (12.3.1887), p. 172; (23.10.1897), p. 690.

50. Gillian Sutherland, 'The movement for the higher education of women: its social and intellectual context in England, c.1840–80', in P.J. Walker (ed.), *Essays presented to A.F. Thompson* (Sussex, 1987), pp. 97–101; Janet Howarth and Mark Curthoys, 'The political economy of women's higher education in late nineteenth and early twentieth century Britain', *Bulletin of the Institute of Historical Research* (June 1987), LX, no. 142, pp. 213–14.

to Bedford, a sum of money he would cheerfully give for a dance at University College.[51] Elizabeth Reid drily remarked to him that it was difficult to find a gentleman 'who is deliberately of the opinion that Female Education, the improvement of the Moral and mental education of women, is of any importance to society; while all the time the good man may be teased by a very silly and tiresome wife himself, who is spoiling the minds of his children'.[52] Yet, although she determined on a college not a school, her aims hardly appear excessive today. She wished to save young women of the 'professional and upper middle-classes' from the 'dreary futility of life' they were condemned to, hoping that by raising the 'moral and intellectual character' particularly of mothers an 'improved state of society' and 'better men' would be created. But even this proved to be revolutionary for the day. On the practical side, many of the first students had too low a standard for advanced study, and thus in 1853 a Junior School was started and in 1856 a more systematic course of study became the norm in the college. By 1858 this comprised four years of history, three of Latin and at least three extra subjects a year from modern languages, mathematics, science and others. Despite the setbacks, it was recognized that at least many young women had been given 'habits of industry, a desire for solid improvement and a love of knowledge which must have a beneficial influence on their future lives'. The sad counterpoint to this was that the importance of advanced education for women was 'as yet very imperfectly recognised' and the principle of non-sectarian education even less so. The latter was a reference to the numerous instances whereby either the college's Unitarian associations or, conversely, the unorthodox religious writings of male professors had exacerbated the staffing difficulties of the institution.[53] Such events were both reminiscent of the fate of other educational ventures of Unitarians, including Manchester College, and a foretaste of some of the challenges awaiting girls' high schools and university colleges.

In reality, it would have been too soon for even those Unitarians who did help women gain some form of higher education to look for equality with male provision. Lant Carpenter, for example, despite all his pioneering work in this regard, detected a general distinction in intellectual powers and capabilities between the sexes, although he refused to be drawn on the part education played in this.

51. Edith Morley, *The Life and Times of Henry Crabb Robinson* (New York, 1970), pp. 118–20; Thomas Saddler (ed.), *Diary, Reminiscences and Correspondence of Henry Crabb Robinson*, 2 vols (1872), I, p. xii.

52. Tuke, *Bedford*, p. 14. 53. Ibid., *passim*.

He believed the weaker physical structure of females debarred them not only from continuous bodily exertions but also 'the struggles of public life' and 'that persevering energetic research, that long-continued closeness of investigation, by which the mighty processes of human improvement have been carried on'.[54] Carpenter thought women capable of much, especially the gentleness, cheerful self-sacrifice, patience and compassion which made a man's home the 'dearest place on earth'. Indeed, he believed men could not equal the moral and spiritual writings respectively of Maria Edgeworth and Anna Barbauld, but they could equal the intellectual excellence of women such as Mary Somerville, who should be admired most because she coupled her gifts with domestic duties and a meek and modest spirit.[55]

Such fears of women rivalling men in intellectual pride came well from a gifted, sensitive man unstintingly supported through many bouts of nervous debility by a calm, practical wife whose inner intellectual and spiritual longings were only known to her family in her secret journal found after her death.[56] Carpenter's distinctions between the taste, perception and discrimination of women and the logic and application of men were not unusual among educational reformers. Some of these were reiterated by William Johnson Fox, but Fox stressed further the supreme object, common to all, of achieving everyone's full potential. He deplored the legal and domestic subordination of females to males which led all too often to the wastage of many fine human qualities, including those 'which have guided man to his best exertions and his loftiest condition'. Accepting that a man's brain might be heavier than a woman's, he added: 'a head as heavy as an elephant's may only be a lump of leaden ignorance.'[57] In crippling female intellect, man has 'thereby enfeebled his own', he said, and had deprived himself of so much comfort and stimulus by 'claiming science, politics, philosophy, and all the higher regions of thought for himself, and warning off intrusion by placarding them with the word unfeminine'.[58]

James Martineau, whose own wife attended his lectures to 'ladies', did much for women's education and later wished that all professions and activities 'deemed honourable for men' should be open to

54. Lant Carpenter, *Sermons on Practical Subjects* (1840), p. 263.
55. Ibid., pp. 263–5.
56. Jo Manton, *Mary Carpenter and the Children of the Streets* (1976), p. 23 and *passim.*
57. W.J. Fox , 'Five lectures on education', *Collected Works* (1865), VIII, pp. 168–9; *MR* (1832), NS 6, p. 640.
58. R. Garnett, *The Life of W.J. Fox* (1909), p. 112.

them so that they could prove naturally what they could do. Yet he considered women's roles in life would be little altered by this and was later to speak against married women's suffrage as spoiling household union. Earlier he certainly appeared to have difficulties with his sister Harriet's fame.[59]

Harriet Martineau, however, like many of those involved in Bedford College, was a pioneer generally on the issues of women's opportunities and rights. She, Fanny Wedgwood and others from Bedford also supported Queen's College, which likewise educated a number of pioneering women although it generally appealed to those from more orthodox religious backgrounds. Educational reform was thus basic to the origins of feminism. It was to be seen from the 1860s that the growing movement for girls' high schools, for girls to take part in public examinations, for women to enter higher education could not be divorced from other campaigns concerning the rights of women, although certainly not all those involved were radical feminists.

In the earlier period too the issues were inextricably entwined and many of those who were engaged across a range of reforms for women were Unitarians. Amongst the women, like the men, there were differing shades of opinion, but in general it can be seen that by the mid 1850s the middle classes were beginning to gain those opportunities in higher education demanded so insistently by Unitarians. The latter had played no small part in this achievement, and more than others among the middle classes had involved themselves in educational opportunities beyond schooling for women. On the other hand, in this period the priority for most Unitarians was male education, on which an enormous amount of expertise, time, effort and money was expended. The results were extraordinary, with men from this small religious group becoming prominent in some of the fastest-developing towns of the leading industrial nation on earth. Unitarians were unable to achieve their ultimate aims even for males, however. Their interrelated aims for women were affected by both their successes and their failures. For the many Unitarian women who were well educated for their day there was the further problem of what effect this had on their lives, including their thinking on gender issues.

59. Joseph Carpenter, *Martineau*, pp. 275, 431–2, *passim*.

CHAPTER EIGHT

Unitarians and education for the working class: a gendered concern?

The debate over women and higher education was partly about to what use a woman could put advanced learning. Within the tightly knit Unitarian community many women seem to have been deeply committed to the intellectual culture and religious, social, economic and political aspirations of their group. Such commitment might take them beyond the usual bounds of female action and give them a place where they might utilize their developed understanding. Unitarian aspirations, at both local and national level, permeated the class power struggles waged politically, economically and socially among the middle classes and against both the upper and working classes, although there were important pockets of working-class Unitarianism. It will be shown that women and men were often involved in the same issues and yet experienced both the participation and the outcomes differently. This will be seen particularly in the educational activities run by chapels and individuals.

Most of the discussion has so far centred on the aspirations of Unitarians of the middle class, which was where most Unitarians originated. But this category ranges widely. For example, both the Unitarians John Relly Beard, son of a poor tradesman and enjoying a ministerial salary ranging between £45 and £120 a year, and his fellow committee member at the Manchester Free School in 1854, Mark Philips, member of a rich, very significant manufacturing family in Lancashire, would have called themselves middle-class.[1] The 'working class', of course, was not a homogeneous group either, although its members shared a common financial insecurity. The varying layers of poverty produced different educational responses

1. DWL, James Beard, Duplicate typescript of collection of notes and materials for life of John Relly Beard DD (undated), *passim*; I am indebted to Don Jones for information on who the committee members were.

from the Unitarians, although the latter did not always make their references explicit. Some of their writings were obviously directed to the artisan class, the working-class élite admired deeply, for example, by Harriet Martineau and William Johnson Fox.[2] This was particularly important for the Unitarian contribution to working-class education, which will be examined briefly here in relation to gender issues.

Unitarians, of course, were not the only reformers involved in the education of the working classes. Phrenologists and the Christian Socialists were also concerned, as were some liberal Anglicans and nonconformists, particularly Edward Baines in Leeds, the Congregationalist who led the voluntarist opposition to state education. The writings of Coleridge and Carlyle awakened a new sense of responsibility and care for the working classes generally among the educated classes, although their political effect was usually conservative, as certainly was that of Disraeli. The Anglican Church, revived by its disparate wings of evangelicals and High Church, took an increasingly active role in the education of the poor, although again their education aimed to preserve a conservative, hierarchical, deferential society.[3]

Unitarians and education for the working classes

Unitarian involvement in working-class education was more complex. Logically their environmentalist educational philosophy could hardly be confined to one section of society. John Relly Beard, for example, fervently wished all to gain the liberty, even the power, which comes from knowledge. He despised any class hanging on to power if they could only do so 'by holding others in the degrading vassalage of ignorance' and pronounced himself 'a friend to unlimited education, the widest possible education to all of all ages and of all ranks'.[4] This was knowledge for personal autonomy, as David Vincent has described,[5] and the astonishing involvement of so many Unitarians in almost every conceivable aspect of education would seem to testify that many other Unitarians agreed with Beard. They

2. Harriet Martineau, *Household Education* (1870), pp. 41–3; Margaret Parnaby, *William Johnson Fox and the Monthly Repository Circle* (Ph.D. thesis, Australia National University, 1979), pp. 94–104.
3. 'Edward Baines', *DNB*, XXII, Supplement, pp. 100–1; Ben Knights, *The Idea of the Clerisy in the Nineteenth Century* (1978), pp. 36–99.
4. *UC* (1832), pp. 8–9.
5. David Vincent, *Bread, Knowledge and Freedom* (1981), pp. 109–95.

were concerned in a wide range of educational experiments and institutions for both children and adults and ran various types of school themselves. As they constituted such a small proportion of the population, some of their actual provision was outnumbered by that of other denominations, the number of working-class children in their day schools in 1834 being estimated at 2,900, with 14,350 in their Sunday schools.[6] Much of this provision, however, has been recognized as being both deeper and wider than that commonly given. In Birmingham, for example, even the atheist George Holyoake commended the way that Unitarian Sunday schools turned out young people who were very 'superior' in learning to those taught by evangelicals. This would be partly because Unitarian ones were non-denominational and, whether large or small, taught not only the three Rs but also subjects such as geography, history and science, often with weekday evening schools, adult schools, libraries and a wide variety of activities attached. Above all, many of them wanted to 'embrace the elements of a liberal education' and tried to teach their pupils to think.[7]

The educational activities of a small sect were hardly enough, however, to redress the deficiencies in education of the working classes. Lant Carpenter praised Sunday schools as the spiritual parallels of steam engines, but these, like factory and evening schools and mechanics' institutes, confined education to a time when the working classes were not earning a living. Thus Unitarians got involved in other initiatives, including enthusiastic support of *Lancasterian and British schools, before their increasing estrangement from orthodox dissent. Most, however, bitterly opposed any attempt to extend education by increasing Anglican educational control. John Relly Beard, for instance, fiercely attacked elementary education by the opulent Established Church for being 'almost as bad in kind as it is deficient in extent'.[8]

The answer seemed to lie in non-denominational state provision of some kind such as they saw the Unitarian Horace Mann, secretary of the Massachusetts Board of Education, establish. Unlike nonconformists generally in this period, therefore, most Unitarians became whole-hearted supporters of various moves towards state education, not least helping the American system to influence the

6. *CR* (1834), I, pp. 542–3.

7. Angus Easson, *Elizabeth Gaskell* (1979), pp. 18–19; James Luckcock, *Moral Culture* (Birmingham, 1817), pp. x, 3–14, 274–5, 282.

8. *UC* (1834), p. 216; *CR* (1834), pp. 542–3; John Relly Beard, *The Government Plan of Education* (1839), pp. 3–32.

emergent state system in England. Unitarians comprised about one-third of the National Public Schools Association of 1850, for example, and eleven of them were on the committee of twenty-five which set up the secular Manchester Free School of 1854. William Biggs' public lectures as mayor of Leicester in 1849 and William Johnson Fox's education bill of 1850 when MP for Oldham were typically strong demonstrations of support for such ideas.[9]

Such public action on education was not possible for those who could become neither mayor nor MP. Primarily a woman's role was still seen within the household as wife, mother, daughter, sister or maiden aunt – always as a relative creature serving the needs of her family. Young men might also find their career limited by family expectations but they certainly had greater choice and freedom and would be defined more by what they did outside the home and not by a relationship contingent upon their sex. Unitarian educational philosophy so emphasized the importance of early education upon associationist lines that the role of carers of children was enhanced both at an affective and at an intellectual level. This strengthened the caring, familial role of men but could have the effect of containing women further in the home even whilst the better education they received might be giving them the tools to enter new roles outside of it.

However, although the first concern of Unitarian women often was to use their education within the family and home, many fulfilled the compelling ethic of radical dissent to turn talent and experience outward by social work. This was not unusual: philanthropy was generally held to be peculiarly permissible for ladies. As Frank Prochaska has shown, Evangelicalism especially, with its religious fervour and stress on duty and women's moral mission in society, drove many women into philanthropic work of all kinds. Here they used their domestic skills in work supposedly ideally suited to their role in society. The voluntary female sector generally was substantial, but Unitarian women differed in that both religious principle and a more rational outlook led them to ban religious indoctrination and to doubt the value of the emotional proselytizing among the poor by what they saw as enthusiastic but ill-informed evangelicals.

9. S.E. Maltby, *Manchester and the Movement for National Elementary Education* (Manchester, 1918), pp. 68, 154; D.K. Jones, 'Working-class education in nineteenth-century Manchester: the Manchester Free School', *VASFE* (Spring 1967), XIX, no. 42, pp. 22–33; *CR* (1834), pp. 13–22, 188–202; *UC* (1834), pp. 33–6; Leicester PRO, 5D61, *John and William Biggs Scrapbooks*, 3 vols (undated), III: 'Lecture on Education' (1849), p. 133; I, II and III, *passim*; Parnaby, *Fox*, pp. 566–8.

Unitarians, though not always lacking in spiritual fervour, preferred, like their menfolk, a more practical approach based on firm statistical knowledge and organization. The outstanding pioneering work by women like Catherine Cappe and Elizabeth Rathbone in hospital management and schooling for the poor were good examples of the value of their attitudes.[10]

In these ways Unitarian women found their own way of expressing their social concern, although mostly they demonstrated the latter through education. They usually tried to participate 'within their sphere' but, as in other areas, they widened this a little. Sarah Austin, for example, used her scholarly talents to produce an able and widely influential translation of Victor Cousin's report on public education in Prussia. Her own preface, however, powerfully and clearly argued the case for national education, dismissing both laissez-faire ideology in the case of children's education and fears of a totally despotic, anti-religious state system. Her view of a centrally directed, but locally controlled system, with well-trained teachers developing to the full the minds and characters of their eager pupils, was welcome to radical educationists such as William Fox and his circle.[11] In Liverpool Elizabeth Rathbone worked with her husband William and other Unitarians to secure the Hibernian system whereby Protestants and Catholics were educated in the same schools but given separate religious instruction. Virulent opposition prevented a lasting success but Elizabeth Rathbone never gave up, as she sent a memorandum on the schools to William Forster in 1870 to help guide his thoughts on religious education.[12]

Sunday schools

It was in the local provision of schooling, particularly that centring on the chapel, that women chiefly participated. Sunday schools, for example, especially offered a rare field of warm, personal, yet public service. Members of leading Unitarian families, including Harriet

10. F.K. Prochaska, *Women and Philanthropy in Nineteenth Century England* (1980), *passim*; Anna le Breton (ed.), *Correspondence of Dr Channing and Lucy Aikin* (1874), pp. 396–8; MSS Liverpool University, *Elizabeth Rathbone: Correspondence with Lady Byron*, VI. 1.264; VI. 1.277; VI. 1.283; *passim*; Catherine Cappe, *Memoirs* (1822), pp. 416, 430–1.

11. Sarah Austin, *Report on the State of Public Instruction in Prussia by M. Victor Cousin* (1834), *passim*; Parnaby, *Fox*, pp. 375, 389–94.

12. Eleanor F. Rathbone, *William Rathbone* (1908), pp. 48–51; MSS Liverpool Reference Library, EDU/1/36/1, *Hibernian Schools Minute Books*, *passim*.

Martineau and Elizabeth Gaskell, wrote for Travers Madge's *Sunday School Penny Magazine*, thus supporting an almost unique publication. In Unitarian Sunday schools, women served as teachers, visitors to scholars and parents, and superintendents, as in the case of Mary Carpenter and Catherine Turner.[13] Women often effectively ran the girls' schools although men retained overall control. For instance, at High Pavement, Nottingham, the male vestry committee prevented the ladies' committee from giving surplus funds 'to relieving the distress . . . they frequently witness[ed]' as the men deemed this 'would be productive of very little good – and would be attended with many evil consequences'. In turn the women won the rather dubious victory of stopping the 'impropriety' of girls sitting in the choir.[14]

These Unitarian women were certainly not using Sunday schools to break all traditions. Similarly, in provision for girls, Unitarians followed the prevailing norm to some extent as they had more places for boys. In 1832, certainly, the *Unitarian Chronicle* survey showed that although the majority of the nineteen schools which returned boys and girls separately appeared to have more girls, these were smaller schools. Those which had more boys were mostly much larger and had a considerably greater imbalance.[15]

Yet if there was some discrepancy in numbers and aspirations for girls, there were also examples of unexpected attitudes for this time. From the extra provision Elizabeth Gaskell gave to the older girls of Cross Street and Mosley Street Sunday schools in her own house to the working woman Jane Stallard teaching Shakespeare to the older girls at Shepton Mallet at five in the morning before they went to the mill, there was an array of activities that attempted to take females of the working classes beyond the mere literacy and sewing skills usually allotted them.[16] Unitarians scorned other religious bodies for giving the 'mere rudiments of an education' to the poor or not having open access to all, regardless of belief. They typically not only taught writing, uncommon in the Sunday schools of many other religious bodies, but encouraged a wider education. Their different practices earned them little respect amongst the

13. Brooke Herford, *Travers Madge: A Memoir* (Hamilton, Adams & Co., 1867), pp. 7–15, 20–1, 51–65; Joseph Estlin Carpenter, *The Life and Work of Mary Carpenter* (1879), pp. 5, 36; 'Catherine Turner', *Inquirer* (19.5.1894), p. 319.

14. MSS University of Nottingham, HiM, *Minute Books* (9.1.1803; 28.9.1823; 12.5.1816; HiW24, *J.C. Warren's Papers, Written History of HP* (1815).

15. *UC* (1832), pp. 145–7, 197–9; e.g. Luckcock, *Moral Culture*, pp. 274–5.

16. 'Elizabeth Gaskell', *Inquirer* (18.11.1865), p. 742.; Henry Solly, *These Eighty Years*, 2 vols (1893), II, p. 30.

more orthodox. In Cheltenham, for instance, Unitarian Sunday school pupils were publicly insulted in the streets by both clergy and laity and several 'Evangelical ladies' paid for some pupils to attend a non-Unitarian day school in preference.[17]

The 'dangerous' Unitarians were thus rarely found in the various Sunday school unions. On the other hand, many of them were very popular with the working classes, a number of whom became teachers in the schools, some succeeding further like John Ashworth, later a cotton manufacturer, member of the town council and school board. The emphasis was on teaching pupils to think. This was exemplified by working-class Unitarians such as the Methodist Unitarians, especially Joseph Barker's Christian Brethren, who developed excellent Sunday schools with libraries and reading-rooms.[18] Further examples were demonstrated by the Brotherly Society and later the Newhall Hill schools in Birmingham, where the teachers recognized their type of education as differing from evangelical instruction, which was 'debasing, instead of improving the people . . . the greater part of popular education tends to stunt the growth of the mind . . . and poisons instead of nourishing the heart'.[19]

Most of the more startling recorded achievements from Unitarian schools are of men, however. Although many girls were educated in the Birmingham schools, for example, there were fewer of them than boys and they were not included in the Brotherly Society. On the other hand, some well-connected women in Unitarian circles, like Sarah Crompton at the Old Meeting, quietly worked for many years in the Sunday and evening schools. Sarah, indeed, wrote books to help the instruction of children and illiterate adults.[20] At the New Meeting there was a flourishing group of women visitors to the girls' schools, who held quarterly meetings at each other's houses and monthly business meetings where they also made and repaired caps and tippets for the girls. They also visited the families of scholars. From 1850, it seems, the girls' school run by the New Meeting sought greater recognition for its work. As in Nottingham, these lady visitors opposed a plan for girls being in the choir, but this did not appear to lose the schools any popularity for apparently girls often stayed until they were women and then sent their own children.

17. *MR* (1832) NS 2, pp. 234–7; *CR* (1841), p. 714.

18. H. McLachlan, [1] *Essays and Addresses* (Manchester, 1950), pp. 226–7; [4] *The Story of a Nonconformist Library* (Manchester, 1923), pp. 164–83.

19. *CR* (1841), pp. 519–20; Birmingham Reference Library L18.4, *New Meeting Sunday School Reports* (1817–46), *passim*; Luckcock, *Moral Culture*, *passim*.

20. Catherine Hutton Beale, *Memorials of the Old Meeting House and Burial Ground, Birmingham* (Birmingham, 1882), 'Gravestones', p. 12.

Sometimes, possibly, as at the Leicester Girls' School, admission was eagerly sought because people from well-known local families were involved in the schools.[21]

These examples show how complex is the argument between Malcolm Dick and Walter Laqueur over whether Sunday schools, at least in the earlier nineteenth century, were essentially conservative and patriarchal institutions or central institutions in the religious and recreational life of the working-class community itself, creating a working-class culture of respectability and self-reliance. Unitarian Sunday schools exemplified both premises, partly because of the gender imbalance, although it was always openly affirmed that knowledge could lead to power and that no knowledge should be denied the working class.[22]

Furthermore, although for both sexes the schools served to give an outlet for the reforming and social energies of the patrons as well as educating their pupils – John Fielden and Joseph Chamberlain are only two of the number of Unitarian manufacturers who enthusiastically taught in Sunday schools – this was particularly so for women, who often had little other outlet for such energies. They were sometimes able to get closer to their working-class protégées too and even to take the initiative in policy making. In Nottingham, for example, Anne Enfield, long superintendent of the girls' Sunday school, promoted music and the 'costly provision of gardens for the scholars'.[23]

Perhaps the best instance was at Bristol where Mary Carpenter followed as far as she could, as a woman, in the footsteps of her father Lant. He had opened the doors of the opulent Lewin's Mead Chapel to the poor, who, drawn by the warmth of his manner, preaching and consideration, came to fill the galleries. He happily depended on women to further his ideas and overcome the initial reservations of many of the congregation to establish Sunday schools which soon were flourishing with large, spacious accommodation. In the following decade it was Mary Carpenter, long a teacher in the schools and more or less the superintendent of the girls' school,

21. Herbart New, *Centenary of the Church of the Messiah (formerly New Meeting) Schools* (Birmingham, 1888), pp. 15–16, 19–20; Edith Gittins, *The Centenary Book of the Great Meeting Sunday Schools* (Leicester, 1883), pp. 8–9.

22. Malcolm Dick, 'Religion and the origins of mass schooling: the English Sunday school c.1780–1840', *The Churches and Education* (HofE Society, Conference papers, Dec. 1983), pp. 42–6.

23. MSS MCO, 'Todmorden' (5.1.1889), *Presbyterian Chapels,* I, p. 179; Solly, *Eighty Years,* II, pp. 83–8; MSS HP, Hu2Su1, Rev. P.W. Clayden, *An Address . . . on . . . Mrs Enfield.*

who extended the role of women by establishing a Working and Visiting Society to visit the homes of the poor of the congregation and of the Sunday school. She was the tireless secretary of this society of about thirty ladies which met monthly at each other's houses to sew for the poor and try to visit them as friends, relieve the sick and unemployed and enable them to help themselves. Their society was very carefully organized in what might have been termed a 'masculine system' of five visiting districts and twelve visitors.[24]

The women soon perceived they needed to promote their society's objects and plans amongst other members of the congregation. Their reports demonstrate their growing awareness both of their own great 'pleasure and improvement' from their active role and of the difficulties even employed and provident working people faced when trying to raise a growing family or hit by sickness or unforeseen misfortune. Growing understanding of these problems led the women to subscribe to the Dispensary so that medical advice and medicine could be given and to investigate better provident societies than the ones in Bristol. They also persuasively argued for a minister who could devote his time exclusively to the poor and visit the most 'wretched habitations' where ladies 'should not go alone'. 'Ladies', after all, were limited to visiting congregational members and those with children in the schools whether they belonged to any religion or, more often, none at all. Their religious beliefs were left alone by their Unitarian visitors, although both the services at Lewin's Mead and the education provided appear to have been increasingly attractive to the poor. Significantly, the ladies were sure that their efforts were developing mutual understanding between the classes, although their deliberations on who deserved practical help smacked of superiority rather than equality.[25]

Charity and day schools

Women of Unitarian congregations elsewhere often demonstrated similar initiative in the running of charity or day schools at their chapel. From 1813, indeed, the Birmingham charity school was for girls only and effectively superintended by a ladies' committee of

24. Russell Lant Carpenter, *Memoir of the Revd. Lant Carpenter* (1842), pp. 242–3, 474–5; Bristol Central Library BL 2d B7054, *The First Report of the Lewin's Mead Chapel Working and Visiting Society* (1836), pp. 2–8.

25. *Second Report* (1836), p. 1; *Fourth* (1839), pp. 3–5; *Fifth* (1841), pp. 1–2; *Third Report* (1837), p. 2.

the Old and New Meetings. This committee, however, had no constitutional standing and until 1867 was nominated by the men while its minute books were inspected by the ordinary committee. Ladies could vote for which children might attend the school but only by proxy. Within the limits of charity schooling they established a caring establishment based on elementary learning and useful work, even being castigated by the government inspector whom they secured in 1849 for being 'lavishly sufficient', more like a boarding than an industrial school. Subsequently, therefore, the girls did all the housework of the school under the direction of the matron and a new governess was appointed on lesser pay. This education was hardly either wide or deep, the ladies deeming even music unnecessary in 1840, but much care was taken over the general well-being and health of the girls and many educational visits to exhibitions and other treats were arranged. The ladies' committee kept tight control over the placement of the girls in service – the goal of their education. They usually would not allow girls to go to a house where there was only one servant in case they were lonely.[26]

Similar caring attitudes within a class framework were shown by Unitarian middle-class women elsewhere, for example at Leicester and Nottingham. At the former it was the ladies' committee who decided to put the girls' school under government inspection in 1858, although they had to ask the male vestry's permission.[27] At High Pavement in Nottingham, free admission ended in 1848 when the charity schools were placed under inspection as British Schools. The girls also lost their free clothing, but from 1850 to 1860 only the girls' school had a certificated teacher. The rules and curriculum – reading, writing, arithmetic, English grammar, history, geography and general religious instruction – were the same for both sexes, although girls also did knitting and needlework. From the beginning the girls' school received very favourable inspection reports and within two years had two pupil teachers. This was quite progressive since at first fewer girls nationally became pupil teachers, a system only started in 1846 to enable the best elementary pupils to gain an apprenticeship into teaching. In both this and other ventures such as the Schools of Design, it was difficult to get equal opportunities for girls. For High Pavement to get thirteen girls passing the School of Art exams in 1859 and eight of them obtaining prizes was

26. Emily Bushrod, 'The history of Unitarianism in Birmingham from the middle of the eighteenth century to 1893' (MA thesis, Birmingham University, 1954), pp. 155–75.

27. Leicester PRO, *Great Meeting Vestry Book*, Book II (5 Oct. 1858, 5 Oct. 1859).

therefore very good. (Twenty-five boys passed with twelve prizes from the boys' school.)[28]

As with Sunday schools, so in the provision of charity and day schooling Unitarians often educated more boys than girls, although this did vary. At Nottingham, for example, there were more boys than girls until 1850 when the boys doubled to 80 and the girls more than trebled to 90, but still more was spent on the boys. The master was paid about a third more than the mistress until the 1850s when his salary was 50 per cent more, yet the mistress at that time appears to have been far more go-ahead.[29] Apart from women teachers consistently being paid less, men were usually in ultimate control. Bristol was ahead of other Unitarian chapels (and, indeed, anywhere else) in its inclusion of women on committees and equality on finance. At the Leicester Great Meeting two ladies were added to the committee of eleven in 1828 to help carry out educational resolutions but the separate ladies' committee which ran the girls' schools had to defer to the male vestry on accommodation and financial matters. In 1858 they asked unsuccessfully to have 'the pecuniary management of their own school'. On the other hand the ladies' committee at Mosley Street, Manchester appear to have ignored the 'respectful request' of the general committee for the 'favour' of half-yearly reports.[30]

The charity schools tended to evolve into inspected day schools where the patrons had less control. Only the larger congregations could provide charity schools anyway. While the schools remained under Unitarian patronage they tended to be popular, and there is much evidence to show that some of the boys' schools and their teachers, such as Mosley Street School, were excellent among elementary schools of the day. Again a number of ex-pupils rose in society. For example, J.C. Robinson of High Pavement School was later knighted and became Inspector of Pictures for the Sovereign.[31] Yet again for women ex-pupils no such examples have been

28. HP MSS, William Hugh, *The High Pavement Day Schools Nottingham and Mrs Fisher's Bequest* (Nottingham, 1889), pp. 5–9; HiS55 *William Hugh 1861–1905, Day School Papers, Books, References*, 'Rules of the Daily Schools . . . High Pavement Chapel, Nottingham' (1848); HiS54, *High Pavement Charity School Anniversary Services* (1850); (1859).

29. *HP MSS*, HiS9 Charity School Register; HiS54 Anniversary Services.

30. Bristol Central Library BL2D B7054, *Lewin's Mead Meeting Domestic Mission Society: Twelfth Report* (Nov. 1852), p. 2; Leicester PRO, *Great Meeting Vestry Book* (Mar. 1828, Apr. 1837, Feb. 1858; Oct. Dec. 1859; Apr. 1860; Lester Burney, *Cross Street Chapel Schools, Manchester, 1734–1942* (Didsbury, 1977), pp. 32–3.

31. Ibid., pp. 35–9; HP MSS, William Hugh, *Some Notes Historical and Educational Relative to the HP Higher Education School* (privately printed, 1905), p. 3.

found. Their opportunities were more circumscribed, which was why their curriculum, as in other schools, included domestic subjects at the expense of the intellectual. At the Strutt family's Lancasterian schools at Belper, for example, more girls were educated than boys but they spent part of the time sewing, and on Saturdays, whereas boys had extra schooling (admittedly to keep them out of mischief), it was assumed that girls would be helping at home. At the factory schools the girls spent half their time sewing and knitting – useful skills but so often learnt instead of other, more mind-expanding subjects.[32]

Coeducational and infant schools

On the other hand, Unitarians were still more likely to give girls an education broader than that given elsewhere, and they opposed education bills which either left girls out or gave less equal provision. Barbara Leigh-Smith and Frederic Hill advocated coeducation but this was not generally acceptable. In 1854 Leigh-Smith attempted to establish a coeducational, mixed-class 'people's school' in Portman Square, London where fun and excursions were part of the means to make schooling an exhilarating activity. Women from London Unitarian circles helped run the school, with the stimulating first teacher being Elizabeth Whitehead (later Malleson).[33]

Leigh-Smith had been inspired by the infant-school philosophy of practical, moral and spiritual development in a happy, non-doctrinal atmosphere which she had seen in action in the Westminster Free Day Asylum, financed by her father after the Benthamites had abandoned it and run by James Buchanan, a former teacher for Robert Owen at New Lanark. Unitarian chapels at Salford, Manchester and Newcastle also established infant schools, but generally evangelicals gradually took over the movement and by the 1840s the schools were more formal in method, more limited in curriculum and more doctrinaire in religion. Most infant schools were for the poor but the very concept of them did have implications for women. Henry Ashworth of Bolton, for example, preferred infant schools to be run by females whilst Frederic Hill welcomed them

32. R.S. Fitton and A.P. Wadsworth, *The Strutts and the Arkwrights 1758–1830* (Manchester, 1958), pp. 254–7.
33. *MR* (1821), XVI, p. 115; Parnaby, *Fox*, p. 377; W.A.C. Stewart and W.P. McCann, *The Educational Innovators 1750–1880* (1967), p. 310; Frederic Hill, *National Education*, 2 vols (1836), I, p. 217; Elizabeth Malleson, *Elizabeth Malleson, 1828–1916: Autobiography, Notes and Letters* (printed for private circulation), pp. 45–51.

for allowing working-class mothers the opportunity to go out to work and thus not go on the parish.[34] This was in complete opposition to John Relly Beard, who, despite his liberal views in the education of his own daughters, deplored the 'evils' resulting from the employment of women, especially 'mothers of families' in mills and factories – an interesting selection since even in Lancashire women did many other jobs.[35]

Beard, however, was putting a high status on maternal education. Lant Carpenter too argued that such 'has indisputably the greatest share in the determination of the future character' and the morals of young people especially since the father was 'usually engrossed elsewhere'. Thus, 'on this account, as well as with a view to their own happiness, we earnestly wish to see the cultivation of their judgement made much more an object than at present it appears to be'.[36]

Mary Carpenter

The way that Lant Carpenter's own eldest daughter, Mary, negotiated her beloved father's views on women is interesting. A good linguist, keenly interested in science and fond of poetry, music and painting, she was also a gifted organizer. Yet, unlike her brothers, the cost of whose education was borne largely by the women of the family, the doors of the ministry and of science were closed to her. Nevertheless, despite her obligations to her mother's middle-class girls' school until 1848 when it eventually closed, Carpenter managed in the early 1840s, first with her adored father's support and then after his mysterious death at sea, to establish a domestic mission in Bristol. Her inspiration for this was both the compassion and warmth which the American William Ellery Channing breathed into Unitarianism and the ideas of his Boston friend, Joseph Tuckerman, on non-proselytizing domestic missions to help the neediest in society with respect and sympathy, moral guidance and some practical relief.[37]

34. Stewart and McCann, *Innovators*, pp. 242–53, *passim*; James Beard, *John . . . Beard*, 1832, 1833; Burney, *Cross Street*, pp. 30–2; Church of the Divine Unity, *Grandfather Turner's Fiftieth Year in Newcastle upon Tyne* (1831), pp. 3, 5; Hill, *National Education*, I, pp. 180–96.

35. Herbert McLachlan, *Records of a Family 1800–1933* (Manchester, 1935), p. 111; John Relly Beard, *Schools* (1842), pp. 46–7.

36. Lant Carpenter, *Principles of Education* (1820), pp. 10, 201–2.

37. 'Lant . . . Mary . . . Philip . . . William Carpenter', *DNB* (1887), IX, pp. 157–68; *Reports . . . Lewin's Mead* (1835–41); Bristol Reference Library, B2426, Lant Carpenter and George Armstrong, *Mission to the Poor* (1839); Mary Carpenter, *Memoir of Joseph Tuckerman, DD* (1849), pp. 12–66.

The vivid details of how this angular, repressed middle-aged spinster found sheer joy in working amongst the impoverished, filthy, abandoned, often drunken and violent 'outcasts of society' can be found in her own writings, the warm biography of her nephew and the modern, spirited biography of Jo Manton. There are very significant gender aspects to the way one able Unitarian woman used her education and talents within acceptable bounds and thence beyond them, thereby giving a model to others of what women could do. Her involvement called into play her considerable talents for organization, raising public awareness and writing. Her efforts provoked anxiety from and conflict with her mother for years and were doubted considerably by others. Nevertheless, she overcame opposition at home and persuaded the wealthy 700-strong congregation at Lewin's Mead to back her in 1846 in setting up a *ragged school, or a free school as she preferred to call it, for the very poor in the miserable slum in the neighbourhood. In the running of this, it was her calm authority, respectful sympathy and imaginative teaching approach which tamed the wild, irrepressible children and young people into orderly, but enthusiastic and responsive classes. It was also her beneficence which improved the squalid slum court in which the school was situated, not only by adding water, baths, washhouses and a playground, but also, in a touch of imaginative sympathy, by planting creepers against the walls. Her principles were justified when within two years of the riotous opening of the school, HMI Joseph Fletcher declared that he did not know of any other ragged school 'where there was so large an amount of intellect and well-directed effort exerted to raise the school, to train up self-acting beings'.[38]

Mary Carpenter did not lead the ragged school movement. The first one is historically attributed to John Pounds, who in the 1830s took his destitute pupils from his carpenter's shop in Portsmouth to the Unitarian chapel in High Street because it was the only one which made them feel welcome. Unitarians supported, publicized and extended his work, but, because of their Unitarianism, both he and Carpenter were largely ignored by the ensuing Ragged School Union (RSU), which increasingly propagated conservative theology.[39]

38. Mary Carpenter, *Ragged Schools* (1849), *passim*; Jo Manton, *Mary Carpenter and the Children of the Streets* (1976), pp. 72–96; Joseph Carpenter, *Mary Carpenter*, pp. 76–96, ff.

39. Ibid., p. 92; R. Everett Jayne, *The Story of John Pounds* (1925), *passim*; D.H. Webster, 'The ragged school movement and education of the poor in the nineteenth century' (Ph.D. thesis, Leicester University, 1973), pp. 14–98.

In the Reformatory Movement Mary Carpenter used her incisive writings and excellent organizational talents to greater effect. Working both from intense research and from her own experience and deeply held religious and humanitarian principles, she worked out a system of good free day schools and industrial and reformatory schools which would cater for the three grades of destitution, vagrancy and criminality and be partially state-aided. Against the norm, she pleaded for no degrading or revengeful punishment or child prison sentences, which merely raised better criminals. She believed that every child, 'however apparently vicious and degraded', could be made a useful member of society but that this could only be done lovingly and wisely in schools with a middle-class family-like atmosphere.[40] This was a revolutionary doctrine and the wonder was not that Mary had to face strong, even bitter, opposition, but that she was listened to at all.

Carpenter's obvious deep feelings and overwhelming conviction that child offenders must be treated as children might be perceived as feminine but she had strong masculine support which was often vital for the realization of her plans. Her principal allies were Unitarians – Lady Byron and Matthew Davenport Hill, from 1853 Commissioner for Bankrupts for Bristol, William and Elizabeth Rathbone and Russell Scott junior – but she also had non-Unitarian supporters such as the Hon. Amelia Murray and Lord Shaftesbury. They exploited national disquiet over juvenile offenders to gain the pioneering 1854 Youthful Offenders Act.[41] Carpenter's friends enabled her to establish a model reformatory school, Kingswood in Bristol in 1852, and subsequently Red Lodge, a school for girls only since, through bitter experience, Mary became convinced that girls were harder to reform than boys. Despite difficulties, it became the centre of Mary's life, her deep belief being that delinquent girls, like others, were domestic creatures who could only thrive in loving homes. Such an attitude was also the basis for the later recommendations for girls in workhouses made by Frances Power Cobbe, who lived and worked with Carpenter in 1858–59. As John Seed has

40. Mary Carpenter, *Tuckerman*, pp. 53–5; Mary Carpenter, *Reformatory Schools for the Children of the Perishing and Dangerous Classes and for Juvenile Offenders*, (New York, 1969; 1st edn 1851), *passim* and esp. pp. 38–9.

41. Margaret May, 'Innocence and experience: the evolution of the concept of juvenile delinquency in the mid-nineteenth century', *Victorian Studies* (Sept. 1973), XVII, no. 1, pp. 7–29; Rosamund and Florence Davenport Hill, *The Recorder of Birmingham* (1878), pp. 153–68, 172; MSS *Elizabeth Rathbone*, VI. 1.234–VI. 1.264 *passim*; Joseph Carpenter, *Mary Carpenter*, pp. 121–47.

said, however, the nineteenth-century family was a hierarchy of dependence, and even when Unitarians with their 'rational and personal model of human relationships' used the concept, there were class connotations. There were gender connotations as well, although it was Carpenter's boys' industrial school which became one of her most successful examples of how wild, potential criminals could be transformed by trust, an interesting, useful education, suitable play, and homely care.[42]

Mary Carpenter's work had further implications in gender terms. At first her own family, serious, unworldly, intellectual and religious as it was, had been wary of her almost fanatical involvement with the destitute. Mary herself, however, was very 'proper': at first she wrote anonymously, kept silent at conferences she had worked hard to set up and had her papers read for her. Aware, as her mother said, of 'how jealous the lords of creation are of the interference of women', she very nearly did not attend the Parliamentary Committee of 1852 enquiring into the question of criminal and destitute children. It was evidence of her growing reputation, however, that her controversial opinions were sought in such a place. It is also a measure of her powers of persuasive reasoning that she and her supporters, not exclusively Liberals or Unitarians, were able to gain some state aid in reformatory work and, later, industrial schools, although, much to her disappointment, not for ragged schools. Growing confidence in her own powers enabled her to read papers each year at the National Association for the Promotion of Social Science (NAPSS), established in 1857 (an association which was to provide more than one platform for women). In 1860 Carpenter was given the supreme accolade of being asked to address the statistical section of the British Association at Oxford. She had come a long way from being forbidden attendance of the Association in 1836 because she was a woman.[43]

There were further contradictions in Mary Carpenter's work: the Unitarians around her might extol kindness, industrial training, a family atmosphere to cure delinquents, whom Lady Byron called 'that most injured as well as most wretched class', yet Hill, albeit blaming their circumstances, termed them 'a herd of savages in

42. Ibid., pp. 89–90, 164–6, 185; Manton, *Mary Carpenter*, pp. 120–44; Frances Power Cobbe, *Life of*... (1904), pp. 327–8; John Seed, 'Unitarianism, political economy and the antinomies of liberal culture in Manchester, 1830–50', *Social History* (Jan. 1982), 7, no. 1, pp. 20–23.

43. Joseph Carpenter, *Mary Carpenter*, pp. 48, 121–32, 135, 184–7, 202, 212–13; Manton, *Mary Carpenter*, pp. 75, 103–10, 154–7.

the bosom of civilised society'.[44] Such terminology, used also by Carpenter, as R.J.W. Selleck has pointed out, shifted the focus from the decision-makers in society to the poor themselves. Drink, parental neglect, moral destitution, so often equated with the poor, were ultimately blamed for delinquency, not the economic, political and legislative structure. The very term 'perishing and dangerous', (the phrase is part of the title of Mary Carpenter's book) borrowed from the American Unitarian Theodore Parker, described the poor as threatening.[45] Thus, despite their humanitarianism, Unitarians helped develop that concept of a residuum in society which others increasingly depicted as irredeemable.

Domestic missions

Such a mixture of humanitarian and class concepts was reflected throughout Unitarian initiatives for the working class. For example, other domestic missions were established by Unitarians in many large urban centres such as Manchester, London, Liverpool, Birmingham, Leeds and Leicester, to redress middle-class neglect of the 'uneducated and depressed millions' of England. They were posited as peculiarly Unitarian, non-proselytizing, open to all, eagerly supporting practical good works, self-help, education and almost grimly enthusiastic in striving to breach class barriers to raise the masses from 'degradation, vice and misery, to a sense of their capabilities and dignity as rational, intellectual and spiritual beings'.[46]

To do this, domestic missionaries, men of 'superior mind and character', though not necessarily middle-class, were appointed, whose dedicated ventures stimulated a whole plethora of societies and institutions around them such as non-denominational Sunday schools and chapels (where 'proper' clothing did not matter), ragged schools, libraries, adult and evening classes, mutual instruction societies, sewing classes for mothers, recreational facilities, provident and sick societies. They appear to have particularly attracted females. At Leicester, for example, the night schools had more girls than boys and the missionary Joseph Dare had to provide an adult

44. MSS, *Elizabeth Rathbone*, VI. 236; Hills, *Recorder of Birmingham*, pp. 163, 170–1.
45. Mary Carpenter, *Reformatory Schools*, pp. v, 3; R.J.W. Selleck, 'Mary Carpenter: a confident and contradictory reformer', *HofE* (June 1985), 14, no. 2, pp. 104–6, 113–14; May, 'Innocence', pp. 14–23.
46. le Breton, *Channing and Aikin*, pp. 112, 122, 132–4, 183, 201; *CR* (1841), p. 177.

Sunday school for the many female domestic servants who wanted to learn writing.[47]

These missionaries, however, often found it impossible to counteract the effects of the terrible poverty and hardship endured by the poor. Increasingly they realized and described graphically the miserable destitution which, as Joseph Adshead said in Manchester in the 'hungry forties', crushed even those with 'physical strength, mental cultivation, and moral principle' and left them 'starving in the largest manufacturing town in the world for want of employment'.[48] The relentless, searing factual reports of the different missionaries all discredited the bland, common, middle-class assumption that prudence, temperance and moral reform would be sufficient to assuage the wretched pauperism which surrounded them. They were not trying to restructure society but they highlighted the tensions between liberal political and economic theory and the compassionate, non-proselytizing rationalism which inspired Unitarian educational initiatives.

Such tension could be seen in the sheer difficulty of persuading richer Unitarians to become personally involved in the domestic mission work, as Elizabeth Gaskell complained in Manchester. In Birmingham John Gent Brooks' pleas for someone to act as superintendent of the girls' school in 1850 went unheeded, despite his urging that such an occupation would confer much more pleasure and health than all the 'ingenious fancies' which usually occupied the ladies. On the other hand, Joseph Dare was able to run a flourishing sewing school for both women and girls in Leicester which the ladies superintended in rotation, some of them also teaching the Girls' Instruction Society. This pleased Dare, who believed both that 'the poor require the best of teachers' and that practical knowledge and self-respect were particularly vital for females, for 'wherever woman does not hold her true position in society, its pastimes become barbarous and its morals debased'. He was sure that the later success of social gatherings at the mission were due to the fact that, contrary to general custom, women were present. Nor was only a practical and moral education given – the separate female adult class created in 1850 went beyond learning their letters to lessons in English history and a visit at half-price to the Fine-Art Union

47. Leicester Reference Library, *Domestic Mission Reports* Joseph Dare, 1st *DMR* (1846), pp. 17–18, 2nd *DMR* (1847), pp. 8–9, 13, 16–17; 3rd *DMR* (1848), p. 16; 4th *DMR* (1849), pp. 11–12.

48. Joseph Adshead, 'Distress in Manchester, 1842', in *Conditions of Work and Living: Five Pamphlets 1838–44* (New York, 1972), pp. 28–39.

exhibition. Ladies of the congregation appear to have been donors of books to the library, Miss Paget, for example, giving almost a complete set of Harriet Martineau's *Illustrations of Political Economy*.[49]

Such a gift was symptomatic of the class assumptions of both Unitarian women and men. Educational initiatives for the working class from middle-class Unitarians were marked by a generosity of scope unusual for the age but tempered by economic assumptions which favoured their own position in society. Females were included in this educational generosity but on a lesser scale than men. Middle-class women's work amongst the poor could enable them to realize better their own potential but the interrelated concepts of class and gender were still limiting. Such complex interconnections can be explored further in adult education for the working classes.

49. Seed, 'Liberal culture', pp. 21–3; Emily Bushrod, 'The diary of John Gent Brooks: a Victorian commentary on poverty', *TUHS* (Apr. 1992), XX, no. 2, pp. 103, 106; Dare, 1st *DMR* (1846), pp. 17–19, 22; 2nd *DMR* (1847), pp. 8, 10, 13; 3rd *DMR* (1848), pp. 12–16; 5th *DMR* (1850), pp. 8–11; 8th *DMR* (1853), pp. 6–8.

CHAPTER NINE

Political economy, adult education, class and gender

For middle-class Unitarians, gender disparities in education were most obvious in higher education, the very area into which Unitarian men often poured most effort and resources. Many men, indeed, also devoted much time and money to initiatives for working-class adults. How far the same inequalities recurred and how far the interrelationship of class and gender attitudes, analysed earlier, affected provision for adults will be explored here. Unitarian involvement in working-class education was permeated by class attitudes, not least through the teaching of political economy, and it is important to understand this context before examining more deeply the interrelationship of these attitudes with gender issues. In turn, this interrelationship was significant in the further development of the domestic ideology which impacted on all classes and both sexes.

Political economy, mechanics' institutes and class conflict

Unitarian educational efforts did not necessarily win the popularity they had hoped for among the working classes. This was despite such attempts as Joseph Barker's of the Christian Brethren and John Beard's to produce cheap literature for the working class, and those of others like Harriet Martineau and Frederic Hill against the stamp tax on newspapers.[1] To their dismay, the 'enlightened' Unitarians

1. DWL, James Beard, Duplicate typescript of collection of notes and materials for life of John Relly Beard DD (undated), 1852, 1859, bibliography at end; Herbert McLachlan, *The Story of a Nonconformist Library* (Manchester, 1923), pp. 152, 163–183; Harriet Martineau, *Illustrations of Taxation* (1834), no. v, *passim*; Constance Hill (ed.), *Frederic Hill: An Autobiography of Fifty Years in Times of Reform* (1894), pp. 72–3.

found that working-class people often resisted their efforts to help them be 'wise and virtuous'. This persuaded some Unitarians like John James Tayler to promote educating the poor in the 'axioms' of political economy which would make them realize the futility of fighting against so-called 'natural' economic laws or the middle class.[2]

The promotion of political economy was significant because Unitarians of the new industrial middle class had their own brand of paternalism and materialism. Unitarian factory owners might generally be picked out as the most humane, but they were also among the richest and it was in their interests to appear superior to their smaller competitors. As Engels instanced, those with factories in healthy country districts could show the factory system to advantage yet easily maintain 'patriarchal servitude'.[3] The certainty many Unitarians had of their own enlightenment and their firm intention to impress it on the working class could be oppressive rather than liberating. James Luckcock, the Birmingham jewellery manufacturer, for example, was almost sickeningly condescending in his vision of prestigious prize-winning ceremonies, attended by all classes, to reward good servants and virtuous parents raising large families on scanty means.[4]

Thus, although political economy might be very popular at Manchester College,[5] where the students were from those very families whose position and interests political economy justified, it alienated the working classes. They perceived that worship of the gods of economic individualism and market forces could leave the poor to struggle alone except for imposing on them an education which simply taught them the inevitability of their lot. Increasingly in the 1830s such extreme views as Harriet Martineau's strident championship of the bitterly hated Poor Law Amendment Act of 1834 were loathed and an education which appeared to teach the political and economic selfishness of one class as scientific law was rejected.[6] Dictums such as those of the powerful Unitarian industrialist Samuel Robinson, telling the working-class members of the Dukinfield Village Library that 'the science of political economy would save

2. *UC* (1834), p. 36.
3. S.G. Checkland, *The Rise of Industrial Society in England 1815–85* (1964), pp. 120–6; Frederick Engels, *The Condition of the Working-Class in England* (1969), pp. 214–15.
4. *MR* (1829), NS 3, pp. 28–30.
5. See e.g. MCO MCY, *Address* (1834); MNC, *Address* (1841), pp. 6, 9.
6. Trygve Tholfsen, *Working-Class Radicalism in Mid-Victorian England* (1976), pp. 40–6.

you from many fatal mistakes, many unnecessary evils', were not accepted as necessary and neutral.[7] The searching critique of religion, politics and science advocated by Unitarians was hardly being applied here to the new commercial and industrial order.

The perception that Unitarians were furthering their own ends through the educational institutions they promoted militated against them achieving their aims. This was seen from the 1820s in the mechanics' institutes of which Unitarian men particularly were prime initiators and supporters in many towns. Indeed, they poured enormous resources into the establishment and running of these institutions, founded particularly for male manual workers and especially those of the urban working class. For the most part, however, they failed to convince either manual workers or fellow manufacturers of their utility. At the same time their deep involvement was enough initially to turn many Anglicans against the whole movement.[8]

The prime aim of mechanics' institutes was to teach science, which Unitarians promulgated as enthusiastically as they did political economy, although scientific historians believe that this, too, was motivated by middle-class considerations. Certainly mechanics' institutes gave opportunities both for scientists to gain lecturing posts and for employers to gain superior workmen. Simultaneously the carrot of increased power through increased knowledge was dangled before workmen by men like Benjamin Heywood.[9] In this, however, Unitarians were only echoing what they said to the middle class, and the evidence appears to show that they genuinely believed that a real knowledge of science was useful for all classes. Matthew Davenport Hill supported technical education, for example, only as long as the working class was not limited to industrial training or made into 'tractable tools for the creation of wealth'.[10]

The sad truth became apparent, however, that scientific lectures were beyond the capacity of many workmen. Science did not really succeed in the mechanics' institutes until the examinations of the Society of Arts and the Department of Science and Art in the 1850s.

7. Samuel Robinson, *Two Addresses*, 'Farewell address to Dukinfield Village Library' (1843), p. 21.

8. See e.g. MSS MCO, *CW II*, CW to GWW, 13.11.1828.

9. Ian Inkster, 'The social context of an educational movement: a revisionist approach to the English Mechanics' Institutes, 1820–1850', *Oxford Review of Education* (1976), 2, no. 3, pp. 277–307; Benjamin Heywood, *Addresses delivered at the Manchester Mechanics' Institute* (1843), pp. 2–17, 34, 51–3, 95, 121.

10. Rosamund and Florence Davenport Hill, *The Recorder of Birmingham: A Memoir of Matthew Davenport Hill* (1878), pp. 254–5.

Increasingly a general and moral rather than a scientific education became the aim, with a growing emphasis on recreation and the development of cheaper, more leisure-orientated institutions such as Lyceums. In these developments Unitarian men again eagerly took part, sometimes themselves supplying the recreational facilities.

Once again such moves can be seen as part of the dissemination of middle-class values and for middle-class benefit. In truth, however, conflicts over problems of management and political discussion, exacerbated by financial constraints, long hours and lack of elementary education made it unlikely that many of the working class, beyond a few of its élite, would attend mechanics' institutes. In fact it was often lower middle-class people who provided the clientele, although they too needed further education. Working-class people, thirsty for knowledge, turned to their own solutions, interestingly enough often similar to Unitarian educational ideals. They forged their own ideology partly from their interpretation of those same cultural and political influences which affected middle-class radicals, including the works of Channing, and partly from their own searing experience. They had their own response to the situation, preferring a cooperative, secure society, though, paradoxically, with independent productive workers, to the atomist, unequal one of industrial capitalism. There were, despite many difficulties, many educational advantages for those who joined the mechanics' institutes, including successful schools for workers' children, but when workers did enrol it was without accepting middle-class solutions. Abel Heywood, for example, became a renowned printer imprisoned for fighting for a free press. A 'freelance Unitarian', he later became Lord Mayor of Manchester, but he had hardly been compromised by middle-class values.[11]

Since Unitarians, unlike many other reformers, were also committed to a wide, liberal, rational, modern, non-sectarian education, even if they were orthodox on political economy, they did have a meeting ground with working-class radicals. For many of them, the overriding reasons for mechanics' institutes were, as John Hollings said at the Boston Institute, that the 'true dignity of man consisted in his intellectual capacity', that all that was 'precious in literature, or ennobling in knowledge, or graceful in art' should be freely and widely accessible and that knowledge would raise men from serfdom.[12] Across the spectrum of their liberal views some

11. 'Abel Heywood', *Inquirer* (6.1.1894), pp. 9–10.
12. MSS Biggs *Scrapbooks*, I, J. Hollings' speech at the Boston MI, 1852.

even supported Chartism, one of the most significant working-class movements of the hungry 1830s and 1840s.[13] Although they gave no critique of capitalism, most genuinely believed a generous, liberal education could elevate the working classes from ignorance and narrowness of view. Insofar that even hardened capitalists like Samuel Robinson believed 'knowledge is power' and if such knowledge was justified for one class it should not be denied another, their educational initiatives were generous in concept.[14] Radical even in believing in a wide education for all, many Unitarians could genuinely support self-help through education and cultural and moral reform since this was the means by which *they* had achieved success.

John Seed has depicted the educational initiatives of the liberal bourgeoisie, particularly the Unitarians, in Manchester, as struggles within and between the social classes to achieve cultural power. Unitarian thought and action was honeycombed with contradictory ideas on political economy and liberal ideology.[15] One of the best illustrations of this was Elizabeth Gaskell. Despite Harriet Martineau's example, as a woman she denied having knowledge of political economy or the theories of trade. Nevertheless, she admitted wishing to 'give utterance to the agony . . . of dumb people' through fiction, and was better qualified than many middle-class novelists to do so since, besides her personal experience in Sunday school teaching and as a member of the district Provident Society, her husband was secretary to the Unitarian domestic mission whose searing reports she could read. She let the poor speak for themselves in many of her short stories and later, in 1863, in *Sylvia's Lovers*, where her sympathy was all for gentle Philip Hepburn, who spent years of hard, lonely effort to gain the knowledge he prized so highly.[16] She was obviously appreciated by workers, for apparently cotton operatives clubbed together to buy *Mary Barton*, a story in which her (anti-) hero John Barton, bitterly angry at the callow social irresponsibility of the rich, rejects the argument that the rich know nothing of the trials of the poor:

13. e.g. Margaret Parnaby, 'William Johnson Fox and the Monthly Repository Circle of 1832 to 1836' (Ph.D. thesis, Australian National University, 1979), *passim*; Henry Solly, *These Eighty Years*, 2 vols (1893), I, *passim*.

14. Robinson, [2] 'To the subscribers of the Dukinfield Village Library' (1838), pp. 14, 29, 32–5, 56–62.

15. John Seed, 'Unitarianism, political economy and the antinomies of liberal culture in Manchester, 1830–50', *Social History* (Jan. 1982) 7, no. 1, pp. 12–13, 19.

16. Elizabeth Gaskell, *Four Short Stories* (1983); *Sylvia's Lovers* (Oxford, 1982).

> I say, if they don't know, they ought to know. We are their slaves as long as we can work; we pile up their fortunes with the sweat of our brows; and yet we are to live as separate as if we were in two worlds.[17]

Mrs Gaskell allowed one of her working-class characters to dismiss political economy, arguing that there were circumstances when it was impossible for people to survive by themselves and 'them that is strong in any of God's gifts is meant to help the weak'. She keenly felt and bravely depicted the bitterness felt by the starving at the wilful ignorance, lack of understanding and even ridicule of the seemingly prosperous employers. In her husband's chapel at Cross Street, there were industrialists who bought the book for their workpeople's libraries, but there were others bitterly angry with the minister's wife's perceived betrayal of their interests. William Greg, one of the local industrial and Unitarian élite, argued in print in both the *Edinburgh* and *Westminster Reviews* that if workers like Barton only emulated the virtues of their employers, they could remain self-reliant in times of economic strain.[18] In *North and South* six years later, Gaskell returned to the theme and, although to some extent she gave more of the employer's view, her overwhelming message on industrial relations was still the need for each side to understand more of the other through personal contact.[19] These books, indeed, illustrated the contradictions in Unitarian aspirations particularly as they were modified by changing contexts and understanding.

Women and adult education

Harriet Martineau, too, whilst upholding views of economic liberalism, opposed those who let error thrive on ignorance but kept knowledge and discovery to themselves like some form of property, asking, 'Does the sun shine more brightly when a man thinks he has it all to himself . . . ?' She also said she preferred mechanics' institutes to the universities, where intellectual luxury was reserved

17. Asa Briggs, *Victorian Cities* (Middlesex, 1968), p. 101; Elizabeth Gaskell, *Mary Barton* (Harmondsworth, 1970; 1st edn 1848), p. 45.

18. Ibid., Preface by Stephen Gill, pp. 14–15, 25–8 and 220–1, 455–8 and *passim*; J.A.V. Chapple and A. Pollard (eds), *The Letters of Mrs Gaskell* (Manchester, 1966), pp. 66–73, 118–19.

19. Elizabeth Gaskell, *North and South* (Harmondsworth, 1970; 1st publ. 1854–55), *passim* and pp. 525–6.

to pamper the few while the many starved. So could say Martineau, equally shut out from many such places.[20] The institutes, after all, were established specifically for men and, except for social occasions, stayed that way until a need for numbers, subscriptions and wifely support, together with a growing conviction that education would produce better wives and mothers, allowed women into some of them. Even then, as at Leicester, a woman had to be a relative of a male member. It was not until the 1840s that female classes were established, whilst the Huddersfield Female Education Institute of 1846 was the first of its kind. Such classes proved quite popular in Lancashire and Yorkshire, operating in at least thirty towns in the 1840s, but many of the members were middle class. In Manchester and Liverpool, for example, more women from the lower middle class attended than from the working class, a deliberate decision to effect this having been made in Manchester. Greater numbers of women attended institutes in Yorkshire, Cheshire and Lancashire than anywhere else, although in the southern counties they constituted a higher proportion of the total membership. Working women, however, never attended mechanics' institutes in the same numbers as men because social custom and the demands of home were great handicaps. All women who did attend were given subordinate status, lower subscription rates and limited access to the facilities. Furthermore, their separate provision often meant very basic courses, although admittedly their inferior education meant that these were necessary. In Bradford and Huddersfield, the two chief single-sex female institutes, a wider curriculum was available, but in some institutions, such as Holbeck, courses beyond the basic were reserved for those described as 'ladies'. Girls' schools were established by mechanics' institutes but usually were later and smaller than the boys'. Working People's Colleges were primarily for men, but night schools, in Bristol from 1812 and in the factory areas in the 1840s, became more popular with women, especially once factory legislation had lessened their hours of labour.[21]

Three of the most popular institutes for women as for men were Manchester, Liverpool and Leeds, the first two particularly institutes where Unitarians were prominent in management. The women

20. Harriet Martineau, *Illustrations of Taxation*, V, pp. 110–13; *The History of England during the Thirty Years Peace*, 2 vols (1851), II, pp. 262–5, 412–14.

21. Mabel Tylecote, *The Mechanics Institutes of Lancashire and Yorkshire before 1851* (1957), pp. 263–7 and *passim*; MSS, *Leicester Mechanics' Institute* I, 3.3.1834; June Purvis, 'Working women and adult education in 19th century Britain', *HofE* (Sept. 1980), pp. 193–212; *Hard Lessons* (Oxford, 1989), pp. 100–27.

here as in most other institutes had no vote before the 1860s, although access and membership regulations were equal in the more popular Lyceums. Even in these, however, the curricula varied according to sex and the reading-rooms might be for men only, a situation that only changed gradually in the late 1850s and 1860s. Was this because of fear of mixed company or a presumption that men only would be interested in serious literature and newspapers? Unitarians were largely responsible for the establishment of both boys' and girls' schools at the Liverpool mechanics' institute but the latter was provided seven years after the former and had fewer numbers. On the other hand its wide curriculum included science, singing and callisthenics and it had twelve trained teachers by 1846. The directors did establish a Ladies College in 1856 but its initial popularity was not sustained.[22]

It is difficult to assess how far Unitarians were responsible for the ordinary admission or otherwise of women to adult institutions. Unitarian middle-class women appear to have used the mechanics' institutes but were little involved in their establishment. Their educational initiatives usually remained more connected with their local chapel and children than with public ventures or adults. The tremendous involvement of men like the Biggs brothers and their brother-in-law J.F. Hollings in Leicester, for example, was not matched by work in adult education by their womenfolk, although the men certainly had a high regard for women's abilities and Joseph Biggs was married to Matilda Ashurst and thus connected to the *radical unitarian feminist network.[23] Similarly, Henry Solly's Working Men's Social Clubs of the 1860s were kept exclusively for men even though Solly himself had a high opinion of women's abilities. The language used by Benjamin Heywood and Edward Higginson about mechanics' institutes helping families by enabling the man of the house to be wiser and steadier and thus able to teach his wife and children to rise mentally, socially and morally was to be used later by Solly. The former two, of course, had originally aimed at bringing science to mechanics and artisans so that they could apply it to their various trades, thereby becoming more skilled and better workers and hopefully worthy inventors too. Since women rarely had skilled posts in industry and were not expected

22. Ibid., pp. 117–20, 143–4; Herbert J. Tiffen, *A History of the Liverpool Institute School 1825 to 1935* (1935), pp. 26–31, 66, 103–7.

23. R.H. Evans, 'The Biggs family of Leicester', *Leicestershire Archaeological and Historical Society Transactions* (1972–73), 48, pp. 31, 40–1, 46, 47; Kathryn Gleadle, *The Early Feminists* (1995), p. 40.

to be creative technologists they were not part of the original aims. By the time they were included, middle-class patrons had realized that a more general education and more comfortable surroundings were required to attract working people, but then often feared the licentiousness which might follow if men and women of the 'lower' classes mixed indiscriminately in institutions purposely established to make the working classes more 'respectable'. Solly, for example, like the men of High Pavement Mutual Improvement Society, in 1820, later opposed any mixed dramatic performances, certain that it was female participation that brought in 'destructive and alien elements'. Yet, apparently, the men acting by themselves might be innocent, entertaining and therefore useful.[24]

On the other hand, mechanics' institutes, like Athenaeums and other male societies, opened their doors to women for special occasions and public lectures on a wide range of topics. In the 1840s the latter included many lectures about women and usually given by them, thus opening up a new type of semi-professional career for women like Clara Balfour in Yorkshire.[25] Middle-class Unitarian women certainly attended public lectures: for example, Elizabeth Gaskell preferred Ralph Waldo Emerson's lecture 'On Domestic Life' at the Manchester mechanics' institute to his rather more mystical offerings at the Athenaeum. Caroline Thornley enjoyed a series of lectures at both Liverpool and Stockport Institutes by George Dawson, the brilliant, charismatic social and educational reformer who drew a huge congregation, many of them Unitarians, to his eclectic, non-denominational Church of the Saviour in Birmingham from 1847.[26]

Thomas Ryland, a lifelong friend and supporter of Dawson in Birmingham, wryly remarked on the 'ladies'' preference for Mr Dawson, whose lectures at the Midland Institute in Birmingham in which Unitarians were much involved were certainly a huge draw. This institution also had a very popular class in science for females in 1856, although a chemistry class for female factory workers was not successful. In the following years women won teaching and

24. Solly, *Eighty Years*, I, pp. 58–9, 232, 366–8; II, p. 30; *Working Men's Social Clubs and Educational Institutions* (1867), pp. 264, 290, and *passim*; Higginson, *Observations*, p. 9; Heywood, *Addresses*, 30 Mar. 1825, pp. 3–17; MSS University of Nottingham, Hi I 1, *High Pavement Mutual Improvement Society Minute Books.*

25. Purvis, *Hard Lessons*, pp. 152–3.

26. Jenny Uglow, *Elizabeth Gaskell* (1993), pp. 179–80; Herbert McLachlan, 'A Liverpool ladies journal a century ago', *TUHS* (Oct. 1955), XI, no. 1, pp. 5–6; 'George Dawson', *DNB*, XIV, pp. 221–2.

Council certificates, especially in French, which might indicate a middle-class rather than a working-class attendance.[27]

The Birmingham Institute was one model for the excellent London Working Women's College, instituted by the Unitarian Elizabeth Malleson and other Unitarians in 1864. Malleson was inspired to found her college by the establishment of a Working Man's College in London by Frederick Denison Maurice in 1854. She admired 'the magnificent opportunities of self-development' the college offered and Maurice's ideal of social harmony through the association of university-trained men and manual workers. This vision was inspiring to many Unitarians but once again it was one which omitted women. Through inviting male students and their female relations to evening parties Malleson realized 'the superiority of the knowledge and culture shown by these men compared with the women'. Maurice's Christian Socialism, however, though regarded as dangerous and revolutionary by some of his contemporaries, was not an egalitarian conception between either the social classes or the sexes. He thought the presence of females might actually, indeed, prevent the nobler aims of brotherhood from being realized. For them a better education was desirable, but to make them better wives and mothers not to enrich them as individuals. Such strongly felt views, reiterated by others, effectively kept women either out of the growing number of colleges or with separate, inferior provision and membership even when working-class men begged for their admittance. It was to counteract this that Malleson and her friends established their college.[28]

John Relly Beard, women workers and education

The ambivalent position of Unitarians over the admission of women to mechanics' institutes and later the Working People's Colleges can be exemplified by the views of one of their leading educationists, John Relly Beard. He and William Gaskell were involved in adult male education in Manchester and had established the Unitarian Home Missionary College (UHMB) in 1853 to supply working-class

27. W.H. Ryland (ed.), *Reminiscences of Thomas Henry Ryland* (Birmingham, 1904), pp. 138–43, 147; *Birmingham and Midland Institute Reports* (Birmingham 1857–61), 1856, pp. 3–5, 7; 1859, pp. 4, 7; 1860, p. 9.

28. Conrad Gill, *A History of Birmingham*, 2 vols (Oxford, 1952), I, pp. 394–5; Elizabeth Malleson, *Autobiography, Notes and Letters, 1828–1916* (printed for private circulation, 1926), pp. 57–71, 94; David Young, *F.D. Maurice and Unitarianism* (Oxford, 1992), pp. 188–9; Purvis, *Hard Lessons*, pp. 168–70.

Unitarian preachers for the working-class congregations in the way that the earlier Hackney Academy had been intended. Backed by wealthy Unitarians, it was to become of lasting influence in the Unitarian community.[29] Beard was to support the Working Women's College because it gave women a liberal education for its own sake and for their proper self-development, not because of any position they might hold relative to men or because men's needs seemed to require this. His *Self-Culture* was expressly written for women as well as men and in it he strongly expressed his views on the essential equality of men and women. He condemned 'factitious distinctions between the sexes', for there were 'often greater differences between male and male than between male and female'. All had one human nature in common which required 'a common educational discipline'. Beard had no room for parents who gave sons 'the best educational advantages they can command', but were 'satisfied with something quite inferior for their girls'. Such was 'a relic of a semi-barbarous age' which the Church 'has not yet had self-denial enough to part with and cast away'. For Beard nothing should be 'Good enough for a girl?' unless it was also good enough for a boy and, if possible, girls should have 'the highest University learning no less than boys'.[30]

After such a bold and advanced statement, however, Beard qualified his assertion by stating that he had no wish 'to see women leave their *own sphere* [my italics] in a vain attempt to displace men'. Like William Fox he was sure that particularly in work where 'taste and grace' were demanded, women were likely to be better than men. He desired a 'free field' where male and female could compete equally and 'character and skill' be the only condition for success. He urged that for this women needed a much improved education both at home and at school. He wanted a good general education for individual development, but he immediately moved on to what women needed as housewives and mothers. Admittedly in this he wanted the *science* of cookery and the laws of health and mental and moral education, but, nevertheless, he was asking for a gendered curriculum. He inflated the role of women by arguing:

> Custom forbids her to enter the senate, and rarely allows her to occupy your pulpits, nevertheless she is the mother of your senators and the educator of your preachers. To her your heroes owe their prowess, and from her your poets imbibe their inspiration. That

29. Herbert McLachlan, *The Unitarian Home Missionary College* (1915), *passim.*
30. John Relly Beard, *Self-Culture,* pp. 61, 256.

> which makes each man what he is he owes to the genial and fostering influences of home . . . And is it not, then, of the last importance that that centre should be light as well as warm? And strong no less than wise and cherishing?[31]

Such views could inspire women and stimulate a demand for their better education whilst the more firmly entrenching them in their traditional roles. Beard in fact had earlier asked for institutions for young women in manual labour, presided over by matrons who could instruct them in their future duties as domestic servants or mothers of labouring families – a limited view even of women's typical work.[32]

Such a domestic emphasis aided the rhetoric against married women working in factories used by men as far apart in political thinking as Engels and Lord Shaftesbury. Beard, who did not share Shaftesbury's fear that factory women were 'gradually acquiring all those privileges which are held to be the proper portion of the male sex', and thus turning from their rightful wifely obedience, nevertheless wanted legislation to prevent at least mothers from working in factories, believing it impossible for labourers to be happy 'until a new and improved race of mothers appears'. He thought working-class women educated in moral and domestic economy would somehow turn their homes into a delight. He constantly reiterated his theme that factory girls, when married, rendered their homes 'filthy and miserable' by their 'ignorance and sluttish habits' so, unsurprisingly, their poor husbands sought refuge in pot-houses. Even Elizabeth Gaskell repeated such views on factory girls in *Mary Barton.* This, despite the fact that work amongst the very poor drove both to understand the 'overwhelming devastation that extreme poverty commits' and the lack of elementary facilities required to create a good home. Gaskell especially knew well the economic fact that most women had to work for either their own or the family income even if many, particularly those who were married, often had temporary, as well as low-paid and unskilled jobs.[33]

Reformers who wished to raise men's wages so that their wives did not have to work, however, were in tune with traditional working men's demands. The latter feared women undercutting their wages, for women were always paid at lower rates, which, as far as

31. Ibid., pp. 257–8; William Johnson Fox, 'Five lectures on education', *Collected Works* (1865 but taken from Finsbury Lectures 1835–40), IV, pp. 167–9.
32. Beard, *Schools*, pp. 47–8.
33. Ibid.; *MR* (1832), NS 6, pp. 164–5, 236–8; Gaskell, *Mary Barton*, pp. 43–4, 165–6.

William Greg was concerned, justified their employment: 'It is clearly a waste of strength, a superfluous extravagance, an economic blunder, to employ a powerful and costly machine to do work which can be as well done by a feebler and cheaper one.'[34] Although some Unitarians particularly had a good name for their caring, if rather paternalistic, employment of women, they were hardly feminists on the matter of employment.

Traditional arguments against women being breadwinners paid far less attention to jobs involving sweated labour where women worked in conditions that were as bad as, if not worse than, those in factories, but were less independent of men. Harriet Martineau, in contrast, wished women to be able to gain independence in respectable, decently paid jobs, although her wish for the bastardy provisions of the 1834 Poor Law to throw the whole charge of illegitimate children upon the mother took this independence rather far. Making a woman 'the guardian of her own mind and morals, instead of the ward of man' did very little to make men more responsible in sexual matters. In 'The Scholars of Arneside' (a short story), however, Martineau showed the difficulties for women both of ignorance and of early marriage and motherhood.[35]

Working-class women, reform movements and the domestic ideology

It is not easy to find direct evidence of what working-class women thought about these various views, since, in this period, they had not gained sufficient self-confidence to write about their ideas, as many of their menfolk did, nor have historians always concerned themselves much about them. Women did play a part in working-class movements although not necessarily fighting for or even thinking of feminist ideas. Male working-class reformers, such as Rowland Detroisier, tended to express views similar to Beard's.[36] Better-educated maternalism within a patriarchal system was usually the aim for working-class as for middle-class reformers. Chartists, for example, did not include female suffrage in the final draft of the Charter, as a newspaper letter addressed to the Chartists, probably

34. William Rathbone Greg, *Literary and Social Judgements* (1868), p. 371.

35. Harriet Martineau, *Society in America*, 3 vols (1837), III, pp. 147–51; *Thirty Years Peace*, II, p. 86; *Illustrations of Taxation*, V, p. 22.

36. R. Detroisier, *An Address on the Advantage of the Intended Mechanics' Hall of Science* (Manchester (31.12.1831), p. 7; *MR* (1830), NS 4, pp. 710–1.

from the Leicester Unitarian William Biggs, strongly protested in 1840. Even so, William Lovett did aim at the harmonious development of the physical, moral and intellectual powers of every child, whether boy or girl, and wanted high schools for both, teaching a wide range of sciences, including applied ones, social science, physiology and health, and the first principles of the most useful trades and occupations according to sex.[37]

It was not surprising therefore that, on their education ideals at least, many of the most progressive Unitarians felt close to the 'moral' Chartists, as they did to other working-class collectivist movements of this period, especially the Cooperative Movement. A few supported the Socialist ideas of Owenism. The latter two movements offered the fullest opportunities, both generally and in education, to women although neither of them was able to overcome the obstacles of lack of resources, good teachers, time and support. In the Cooperative schools, the Halls of Science and Owenite communities women received and took greater chances of equality. Yet the attention given to collective self-improvement instead of male-orientated 'low and debasing amusements', and to a sober, gentle, family-orientated way of life, whilst in one way enhancing women's status and participation, in another, once again, increased the emphasis on their domestic role and their relative virtues. The weaknesses of the Owenites and Cooperators in a capitalist, patriarchal world were not helped by their freer position on marriage. Furthermore, tensions did arise over the position of women, and the general support for equality in early British Socialism was soon diluted.[38]

The general Unitarian view for all classes to emphasize the importance of mothers and the equal rights and capabilities of women, although not necessarily in the same spheres as men, was therefore quite advanced for the day. John Relly Beard supported women's rights and the better employment of unmarried women alongside his central plea for intelligent, educated wives and mothers, the 'sap and marrow of our national strength'. Indeed, he argued cogently, 'To educate a mother is to educate a family, and the education of families is the education of the race.'[39]

37. William Lovett, *Life and Struggles of . . .* (1967; 1st edn 1876), pp. 31–4, 81, 116–20; MSS, *Biggs Scrapbooks*, I, 9.5.1840.

38. Barbara Taylor, *Eve and the New Jerusalem* (1983), *passim*; William Thompson and Anna Wheeler, *Appeal of Half the Human Race, Women, against the Pretensions of the Other Half, Men, to Retain them in Political and thence Civil and Domestic Slavery* (privately printed, 1825), *passim*.

39. Beard, *Self-Culture*, pp. 258–60.

This domestic ideology was not altogether to working-class women's disadvantage since domestic training gave them a way into their largest source of employment, and the ability to sew, make and mend was a financial boon to a household. There were many working-class women who could appreciate Beard's view and prefer the status and influence he conferred on educated mothers at home to the unskilled, low-paid, second laborious job they might have in a highly disciplined, dirty factory. Yet at the same time such views would keep women in the home which for most was an 'unremitting round of domestic chores', emotionally draining, worsened by continuous child-bearing and with little escape. The educational ideals of Unitarians and other educationists such as Pestalozzi and the Phrenologists concerning the moral and domestic influence of women could be simply an added strain.[40] Catherine Barmby, for example, a Unitarian Owenite feminist, grandly described the domestic sphere as including customs, private and public behaviour and assigned to women's rule by God and thus requiring a greater educational basis. At the same time her blaming uninteresting drudges of wives for their men leaving home at night did little for men's moral responsibilities in the home and less to lighten their wives' toil.[41]

This is interesting, for Barmby was one of those radical unitarians[42] born out of William Fox's ministry at South Place and his *Monthly Repository* group which in the 1830s and 1840s wanted, as Kathryn Gleadle has compellingly argued, 'a radical evolution in the existing culture'. Wider views of women's roles, enlarged employment opportunities and greater equality with men were fundamental to this but so was their domestic ideology, which was integral to their holistic concept of democracy. In contrast to the evangelicals they postulated a 'dynamic model of motherhood', suggesting that homemaking was learnt rather than natural. A corollary to this was their 'progressive notions of fatherhood', seeing men sharing the caring familial role with women. William Shaen, for example, the husband of Emily, who argued for housekeeping to be professional, enthusiastically believed that the 'educating motive of a moral and intellectual man' should be a tender relationship between him and his child. He tried personally to share domestic responsibility, a

40. Janet Horowitz Murray, *Strong-Minded Women* (Harmondsworth, 1984), pp. 77–4 ff.

41. Catherine Barmby, 'Women and Domestics', *People's Journal* (1857), III, p. 37.

42. For an explanation of this term see Chapter 10 below and Kathryn Gleadle, *The Early Feminists* (1995).

prerequisite for the real emancipation of women, as twentieth-century history has shown.[43]

There was much in this with which many Unitarian educators could agree and Gleadle does emphasize the significant connections with mainstream Unitarianism. This is not to say that all Unitarians would interpret the emphasis of the radical unitarians on the domestic role of fathers in the same way. William Enfield in Nottingham, for example, also stressed the crucial educative influence of the father in the family, but as the key figure on whom all depended – an image recognizable to those powerful Unitarian industrialists who regarded their workforces in such a light.[44] The inherent contradictions of a positive domestic ideology were no easier to work out in the nineteenth century than they are in the late twentieth century. The significant point was that Unitarians put an enormously high value on knowledge and understanding and would not deny them to anyone. As the Rev. George Armstrong said when preaching on behalf of the Girls' Daily School at High Pavement, Nottingham in 1845, it was a mistake to suppose that any knowledge, 'however refined, at all indisposes or unfits for the engagements of a toilsome or even a menial life'.[45] This sentiment was equally applied by Unitarians to working-class males and indeed to middle-class males in business. On a previous occasion Armstrong argued that there should be no monopoly of study or subject by either sex – a notion which hardly gained wholesale currency in Britain until the late twentieth century. He enthused on the great benefits of more natural relationships between the sexes, arguing there could be no real respect for woman whilst she was regarded as merely a 'household divinity' and not as 'a noble and intelligent being' who can instruct men. Men could both work and understand about good food so why should there not be 'learned wives and academic cooks'? He was sure that 'the mysteries of confection and the mysteries of theology may dwell in one and the same mind, that the raising of the paste and the raising of the soul are by no means incompatible efforts, and that healthy children and vigorous ideas

43. Ibid., pp. 5–7, 87–106.

44. MSS HP, Hi I 3, *High Pavement Mutual Improvement Society* (23 Oct. 1822); e.g. Samuel Greg, 'Two letters to Leonard Horner Esq. on the capabilities of the factory system', 1840, in *Conditions of Work and Living: Five Pamphlets 1838–44* (New York, 1972), *passim.*

45. Bristol Reference Library, B19568, *Selections from the Writings of the Rev. George Armstrong* (private circulation, 1892), p. 48.

may equally flourish under the same maternal care!'[46] As an example he referred to the Unitarian scientist Mary Somerville, 'mother of a circle of happy children' and with an 'enlightened and far-soaring mind'.[47]

There were contradictions in Unitarian aspirations, therefore, but they were committed to a wide, liberal, rational, modern, unsectarian education and, in this, did have a meeting ground with working-class radicals. Their paternalism put an emphasis on maternalism which, in the way individuals, both men and women, internalized it, had profound meanings for women of all classes.

46. Ibid., 'Address from the Chair of the Literary Conversation Society, Dublin, 1st June, 1837', pp. 118–25.
47. Ibid., p. 125.

CHAPTER TEN

Unitarians and gender issues in the 1850s: the seeds of feminism

This book has argued that the religious and educational beliefs of the Unitarians led them to adopt far more pronounced egalitarian views on women and their education than was the norm. This, in turn, helped to produce women who achieved much in public life, set new role models for others and were in the forefront of those creating better educational provision for females. At the same time Unitarians were fighting for reforms and expansion in male education and to be the political and cultural leaders of the urban middle class, despite the deep hostility of most others in society to their religious views. Such struggles necessarily lessened any focus on female issues, whilst class attitudes complicated views on gender roles. Unitarian emphasis on unlimited and rational education for all and the dignity and self-respect owed to each individual had great appeal to aspiring autodidacts whatever their class or gender. The role some of their wealthiest and most well-known families played in the bitter industrial conflicts of the day, however, and the way their educationists upheld the so-called economic laws underlying such fights, militated against their popularity among the working classes. Their gendered domestic ideology, although ironically based on greater educational and working opportunities, was more congenial both across class aspirations and in the context of the deepening divisions of gender generally in Victorian life. Yet at the same time middle-class Unitarians, both men and women, became engaged publicly in attempts to win greater rights for women. This chapter aims to bring these threads together with particular reference to the 1850s.

Respectability and 'home duties'

As the nineteenth century progressed, the lives, particularly of more prosperous middle-class women, became more, rather than less, circumscribed. Unitarians were caught by the assumptions of their age in this and many of the women themselves did not wish to break the code of respectability: Harriet Martineau and Harriet Taylor cut their hitherto warm relationships with William Fox when he left his wife and started living with Eliza Flower, for example. Yet, at the same time, Martineau, in her writings on political economy and slavery and in her independent journalism, and Taylor, in her relationship with John Stuart Mill, were themselves among those who pushed at the boundaries of what was deemed 'proper'. This was typical of Unitarians. Caroline Thornley's father, for example, would not go to the Liverpool Philharmonic in 1858 to hear Charles Dickens read when the latter separated from his wife, although Caroline went despite her mother's shock.[1] Elizabeth Gaskell, seemingly fussily anxious over whom her daughters should be friendly with, including some Liverpool Unitarians, worried about Charlotte Brontë's seeming 'coarseness' in *The Professor* and wished the brilliant *Adam Bede* had not been written by Marian Evans (George Eliot) since her private life did 'so jar against the beautiful book'. This 'beautiful book', nevertheless, took the part of an unmarried mother against the careless father. Often unconventional in her own writings, Gaskell was to uphold right action over propriety for her fictional heroine Molly Gibson in *Wives and Daughters.* She became a fervent friend of Fox's daughter, Tottie, and would not cut Harriet Martineau off as others did when she published the atheistic *Letters on the Laws of Man's Nature and Development* with Henry Atkinson.[2]

Propriety and respectability were severe limitations to freedom of opportunity but the lack of them would further prevent social acceptance for those already marginalized by their religion. At the same time many Unitarians accepted gendered differences in personality to some extent. By the mid nineteenth century fewer of them were extreme environmentalists, so that it was easier for someone like William Rathbone to subscribe to the idea of women having

1. Josephine Kamm, *John Stuart Mill in Love* (1977), pp. 44–7; Herbert McLachlan, 'A Liverpool ladies journal a century ago', *TUHS* (Oct. 1955), XI, no. 1, p. 19.

2. Brenda Colloms, 'Tottie Fox, her life and background', *Gaskell Society Journal* (1990), 5, pp. 17–18 and ff.; J.A.V. Chapple and A. Pollard (eds), *The Letters of Mrs Gaskell* (Manchester, 1966), pp. 206, 259–60, 410–17, 531–3, 566.

'natural' characteristics of self-sacrifice and gentleness, although he tempered this with the thought that 'their life is generally free from that struggle for existence which unless carefully watched hardens men's character'. He evidently was not thinking of the majority of women below the wealthy nor of the hardships of frequent pregnancy and childbirth suffered by mothers of all classes. His advice for his daughter if she married was to put her husband first in everything, remembering her attention, cheerfulness and open affection would be unlikely to be reciprocated. The only underlined words in his text were *'never excuse yourself when he is angry'*, yet he added that wives should preserve their own self-respect by gentle dignity under all circumstances. Such strictures, coming from the son and grandson of Elizabeth Rathbone and Hannah Greg respectively, who himself, according to his famous daughter, held an exhilarating and invigorating high standard of expectation for women and was the founder of district nursing, indicated how patriarchal even a reformist Unitarian could sound.[3]

It would be foolish to ignore the deep desire that many women have for motherhood and the limitations this may have on career aspirations even now until the duties of parenthood are shared more equally by both sexes. These restrictions seemed inevitable in a period when few used birth-control and the methods available were unreliable. Continuous child-bearing was the norm for most married women and 'household duties' correspondingly were enlarged, especially in the days before labour-saving devices and public schooling for all. Housework varied as to wealth, but Elizabeth Gaskell, for instance, even when moderately well-off partly through her own earnings, found it difficult to find private space or sustained time to concentrate on her writing. In contrast, her husband William could retreat to his beloved study to attend to his ministerial and educational work. On the other hand Elizabeth delighted in both her maternal and domestic responsibilities. She perceived motherhood as the role *par excellence* whereby women achieve knowledge, autonomy and power. As exemplified in *Ruth*, her emphasis on the nurturing role of women was part of that Unitarian thinking which wanted all people to respond to family and community values. Men were included in this, as Gaskell's most sympathetic male characters, usually fathers or doctors, illustrate.[4]

3. MSS University of Liverpool, *William Rathbone VI Papers* IX.9.9 (6.8.1861); Eleanor Rathbone, *William Rathbone: A Memoir* (1908), pp. 155–86, 359.

4. Elizabeth Gaskell, 'My Diary', in J.A.V. Chapple and Anita Wilson (eds), *Private Voices* (Keele, 1996), pp. 11–71; Elizabeth Gaskell, *Ruth* (1967; 1st publ. 1853).

For women to be at the vanguard of the moral evolution of the family and the community was seemingly to repose much power in them, but, since they were restricted to a domestic role, it severely limited what they could do with the knowledge and experience they possessed. Elizabeth Gaskell was aware of this yet never fully resolved the problem in her own writings or crowded life. To Tottie Fox, with whom she discussed those conflicts between 'womanly duties' and fulfilling one's talent which periodically troubled her, she wrote: 'Women must give up living an artist's life, if home duties are to be paramount. It is different with men, whose home duties are so small a part of life.'[5] Nevertheless, she wished to blend these home duties with the development of the individual despite the difficulties inherent in so doing. Her books were very much about the education of women in the wider sense, although *Wives and Daughters* particularly concentrated, according to Patsy Stoneman, on the 'education of daughters by wives to be wives'. But wives were legally and by their marriage vows subordinate to their husbands. They ran households, but since knowledge of housewifery was not generally accorded high status, the domestic role of women had more rhetorical value than real. On the other hand, Elizabeth Gaskell, like other Unitarians, believed women should have moral responsibility for themselves, should speak out when necessary as she did, share in the creation of values and do their own appointed work.[6]

This was significant, for men were increasingly defined by the work they did, as, indeed, Priestley had hoped. Generally, however, a 'lady' was defined by the fact that she did *not* do paid work, such attitudes necessarily making most 'ladies' dependent on some man, as Davidoff and Hall have exemplified.[7] Harriet Martineau's hero in *Deerbrook* fought against such attitudes by inveighing against his grandfather's decision to leave money to his grandsons but not his granddaughters, for example.[8] A Unitarian example of the more customary stance was John Yates of Liverpool, who left a fifth of his sizeable fortune to each of his four sons and one fifth to his two unmarried daughters to share. Richard Vaughan Yates was able to give Princes Park to Liverpool, but his sisters Anna and Jane had to live a life of frugality in order to give to Manchester College, the

5. Chapple and Pollard, *Gaskell*, p. 106.

6. Ibid., pp. 107, 598; Elizabeth Gaskell, *Wives and Daughters* (Harmondsworth, 1969; 1st publ. 1864–6); Patsy Stoneman, *Elizabeth Gaskell* (Brighton, 1987), pp. 172, 50–2, 196–200.

7. Leonore Davidoff and Catherine Hall, *Family Fortunes: Men and Women of the English Middle-Class 1780–1850* (1987), pp. 205–19, 275–9.

8. *Deerbrook*, (1983; 1st publ. 1839), pp. 74, 466–7,

Unitarian Home Missionary Board and the many charities they supported. All were well educated, Anna, for example, attending William Shepherd's school as did her three elder brothers, but higher education, the ministry, business and politics were for the latter only. As Anna noted, their brother John discovered that women in Paris were 'more on a footing with the men than in England'.[9]

The intersection of class and gender often militated against the greater freedom of women. Middle-class women were supposed to be private not public persons, but as William Fox said of the Unitarian radical publisher Benjamin Flower, a man's character was perceived, especially by Unitarians, to be only fully developed when he acted in public, for the public good was the 'noblest object'.[10] On the other hand, it was Unitarian women who often transformed this view of womanhood, partly because some Unitarian policies had unexpected results. For example, neither Mary Carpenter's nor Harriet Martineau's family educated them expecting them to play a public role, but the education they had had motivated and empowered them to do so.

In practice, the distinction between the public and private world was often blurred, especially when, through religious, social or sometimes political concerns, women of all religious groups strove to make their voice heard in those familial and community matters which *had* been considered part of their prerogative. But many, especially the more conservative, evangelical women engaged in philanthropic or even political reform, were not feminists in the sense of wanting equality with men. Women of wealth and status already exercised considerable authority within their 'private' sphere which they were reluctant to relinquish. This caused a very real tension within the women's movement. Women's espousal of philanthropic causes could give a semi-public role at least to those involved yet might further reinforce feminine stereotypes especially when these 'activists' imposed their internalized values of domesticity and middle-class morality upon the victims of their charity. On the other hand, within the anti-slavery movement particularly, in which women played such a significant and often innovative part from the 1820s, many Quaker and Unitarian women found both text and experience for future struggles for women's rights.[11]

9. Liverpool Public Library, H920 YAT, Samuel Yates, *Memorials of the Family of the Rev. John Yates* (privately printed, 1890), pp. 11–13, 16–23, 37–9, 69.

10. W.J. Fox, *A Sermon Preached at Finsbury Unitarian Chapel March 1st 1829 on the occasion of the death of Mr Benjamin Flower* (1829), p. 15.

11. e.g. Clare Midgley, *Women against Slavery* (1992), pp. 43 ff.

Radical unitarians

Furthermore, not only were Unitarian women to the fore in a wide variety of educational and social concerns but the political activities of women such as Bessie Parkes and Clementia Taylor worked directly to extend the rights of women. Both of these were deeply influenced by what Kathryn Gleadle has termed the 'radical unitarians', a coterie whose origins lay in Unitarianism and *communitarianism and who continued to draw from Unitarians throughout their existence in the 1830s and 1840s. Committed to liberal education for all, fascinated by science, German Romanticism and political radicalism, and maintaining a close relationship with literary circles, their closeness to Unitarianism was easily apparent. But they also drew from liberal Anglicans and those who sought a religion based on the heart of Christian ethics. Some, indeed, became humanists. By the late 1840s they had 'developed a powerful social, political and cultural critique of modern society, and women's role within it'. Intellectual and dynamic, they became involved in specific legal campaigns, trying to push female suffrage into Chartism, to tackle the problem of prostitution and to introduce a programme of adult education. They used journalism and fiction to argue their ideas, thus enabling women amongst them to find satisfying paid public work at the same time. Gleadle argues convincingly that the radical unitarians established the 'essential ideologies and personal networks which were to determine the feminist movement of the succeeding decades'.[12]

A number of Unitarians already mentioned were counted amongst the radical unitarians who originated in that eclectic, progressive group centred on William Johnson Fox's South Place Chapel in Finsbury in the late 1820s and 1830s. Fox, first as editor of the Unitarian periodical *The Monthly Repository* and then as owner, attracted eager, liberal reformers, autodidacts and free-thinkers especially from the fringes of the middle and working classes. Enthusiastically exploring poetry, the theatre, science and education for the young, they were called the '*Monthly Repository* Circle' by their historian, Margaret Parnaby. She termed them unique in their explicit Pestalozzian ideas on the rearing of children and elementary education, their vision of the theatre as an instrument for expressing ideas of social progress and their claims for improving the educational, social, sexual and political status of women. The gifted Flower sisters, Eliza

12. Kathryn Gleadle, *The Early Feminists* (1995), pp. 1, 6 and *passim.*

and Sarah, daughters of Benjamin and Eliza, were pivotal to this group, and Harriet Martineau and Harriet Taylor were close friends at first, but others, like Mary Leman Grimstone, were not Unitarian whilst mainstream Unitarians looked askance when the group began to advocate divorce. Leading Unitarians such as Lant Carpenter and John Estlin were happy to promote equal education for females and even better employment for them thereafter but were horrified by arguments for marriage as a civil contract or radical changes 'in the constitution of our female society' respectively. Thomas Southwood Smith's *The Philosophy of Health* equally stimulated praise for its analysis of the evils of existing female education but anathema for his sweeping proposals for female emancipation. Yet Dr Smith, social reformer, unconventional father of Caroline Hill and grandfather of Octavia, was a leading Unitarian too and many mainstream Unitarians continued to frequent South Place Chapel.[13]

Such a mixture of both allegiance to and divergence from Unitarianism continued as the circle broke up but the central group of feminists was augmented by individuals such as the writer Anna Jameson and the group of radical lawyers around William Ashurst, whose family and friendship connections drew in reformers and feminists from both London and the provinces. Many of these were either originally or lifelong Unitarians – for example, the Leicester Biggs family, the Coventry Brays and Hennells, who so influenced Marian Evans, the Wakefield Gaskells, George Dawson, Clementia and Peter Taylor, William Shaen, James Stansfeld, Elizabeth Malleson, née Whitehead, Catherine and Goodwyn Barmby. Shaen, who was at John Malleson's school in Brighton with Taylor and London University with Stansfeld, was to work tirelessly for women's higher education and legal emancipation. As the *Pall Mall Gazette* noted on his death in 1887, Shaen 'as a lawyer and as a man' never ceased 'arraigning the injustice to which women were subject' and 'toiling' to amend this even 'when the legal barbarities . . . heaped upon women were almost unnoticed, even by women themselves'. With Stansfeld he was to fight against the Contagious Diseases Acts, as did the Mallesons. Stansfeld, indeed, at the age of seventy-five, received a testimonial from the women of England for his services to morality and female suffrage.[14]

13. Margaret Parnaby, 'William Johnson Fox and the Monthly Repository Circle of 1832–1836' (Ph.D. thesis, Australian National University, 1979), pp. x–xi and *passim*; Gleadle, *Early Feminists*, pp. 33–8.

14. Ibid., pp. 38–43, 175–6; *Inquirer* (12.3.1887), pp. 171–3; *DNB* (1898), XXII, pp. 1224–5; Hope Malleson, *Elizabeth Malleson, 1828–1916: Autobiographical Notes and Letters* (printed for private circulation, 1926), pp. 37–41, 93–4, 125–7.

Others whom Gleadle has termed radical unitarians, such as Eliza Cook, Eliza Meteyard, Douglas Jerrold and John Chapman of the *Westminster Review*, were not actual Unitarians, although the popular and successful writers William and Mary Howitt apparently were drawn from Quakerism to Unitarianism. The group provided the most significant participants of Douglas Jerrold's Whittington Club in London, which deliberately set out to include women, as well as lower-class men, as full members. It provided a much-needed service to independent women not only for its educational facilities but also as a rare, respectable public dining place. Four hundred belonged in 1850 (about a quarter of the membership), before rising fees dramatically reduced numbers. Despite the chairman William Shaen's care of the business and legal matters, however, financial difficulties and external and internal opposition to the educational and social experiments led him and others to resign. From the beginning, indeed, there had been different interpretations of women's place in the club, the feminists who founded the club failing to convince particularly those men of the lower middle class who attended of the need to overturn traditional ways of social behaviour and help women to become active, independent beings. Thence the club became an ordinary men's club. Similar experiments in Liverpool and Birmingham were even less successful.[15]

The Women's Movement

The radical unitarians as a group gradually split up by the 1850s after the death of several of their most inspiring members – the Flower sisters, Eliza Ashurst and Mary Leman Grimstone. Nevertheless, they provided both key concepts and people to the burgeoning Women's Movement of the 1850s which began with a small group of intellectual and energetic women in London, led by Barbara Leigh-Smith, cousin of Florence Nightingale and granddaughter of the Unitarian, William Smith MP, and by Bessie Parkes, great-granddaughter of Joseph Priestley. Both of these had links from their early years not only with Unitarian intellectual and political circles but also with the radical unitarians. Bessie Parkes was also excited by the feminist arguments she heard in George Dawson's popular lectures in Birmingham. This group first made a spirited,

15. C. Kent, 'The Whittington Club: A Bohemian experiment in middle-class social reform', *Victorian Studies* (Sept. 1974), 18, no. 1, pp. 31–56; Gleadle, *Early Feminists*, pp. 42–5, 140–70.

although unsuccessful, bid to alter the Married Women's Property laws but were more successful in establishing the first employment bureau for women and in publishing a newspaper, *The Englishwomen's Journal*, organized and written solely by women. Later they tried to widen women's educational opportunities as a way of raising their whole status and helped both Elizabeth Garrett to train as a doctor and John Stuart Mill's 1867 attempt to obtain female suffrage. The latter's article of 1851 'The enfranchisement of women', written together with his wife, the Unitarian Harriet Taylor, powerfully castigated the inferior status of women and argued for equal rights in every sphere of life.[16]

Although both Parkes and Leigh-Smith abandoned the religious basis of Unitarianism for liberal humanism, many Unitarians were involved in their work. For example, Matthew and Frederic Hill (helped by his wife Martha), like William Shaen, helped Barbara Leigh-Smith in her fight against the property laws. Unitarians such as Lady Byron and Elizabeth Gaskell supported the 1856 Petition. It is not always easy, indeed, to divide 'mainstream' from 'radical' Unitarians. Generally the former had been the first to fight for many women's rights, as Thomas Talfourd and Matthew Hill had proved. Later in the century, Unitarians such as Frances Power Cobbe played an important role in securing other rights for women.[17] In a less dramatic way, Unitarians had slowly and gradually opened up their church committees, especially Sunday school ones, to women, although men often remained in overall control, particularly of the money. Lant Carpenter had consistently argued for female representation in such matters.[18]

The Englishwomen's Journal, incidentally, was highly praised by John Relly Beard for its wise treatment of women's rights and employment, although he added that neither of these could ever be achieved until women acquired, probably 'by as well as for themselves', far better education.[19] This was an important truth that the reformers of the 1850s were to realize, and in the 1860s and 1870s much of their energy was channelled into securing quality schooling for middle-class girls and higher education for women. Yet the reformers of these three decades retained deeply ingrained class

16. Ibid., pp. 171–83; Kamm, *Mill*, pp. 83–91.

17. Gleadle, *Early Feminists*, pp. 126–9, 176; Constance Hill (ed.), *Frederic Hill* (1894), pp. 305–7, 309; Chapple and Pollard, *Gaskell*, p. 379; *DNB* (1912), 2nd Supplement, I, pp. 378–9.

18. *CR* (1836), pp. 203, 583; (1841), p. 522, but (1840), pp. 543, 549; *MR* (1831), NS 5, p. 428.

19. John Relly Beard, *Self-Culture* (3rd edn; 1st edn. 1859), p. 260.

ideas about gender roles, thinking only middle-class women bereft of male support needed to gain rewarding work. Change in attitudes towards women and their role was indeed slow. Nevertheless, through their ideals and often their practice, Unitarians did help to moderate patriarchy, Elizabeth Gaskell's scorning the use of her husband's first name by his wife being one significant instance of this.[20]

Unitarian networks

There was a continuum throughout and beyond the period 1760–1860. For example, Hartleyan associationism inspired Harriet Martineau, Lant and Mary Carpenter (and John Stuart Mill) in the nineteenth century as it had Priestley and others in the eighteenth. The same families were responsible for educational reform: the Aikins intermarried with the le Bretons, stalwart workers for the admission of women to London University, like James Heywood, the grandson of Thomas Percival. From the Beard, Roscoe and Herford families came leading educational reformers in later nineteenth-century Lancashire, many of them eager like other Unitarians for women's entrance into higher education.[21]

The networks helped educational ideals to continue. To take just one example, William Turner of Newcastle's daughter, Mary, was to marry John Gooch Robberds, a fellow minister in the nineteenth century at Cross Street, Manchester with William Gaskell, whose uncle had been at Warrington and whose wife Elizabeth was daughter of William Stevenson, ex-Warrington and briefly a tutor of Manchester Academy. Both Robberds and Gaskell were students at Manchester New College, the successor to Manchester Academy at York, and were taught mathematics and science by William Turner's son William. Elizabeth Gaskell spent the two years before her marriage living in William Turner senior's house in Newcastle. William Gaskell, deeply involved in the Manchester cultural scene, was a first-class educator especially in English literature and engaged in higher education, women's education and the teaching of mechanics. With John Relly Beard he taught at both Owens College and the Unitarian Home Missionary Board. Elizabeth Gaskell was a brilliant author of fiction whose writings explored social questions including the position

20. Chapple and Pollard, *Gaskell*, p. 40.

21. Herbert McLachlan, *Records of a Family* (Manchester, 1935), *passim*; Henry Roscoe, *The Life and Experiences of Sir Henry Enfield Roscoe, DCL, LL.D, FRS* (1906), pp. 102 ff.

of women, scientific education and the liberalization of businessmen. She was very much enmeshed in humanist and reformist circles both amongst Unitarians and in London, reminiscent of those explored above.[22]

Elizabeth Gaskell

The life and work of Elizabeth Gaskell can be used as an example, indeed, not only of the continuing networks which were so important to the development of Unitarian ideas and activities but also of the issues explored previously. Her own family, education and upbringing brought her into early contact with those scientific and medical circles of the new professional and intellectual middle classes in which Unitarians figured so prominently. These fired that understanding of the significance of scientific and technological discovery expressed in *Cousin Phillis* and *Wives and Daughters.* They also gave her knowledge of semi-rural life in Knutsford and Warwickshire to contrast with the smoke of Manchester where she lived out her married life. There, through Cross Street and Mosley Street Chapels, she and her husband knew the leading industrial and commercial families in the foremost city of a new age. Many, like the Gregs and Darbishires, were close personal friends. At the same time she and William, involved with the domestic mission and Sunday schools, were deeply concerned with the plight of the workers on whose backs lay most of the work but little of the profits for the industrial miracles of nineteenth-century Britain. Elizabeth's 'industrial' novels reflected those tentative moves towards cooperation and consensus which some of the more sensitive reformers among both middle and working class were seeking in mid century. The horror which some of her husband's congregation felt at her views on capitalist relationships, combined with the way they did not deny her right to express them, is indicative of both their economic ideology and their equally heartfelt commitment to freedom of thought and speech.[23]

At the same time, through Manchester College, Gaskell was connected to the intellectual aristocracy of Unitarianism and an exciting range of religious and educational as well as political and social ideas. Her own husband was a brilliant teacher in all the chief

22. MSS MCO, MS C2, John Reynall Wreford, *Statistics on Dissenting Colleges* (1820, presented to MCO 1916); Jenny Uglow, *Elizabeth Gaskell* (1993), *passim.*

23. Ibid., *passim*; Chapple and Pollard, *Gaskell, passim.*

educational institutions in which Unitarians were involved, whilst at home his tutoring of the intellectual Winkworth sisters brought Elizabeth some of the most satisfying friendships of her life. Emily Winkworth was to marry William Shaen, whose sisters were eager political and social reformers like himself and similarly great friends with Elizabeth. Gregarious and full of fun, the latter enjoyed the cultural life of the ebullient town, yet, rather like the College, became disappointed with Manchester in the 1850s and sought wider mental satisfaction elsewhere. From her visit to Germany with William in 1849, she began her love of European travel which the sale of her books was able to finance for the rest of her life.[24]

From the late 1840s Gaskell's writings gave her contact with Dickens and literary circles in London. It also brought her friendship with other authors who were exploring ideas about women – namely Charlotte Brontë and the Howitts. Through her Unitarian contacts she knew radical unitarians such as the professional artists Barbara Leigh-Smith (whom she admired but thought rather bold) and Tottie Fox. She knew Leigh-Smith's cousin Florence Nightingale personally and deeply admired her work and dedication as a nurse, although she noted that her sister Parthe had to take on all Florence's 'home duties' to enable her freedom. Gaskell was happy for her own daughter Meta to become an artist or nurse like these women and depicted the dignity of nursing in *Ruth*, yet was not keen on the idea of women doctors, another glimpse of the depths of conditioning that had to be plumbed even amongst quite radical women.[25]

On the other hand Elizabeth Gaskell was not afraid as a married woman to be a writer as well or to raise controversial views on class relationships and gender. In 1853, in *Ruth* itself, for example, she counterpoised the rigid, one-sided views that dominated the problem of prostitution in Victorian England, a problem which, as Gleadle points out, was long assumed to become a feminist issue only in the 1870s. Gleadle argues that it was the radical unitarians who first raised the issue, but it can be seen that other Unitarians were concerned too. Elizabeth Gaskell, like William Biggs, who helped 'penitent' females in Leicester, had an awareness, unusual for the time, that girls were safer through developed intelligence and common sense than through a hopefully innate virtue. She rightly anticipated criticism for tackling such a subject, drily commenting, 'I have taken leave of my *respectable* friends' and that many women especially expressed disapproval 'at considerable pain to

24. Ibid. 25. Ibid.; Gaskell, *Ruth*, pp. 384 ff.

themselves'. William Greg, however, did not think that Gaskell went far enough.[26]

Gaskell went further than Greg, however, in realizing that women derived strength and dignity from independent work, not just as he wished in 'completing, sweetening and embellishing the existence of others'.[27] This was illustrated by Mary Barton, Libbie Marsh and others of her working-class heroines, who, admittedly, tended to be single or widowed. Gaskell's view was not a general one, even among Unitarians, although a number of the women appear to have had warm relationships with their female servants – for example, Mary Carpenter was a bridesmaid to Harriet Martineau's maid Martha, who married the master of her ragged school.[28] Nevertheless, it was within the Unitarian context that Gaskell held up an ideal of independently minded, deeply educated women who needed to grow sexually as well as mentally, and her heroines were capable of courage and making their own decisions (sometimes more so than her male characters).

Elizabeth Gaskell, indeed, did not present woman's position in society as unproblematic, the 'Amazons' of *Cranford* in truth telling the reader more about the marginalization of women than their dominance. Her awareness of the ambiguities of women's position was seen in the lives of her daughters, who were exceedingly well educated for the times yet of whom none, not even the talented Meta, either attended Bedford College or had independent careers of their own. Gaskell's own life showed similar contradictions. Her writings, with their many easy biblical, literary and historical allusions, reflect her upbringing among the cultured, knowledge-thirsty Unitarians. Married to the 'bishop' of Unitarians, she held a deep religious conviction herself which manifests itself as typically Unitarian in her writings – moral, tolerant, undogmatic, compassionate and searching and stressing action rather than creed. Delighting in womanliness and being a mother, she shared an affectionate companionship of mutual interests and enjoyments with her husband, whose active support was often vital when her books aroused storms of criticism and even legal action.[29] Her work was of particular

26. Chapple and Pollard, *Gaskell*, pp. 98–100, 205, 220–8, 235–7; MSS *Biggs' Scrapbooks*, I and II – many letters of William Biggs in the *Leicester Mercury* 1846 and 1859; Gleadle, *Early Feminists*, p. 108; W.R. Greg, *Literary and Social Judgements*, 'False morality of lady novelists' (1868), pp. 133–6.

27. Ibid., 'Why are women redundant?', pp. 338–9.

28. Jo Manton, *Mary Carpenter and the Children of the Streets* (1976), pp. 113–14.

29. Patsy Stoneman, *Elizabeth Gaskell* (Brighton, 1987), pp. 87–98; Chapple and Pollard, *Gaskell*, *passim*; Uglow, *Elizabeth Gaskell*, pp. 447, 454, 487, 493, 565, 613.

importance because she was expressing and extending Unitarian ideas in accessible form, yet in both her life and writings she ultimately shrank from any alteration of the structure of society which produced inequalities.

Conclusion

It was the paradoxes of this situation which lessened Unitarian achievement in both class and gender issues. Unitarians preached that 'knowledge is power' but how far the enormous effort in education brought about the power they envisaged is a debatable matter. Certainly, as seen, individual Unitarians achieved considerable influence, particularly in what became the great industrial cities of England, despite the antagonism to their religion. Unitarians were prominent in all kinds of social reform; their ideas on social science inspired educationists like James Kay Shuttleworth[30] and ideals of rational and scientific education were absorbed with varying success into the general progressive educational scene of the time. The fact that some working-class Unitarians used their education to successful effect, and, even more unusually for this period, many women also achieved eminence, must testify to the enabling strength of Unitarian beliefs and education. Such examples, however, although there are many of them, do not mean that Unitarians achieved their aims. Their education could empower those who participated in it, but only a few did. Unitarians themselves comprised only a small number of the population, and many of their middle-class schools could be afforded only by the richer of their own congregations. Those of other religious persuasions, including orthodox dissenters, were usually reluctant to entrust their children to such 'heathens'. Similar disadvantages afflicted higher education, which was further affected by the fact that industrialists and businessmen were not persuaded that such an education was needed for their sons. Unitarians fought for access to Oxbridge and for the reform of traditional upper-class education, but when these objectives were won they increasingly ignored institutions run by their own people in preference for the new ones they had helped establish or, later, even for those they had formerly despised. Although they did much to promote science, by the mid nineteenth century the balance of science and the arts originally envisaged by Priestley

30. R.W. Selleck, *Journey of an Outsider: James Kay Shuttleworth* (1994), pp. 48–95.

was not being widely achieved in education. Unitarians were not the only reformers in education in the nineteenth century: they were influenced by others but their own educational views were contested in many ways. The élite of their own movement did win status and power, but if they were enlightened leaders of the new middle class it was in an individualistic and oblique way.

Such limitations also affected their enlightened attitudes to female education, attitudes further complicated by the interrelated concepts of class and gender which evolved in this period. The keen desire for respectability might prevent able, highly intelligent women from speaking up in public, yet, alternatively, they might find that other reformers would not act with them because their Unitarianism was considered irregular and 'not proper'. Henrietta Busk, for example, was mindful of her aunt's injunction that 'Women of *our* family do *not* speak on platforms. Remember!' Only later in the century did she begin the public life in education enjoyed by so many of her male relatives from the Busk, le Breton and Aikin families. Yet she, like them, worked hard for Bedford College, which suffered from its Unitarian connections.[31]

Unitarians did help change gender conceptions, however. They were not the only ones to do so but both their ideas and actions usually went further than others. Quakers were the closest to Unitarians in social character and often ideals, as their similar stance within the anti-slavery movement illustrated. They also produced some exceptional women, such as Elizabeth Fry and Priscilla Wakefield, and were responsible for the important adult schools which gave both men and women a chance to gain literacy. Yet, at this time, especially through the somewhat anti-intellectual pietist period, they did less in education. Some Quakers, like the earlier Rathbones and the Howitts, became Unitarian in fact or sympathy, although apparently Elizabeth Heyrick did the reverse, partly because Quakers allowed that women could voice God's word as ministers.[32] Orthodox dissenters were affected by some of the ideas which influenced Unitarians and had some good schools, although chiefly after 1853, but did not promulgate such radical views as Unitarians. Neither did Christian Socialists, although they established Queen's College. Liberal churchmen, like Sydney Smith, sometimes had liberal attitudes on the position of women but such examples are more frequent later in the century. Utilitarians followed the Hartleyan

31. Ruth Young, *The Life of an Educational Worker: Henrietta Busk* (1934), *passim*.
32. Midgley, *Women against Slavery*, p. 111 and *passim*.

philosophy, but, like some individual progressive educationists, lacked the religious element so essential in nineteenth-century society. There was a growing debate in the 1850s about the 'Woman Question': for example, Maria Grey and Emily Shirreff stressed the need for women to have a rational, wide, liberal education to fit them for fulfilling their roles as wives and mothers properly or attaining independence if single. Like Hannah More, however, they explicitly denied women's equality with men, depicted French and German novels as sapping moral strength and, although stressing more than she did women's need to use reason on everything, even the scriptures, also banned some subjects as unsuitable – in their case, anatomy. Many other individuals who helped the Women's Movement, like John Stuart Mill and George Eliot, had links with Unitarians.[33]

It was on women's integral equality that Unitarians perhaps achieved their longest-lasting success, albeit one belatedly acknowledged. Although their priorities were often for male education and their struggle to achieve 'gentleman' status and class leadership might conflict with female aspirations, Unitarians were consistently to the forefront in the increasing debate on women. Their abiding belief in female intellectual capacity and in a liberal, rational education for both sexes as the basis of a new society was inherently egalitarian and revolutionary even if other factors, especially those to do with class, could make them more conservative in practice. An individualistic religion based on freedom of thought was necessarily fluid in both belief and membership and contained a broad spectrum of views. Nevertheless, few, so early and consistently and on such deep principle, advocated such a radical view of womanhood as Unitarians, both men and women, did, or educated women to such a high extent. Thus, by enlarging their self-respect and mental horizons, they enabled women to lead a much fuller life and provide important precedents in what they could achieve. Unitarians, therefore, although limited by the standards of their age and class, were able to teach women to help themselves. Believing that 'knowledge is power', they were not afraid to give knowledge to the hitherto powerless.

33. Sydney Smith, *Selections from the Writings of*... 2 vols (1855), I, pp. 45–73; Maria Grey and Emily Shirreff, *Thoughts on Self-Culture* (1856), *passim.*

Bibliography

This book is partly based on the author's unpublished doctoral thesis, 'The Unitarian contribution to education in England from the late eighteenth century to 1853' (University of Leicester, 1987) and subsequent articles and papers. Throughout the book much material has been garnered from manuscript papers held at Harris Manchester College, Oxford and Dr Williams's Library in London and from journals published by the Unitarians, especially the *Monthly Repository*. The TUHS, *Enlightenment and Dissent* and publications of the Martineau and Gaskell Societies have been very useful. Contemporary writings by David Wykes complement earlier Unitarian historians such as Herbert and John McLachlan and R.V. Holt, *The Unitarian Contribution to Social Progress in England* (1952).

Works used particularly for biographical details are the *DNB*; *Record of Unitarian Worthies* (1896); and D.L. Ouren, [1] *Genealogia Unitariana Britannica*; [2] *Some Ministers and Collaterals: Some Presbyterian/Unitarian Chapels* (presented to MCO in 1975).

The footnotes cite works from which direct references have been taken. The following is a list of titles to enable further reading on the issues discussed in the text. For ease of use, titles are grouped by themes. Place of publication is London unless otherwise stated.

Education

GENERAL STUDIES

Ball, F., 'The Taunton Commission', *Journal of Educational Administration and History* (July 1979), XI, no. 2, pp. 8–11.

Dictionary of National Biography, entry for W. Whewell (LX, p. 455).

Gardner, Dorothy, *English Girlhood at School* (Oxford, 1929).

Hans, Nicholas, *New Trends in Education in the Eighteenth Century* (1951).

Lawson, John, and Silver, Harold, *A Social History of Education in England* (1973).

Pollard, H.M., *Pioneers of Popular Education, 1760–1850* (1956).

Simon, Brian, *The Two Nations and the Educational Structure 1780–1870* (1974).

Simon, Joan, 'Private classical schools in eighteenth-century England: a critique of Hans', *HofE* (Sept. 1979), 8, no. 3, pp. 179–91.

Stewart, W.A.C., and McCann, W.P., *The Educational Innovators, 1750–1880* (1967).

Thompson, R.S., 'The English grammar school curriculum in the eighteenth century: a reappraisal', *BJES* (Feb. 1971), XIX, no. 1, pp. 32–9.

Wakefield, Priscilla, *An Introduction to Botany* (1816; 7th edn).

—— *Leisure Hours* (1812; 5th edn).

—— *The Juvenile Travellers* (1808; 6th edn.).

Williams, David, *Lectures on Education*, 3 vols (1789).

THE DISSENTING ACADEMIES

Ditchfield, G.M., 'The early history of Manchester College', *THSLC* (1972), pp. 81–104.

Fulton, J.F., 'The Warrington Academy (1757–1789) and its influence upon medicine and science', *Bulletin of the History of Medicine* (Feb. 1933), I, no. 2, pp. 66–70.

Harland, John, 'Collectanea relating to Manchester and its neighbourhood. II' (1867), *Chetham Society Remains*, LXXII, pp. 232–41.

Martineau, James, *Essays, Reviews and Addresses* (1890), I, pp. 1–42, 400–14.

O'Brien, Paddy, *Warrington Academy 1757–86* (Wigan, 1989).

Raymond, Jean, and Pickstone, John, 'The natural sciences and the learning of English Unitarians: an exploration of the roles of Manchester College', in Barbara Smith (ed.), *Truth, Liberty, Religion* (Oxford, 1986).

Watts, Ruth, 'Manchester College and education 1786–1853', in Smith (ed.), *Truth, Liberty, Religion.*

—— 'Revolution and reaction; "Unitarian" academies, 1780–1800', *HofE* (Dec. 1991), 20, no. 4, pp. 307–24.

Webster, Charles, and Barry, Jonathan, 'The Manchester medical revolution', in Smith (ed.), *Truth, Liberty, Religion.*

Wykes, David, 'Sons and subscribers: lay support and Manchester College', in Smith (ed.), *Truth, Liberty, Religion.*

UNITARIANS AND EDUCATION

Aikin, John, *Essay on the Application of Natural History to Poetry* (1777).
—— *Letters to a Young Lady on a Course of English Poetry* (1807).
Aikin, Lucy, *Poetry for Children* (1825).
Barnes, Thomas, 'A plan for the improvement and extension of liberal education in Manchester' (9 Apr. 1783), *Memoirs of the Literary and Philosophical Society of Manchester* (1785), II.
Beard, John Relly, *Self-Culture* (3rd edn; 1st edn 1859).
Belsham, Thomas, *Elements of the Philosophy of Mind and of the Moral Philosophy to which is Prefixed a Compendium of Logic* (1801).
—— *The Importance of Giving a Proper Education to the Children of the Poor* (1791).
Byford, Diana, 'Harriet Martineau and didactic fiction 1830–1840' (MA thesis, Leicester University, 1971).
Carpenter, Lant, *Principles of Education* (1820).
Channing, William Ellery, *Self-Culture* (1839).
—— *Lectures on the Elevation of the Labouring Portion of the Community* (1840).
Harris, George, *The Christian Character . . . of the Late Rev. William Turner* (1859).
Heywood, Benjamin, *Addresses Delivered at the Manchester Mechanics' Institute* (1843).
Higginson, Edward, *An Address Delivered on the Opening of the Derby Mechanics' Institute* (1825).
—— *Observations to All Classes of the Community on the Establishment of Mechanics' Institutions* (1825).
Hill, Frederic, *National Education,* 2 vols (1836), I, pp. 109–12.
Hincks, Thomas, *A Syllabus of a Course of Lectures* (1803).
Joyce, Jeremiah, *A Familiar Introduction to the Arts and Sciences for the Use of Schools and Young Persons* (1810).
McLachlan, Herbert, *The Unitarian Home Missionary College* (1915).
Marcroft, A., *Historical Account of the Unitarian Chapel, Oldham* (Oldham, 1913).
MCO, *JK,* III, IV; *Letter-Book, cuttings etc., MC 1824–80; Letters to Lant Carpenter from Glasgow* (10.5.1810); *Shepherd Papers,* V.
MCO, Prospectus (1817); *MC Reports; MNC Report* (1853), p. 4. See also *MR* for regular reports on MC.
MSS Liverpool University, *William Rathbone,* XI.2.1–56.

Priestley, Joseph, *Autobiography* (Bath, 1970, repr. of *Memoirs*, 1806).
—— 'An essay on the first principles of government' (1771), *The Theological and Miscellaneous Works of Joseph Priestley*, ed. J.T. Rutt, 25 vols (1817–31), XXII, pp. 1–144.
—— 'Lectures on history and general policy', (1803), *Works*, XXIV.
—— 'Some considerations on the state of the poor in general' (1787), *Works*, XXV, pp. 315–19.
Sieveking, G., *Memoir and Letters of Francis W. Newman* (1909).
Smith, Barbara (ed.), *Truth, Liberty, Religion* (Oxford, 1986).
Turner, William, *Sunday Schools Recommended* (Newcastle upon Tyne, 1786).

See also Thesis, pp. 77–85, 308–442, for a detailed analysis of the enormous involvement of Unitarians in working-class education.

HIGHER EDUCATION

Burns, J.J., *Jeremy Bentham and University College* (1962).
Cardwell, D.S.L., *The Organisation of Science in England: A Retrospect* (1957).
Haines, G., *German Influences upon English Education and Science 1800–66* (Connecticut, 1957).
Hill, Frederic, *National Education*, 2 vols (1836), I.
New, Chester W., *The Life of Henry Brougham* (1961).
Rothblatt, Sheldon, 'Failure in early nineteenth-century Oxford and Cambridge', *HofE* (Mar. 1982), 11, no. 1, pp. 1–21.
Sadler, Thomas (ed.), *Diary, Reminiscences and Correspondence of Henry Crabb Robinson*, 2 vols (1872).
Simon, Brian, *The Two Nations and the Educational Structure 1780–1870* (1974).
Whewell, William, *On the Principles of English University Education* (1838).

WORKING-CLASS EDUCATION

Cowie, E., 'Stephen Hawtry and a working-class Eton', *HofE* (June 1982), 11, no. 2, pp. 71–86.
Dick, Malcolm, 'The myth of the working-class Sunday school', *HofE* (Mar. 1980), 9, no. 1, pp. 27–41.
Engels, Frederick, *The Condition of the Working-Class in England* (1969; 1st edn 1844).

Frost, Michael Brian, 'The development of provided schooling for working-class children in Birmingham' (M.Litt. thesis, Birmingham University, 1978).

Gomersall, M., Flett, K., and Purvis, J., *HofE* (Mar. 1988), 17, no. 1, pp. 37–54; (June 1989), 18, no. 2, pp. 145–62 [a series of articles on girls' education].

Halevy, Elie, *A History of English People in the Nineteenth Century*, 6 vols (1952), VI, Book II.

Laqueur, Thomas, 'Working-class demand and the growth of English elementary education 1750–1850', in Lawrence Stone (ed.), *Schooling and Society* (Baltimore, 1976), pp. 192–205.

Quarterly Journal of Education (1833), V, pp. 142–53.

Tholfsen, Trygve, *Working-Class Radicalism in mid-Victorian England* (1976).

See also Unitarians and education, above.

MECHANICS' INSTITUTES

Garner, A.D., 'The Society of Arts and the mechanics' institutes: the co-ordination of endeavours towards science and technical education, 1851–4', *HofE* (Dec. 1985), 14, no. 4, pp. 155–62.

Harrison, J.F.C., *Learning and Living 1790–1960* (1961).

Inkster, Ian, 'The social context of an educational movement: a revisionist approach to the English mechanics' institutes, 1820–1850', *Oxford Review of Education* (1976), 2, no. 3, pp. 277–307.

Kargon, Robert, *Science in Victorian Manchester* (Manchester, 1977).

MSS Leicester PRO, 2D39, *Leicester Mechanics' Institute Minute Book 1, 1833–38.*

Reports of the Leeds Literary Institute (Leeds, 1835–40), 1st to 6th Reports.

Thackray, Arnold, 'Natural knowledge in cultural context: the Manchester model', *American Historical Review* (Feb. 1974), 79, no. 1, pp. 673–709.

Tiffen, Herbert J., *A History of the Liverpool Institute School 1825 to 1935* (1935).

Turner, C.M., 'Development of mechanics' institutes in Warwickshire, Worcestershire and Staffordshire' (M.Ed. thesis, Leicester University, 1966).

Tylecote, Mabel, *The Mechanics' Institutes of Lancashire and Yorkshire before 1851* (1957).

See also Thesis, pp. 396–418, for a detailed account of Unitarian involvement.
See also Women: women's education, below.

Women

WOMEN'S LIVES

Austen, Jane, *Emma* (1953; 1st edn. 1816).
Banks, J.A. and Olive, *Feminism and Family Planning in Victorian England* (Liverpool, 1964).
Barker, Hannah, and Chalus, Elaine (eds), *Gender in Eighteenth Century England* (1997).
Berg, Maxine, *The Age of Manufactures* (1994; 1st edn 1985).
Browne, Alice, *The Eighteenth Century Feminist Mind* (Brighton, 1987).
Caine, Barbara, *English Feminism 1730–1980* (Oxford, 1997).
Davidoff, Leonore, and Hall, Catherine, *Family Fortunes: Men and Women of the English Middle Class 1780–1850* (1987).
Davidson, Caroline, *A Woman's Work is Never Done* (1982).
Hall, Catherine, *White, Male and Middle Class* (Oxford, 1992).
Hill, Bridget (ed.), *Eighteenth Century Women: An Anthology* (1987).
—— *Women, Work and Sexual Politics in Eighteenth Century England* (1994).
Holcombe, Lee, 'Victorian wives and property: reform of the married women's property law, 1857–1882', in Vicinus (ed.), *A Widening Sphere*, pp. 3–28.
Jones, Vivien (ed.), *Women in the Eighteenth Century: Constructions of Femininity* (1990).
Malmgreen, Gail (ed.), *Religion in the Lives of English Women* (Indiana, 1986).
Martineau, Harriet, *Society in America*, 3 vols (1837).
Murray, Janet Horowitz, *Strong Minded Women* (Middlesex, 1982).
Pinchbeck, Ivy, *Women Workers and the Industrial Revolution* (1930).
Rendall, Jane (ed.), *Equal or Different: Women's Politics 1880–1914* (Oxford, 1987).
—— *Women in an Industrializing Society: England 1750–1880* (Oxford, 1990).
Vicinus, Martha (ed.), *'Suffer and be still': Women in the Victorian Age* (Indiana, 1972).
—— (ed.), *A Widening Sphere* (1977).
Wollstonecraft, Mary, *A Vindication of the Rights of Women* (1792).

WOMEN'S EDUCATION

Binfield, Clyde, *Belmont's Portias: Victorian Nonconformists and Middle-Class Education for Girls* (1981).

Burstyn, Joan, 'Women's education in England during the nineteenth century: a review of the literature 1970–76', *HofE* (Feb. 1977), 6, no. 1, pp. 11–19.

Dyhouse, Carol, 'Social Darwinistic ideas of the development of women's education in England, 1880–1920', *HofE* (Feb. 1976), 5, no. 1, pp. 41–58.

Gardner, Dorothy, *English Girlhood at School* (Oxford, 1929).

Hughes, Kathryn, *The Victorian Governess* (1993).

Kersey, Shirley Nelson, *Classics in the Education of Girls and Women* (1981).

Pedersen, Joyce Senders, *The Reform of Girls' Secondary and Higher Education in Victorian England* (1987).

WOMEN AND LITERATURE

Haight, Gordon S., *George Eliot* (Oxford, 1968).

Showalter, Elaine, *A Literature of their Own: From Charlotte Brontë to Doris Lessing* (1977).

Turner, Cheryl, *Living by the Pen: Women Writers of the Eighteenth Century* (1992).

Uglow, Jenny, *Elizabeth Gaskell* (1993).

WOMEN, PHILANTHROPY AND POLITICS

Billington, Louis and Rosamund, 'A burning zeal for righteousness', in Rendall (ed.), *Equal or Different.*

Gleadle, Kathryn, *The Early Feminists: Radical Unitarians and the Emergence of the Women's Rights Movement, 1843–51* (1995).

Lacey, Candida Ann (ed.), *Barbara Leigh-Smith and the Langham Place Group* (1987).

Midgley, Clare, *Women against Slavery* (1992).

Prochaska, Frank, *Women and Philanthropy in Nineteenth Century England* (Oxford, 1980).

Rendall, Jane, '"A moral engine?" Feminism, liberalism and the *Englishwoman's Journal*', in Rendall (ed.), *Equal or Different.*

—— (ed.) *Equal or Different: Women's Politics 1800–1914* (Oxford, 1987), Introduction.

Thompson, Dorothy, 'Women, work and politics in nineteenth-century England', in Rendall (ed.), *Equal or Different.*

WOMEN AND WORK

Bell, Quinton, *The Schools of Design* (1963).

Greg, Samuel, 'Two letters to Leonard Horner Esq. on the capabilities of the factory system' (1840), in *Conditions of Work and Living: Five Pamphlets 1838–44* (New York, 1972).

Neff, Wanda, *Victorian Working Women* (1929).

Parkes, Bessie Rayner, *Essays on Woman's Work* (1865).

Pinchbeck, Ivy, *Women Workers and the Industrial Revolution* (1930).

Rendall, Jane, *Women in an Industrializing Society: England 1750–1880* (Oxford, 1990).

The Unitarians

GENERAL STUDIES

Bolam, C.G., Goring, J., Short, H.L., Thomas, R. (1968), *The English Presbyterians* (1968).

Fitzpatrick, Martin, 'Rational dissent and the Enlightenment', *Faith and Freedom* (Summer 1985), 38, part 2, no. 113, pp. 83–101.

Howe, D.W., *The Unitarian Conscience* (Cambridge, Mass., 1970).

McLachlan, Herbert, *The Unitarian Movement in the Religious Life of England* (1934).

Philp, Mark, 'Thompson, Godwin and the French Revolution', *History Workshop Journal* (1995), 39, pp. 89–101.

Richey, R.E., 'Did the English Presbyterians become Unitarian?', *Church History* (1973), XLII, pp. 58–73.

Saunders, Valerie (ed.) Harriet Martineau Selected Letters (Oxford, 1990).

Seed, John, 'Unitarianism, political economy and the antinomies of liberal culture in Manchester, 1830–50', *Social History* (Jan. 1982), 7, no. 1, pp. 1–25.

Stange, Douglas Charles, *British Unitarians against American Slavery, 1833–65* (1984).

Woodall, R.D., *Midland Unitarianism and its Story, 1662–1962* (Sutton Coldfield, 1962).

INDIVIDUALS

Channing, W.H., *The Life of William Ellery Channing* (Boston, 1880).

The Christian Reformer.

Dictionary of National Biography, entries for: William Carpenter (IX, pp. 166–7), Henry Holland (XXVII, pp. 144–5), Samuel Parkes (XLIII, p. 307), Samuel Robinson (XLIX, pp. 44–5), Samuel Sharpe (LI, pp. 425–7), J.J. Tayler (LV, pp. 399–400), Philip and Richard Taylor (LV, pp. 456–9).

Delbanco, Andrew, *William Ellery Channing* (Cambridge, Mass., 1981).

Fryckstedt, Monica Correa, *Elizabeth Gaskell's 'Mary Barton' and 'Ruth': A Challenge in Christian England* (Uppsala, 1982).

Gaskell, Elizabeth, *Cousin Phillis and other Tales* (Oxford, 1981; 1st edn 1865).

—— *Cranford* (1892; 1st edn 1853).

—— *Mary Barton* (1970; 1st edn 1848).

—— *Four Short Stories* (1983).

—— *The Letters of Mrs Gaskell*, ed. John Chapple and Arthur Pollard (Manchester, 1997). [The 1966 edn has been used here.]

The Gaskell Society Journal (1987–1996), 1–10.

Hoeker-Drysdale, Susan, *Harriet Martineau: First Woman Sociologist* (Oxford, 1992).

Inquirer, passim; 'William Shaen' (12.3.1887), pp. 171–3; 'James Heywood' (23.10.1897), pp. 689–90.

Kenrick, John, *A Biographical Memoir of the Late Rev. Charles Wellbeloved* (1860).

Kenrick, Mrs W. Byng, *Chronicles of a Nonconformist Family: The Kenricks of Wynne Hall, Exeter and Birmingham* (Birmingham, 1932).

Knight, Frida, *University Rebel* (1971).

Lansbury, Coral, *Elizabeth Gaskell: The Novel of Social Crisis* (1975).

le Breton, Anna (ed.), *Correspondence of Dr Channing and Lucy Aikin (1826–42)* (1874).

Litchfield, Henrietta (ed.), *Emma Darwin: A Century of Family Letters, 1792–1896* (1915).

McGuffie, Duncan S., 'William Ellery Channing's religion and its influence', *TUHS* (July 1980), XVIII, no. 2, pp. 42–53.

Martineau, Harriet, 'Lady Byron', *Biographical Sketches*, pp. 317–24. (1870; 1st ed. 1868. Taken from articles in the *Daily News*).

—— *Selected Letters*, ed. Valerie Sanders (Oxford, 1990).

Parnaby, Margaret, 'William Johnson Fox and the *Monthly Repository* Circle of 1832 to 1836' (Ph.D. thesis, Australian National University, 1979).

Potter, Louisa, 'Eighty years ago', *Manchester Guardian* (6.8.1896).

Robberds, J.W. (ed.), *A Memoir of the Life and Writings of the Late William Taylor of Norwich* (1843).

Rodgers, Betsy, *Georgian Chronicle: Mrs Barbauld and her Family* (1958).

Roscoe, Henry, *Life and Experiences . . .* (1906).
Ross, Janet, *Three Generations of Englishwomen,* 2 vols (1888), I.
Saddler, Thomas (ed.), *Diary, Reminiscences and Correspondence of Henry Crabb Robinson,* 2 vols (1872).
Uglow, Jenny, *Elizabeth Gaskell* (1993).
Unitarian Chronicle.
Wakefield, Gilbert, *Memoirs,* 2 vols (1792).

N.B. The obituaries of many well-known Unitarians can be found in *The Christian Reformer, Inquirer* and *Unitarian Chronicle.*

JOSEPH PRIESTLEY

Graham, Jenny, *Revolutionary in Exile: The Emigration of Joseph Priestley to America 1794–1804* (Philadelphia, 1995).
Marsh, R., 'The second part of Hartley's system', *Journal of the History of Ideas* (1959), XX, pp. 264–73.
Rossington, H.J., 'Our indebtedness to Priestley', *TUHS* (1933), V, part 3, pp. 239–40.
Watts, Ruth, 'Joseph Priestley and education', *Enlightenment and Dissent* (1983), no. 2, pp. 83–100.

See also Education: Unitarians and education, above.

UNITARIAN DOMESTIC MISSIONS

Bushrod, Emily, 'The diary of John Gent Brooks: a Victorian commentary on poverty (1844–1854)', *TUHS* (Apr. 1992), XX, no. 2, pp. 99–106.
Evans, R.H., 'The Biggs family of Leicester', *Leicestershire Archaeological and Historical Society Transactions* (1972–73), no. 48, pp. 40–1.
Holt, Anne, *A Ministry to the Poor* (Liverpool, 1936).
Packer, B.A., 'The founding of the Liverpool Domestic Mission and its development under the ministry of John Johns', *TUHS* (Apr. 1984), XVIII, no. 2, pp. 106–20.
Simmons, Jack, 'A Victorian social worker: Joseph Dare and the Leicester Domestic Mission', *Leicestershire Archaeological and Historical Society* (1970–71), XLVI, pp. 65–80.
Wilson, H., 'A hundred years of religious and social work in Birmingham: The Church of the Messiah Domestic Mission', *TUHS* (1945), VIII, no. 3, pp. 113–15.

See also Education: Unitarians and education, above.

Religion

Carpenter, Joseph Estlin, *James Martineau* (1905).

Clark, J.C.D., *English Society 1688–1832* (Cambridge, 1985). [A revisionist hypothesis, but even Clark does not present the Church as very spiritual.]

Corfield, Kenneth, 'Elizabeth Heyrick: radical Quaker', in Gail Malmgreen (ed.), *Religion in the Lives of English Women 1760–1930* (Bloomington and Indianapolis, 1986), pp. 41–67.

Dunn, Waldo Hilary, *James Anthony Froude 1818–56* (Oxford, 1961).

Gilbert, A.D., *Religion and Society in Industrial England* (1976).

Malmgreen, Gail (ed.), *Religion in the Lives of English Women, 1760–1930* (Bloomington and Indianapolis, 1986).

Richey, R.E., 'The origins of British radicalism: the changing rationale for dissent', *Eighteenth Century Studies* (1973–74), VII, no. 2, pp. 179–92.

Sellars, Ian, *Nineteenth Century Nonconformity* (1977).

Watts, Michael R., *The Dissenters*, 2 vols (Oxford, 1978, 1996).

Wykes, David, 'Religious dissent and the penal laws: an explanation of business success?', *History* (Feb. 1990), 75, no. 243, pp. 39–62.

Intellectual, social and cultural history

Berlin, Isaiah, *The Age of Enlightenment* (New York, 1956).

Briggs, Asa, *Victorian Cities* (Harmondsworth, 1968).

Carpenter, Joseph Estlin, *The Bible in the Nineteenth Century* (1903).

de Guistino, David, *Conquest of Mind: Phrenology and Victorian Social Thought* (1975).

Dunthorne, Hugh, *The Enlightenment* (The Historical Association, 1991).

Fraser, Derek (ed.), *Municipal Reform and the Industrial City* (Leicester, 1982).

Garnett, R.G., 'E.T. Craig: communitarian, educator, phrenologist', *VASFE* (1963), XV, no. 31, pp. 135–42.

Hartley, A.D., *Observations on Man*, 2 vols (New York, 1976), II.

Hollis, Patricia, *Women in Public: The Women's Movement 1850–1900* (1979).

Holmes, Richard, *Coleridge* (Oxford, 1982).

Kamm, Josephine, *John Stuart Mill in Love* (1977).

Knights, Ben, *The Idea of the Clerisy in the Nineteenth Century* (Cambridge, 1978).

Le Quesne, A., *Carlyle* (Oxford, 1982).

McLachlan, Herbert, *Essays and Addresses* (Manchester, 1950), pp. 213–28. [Unitarian support for Chartist and Owenite ideas: see also *Thesis*, pp. 424–7.]

Mill, John Stuart, *Autobiography* (Oxford, 1971).

—— (ed.), *Analysis of the Phenomena of the Human Mind by James Mill* (1878).

Morris, R.J., *Class, Sect and Party* (Manchester, 1990).

—— (ed.), *Class, Power and Social Structure in British Nineteenth Century Towns* (Leicester, 1986).

Nicholson, B., *The Masters: Wright of Derby* (1966).

Orange, Derek, 'Rational dissent and provincial science: William Turner and the Newcastle Literary and Philosophical Society', in Ian Inkster and Jack Morrell (eds), *Metropolis and Province: Science in British Culture, 1780–1850* (1983), pp. 205–30.

Pryke, J., 'The treatment of political economy in *North and South*', *Gaskell Society Journal* (1990), 4, pp. 28–40.

Schofield, Robert E., *The Lunar Society of Birmingham* (Oxford, 1963).

Seed, John, 'Theologies of power: Unitarianism and the social relations of religious discourse, 1800–50', in Morris (ed.), *Class, Power and Social Structure*, pp. 108–56.

Simon, Brian, *The Two Nations and the Educational Structure 1780–1870* (1974).

Stromberg, R.N., *European Intellectual History since 1789* (New Jersey, 1981).

Willey, Basil, *Nineteenth Century Studies* (Harmondsworth, 1969).

Index